P9-DVR-605

Whole
Food
Cooking
Every Day

Amy Chaplin

Photographs by Anson Smart

Whole Food Cooking Every Day

Transform the Way You Eat with 250 Vegetarian Recipes Free of Gluten, Dairy, and Refined Sugar

ARTISAN | NEW YORK

Library of Congress Cataloging-in-Publication Data

Names: Chaplin, Amy, author. | Smart, Anson, photographer.
Title: Whole food cooking every day / Amy Chaplin ;
photographs by Anson Smart.
Description: First printing, August 2019. | New York, NY : Artisan, a division
of Workman Publishing Co., Inc. [2019] | Includes an index.
Identifiers: LCCN 2018039183 | ISBN 9781579658021
(hardcover : alk. paper)
Subjects: LCSH: Cooking (Natural foods) | Natural foods. |
LCGFT: Cookbooks.
Classification: LCC TX741 .C4634 2019 | DDC 641.3/02—dc23
LC record available at https://lccn.loc.gov/2018039183

Design by Toni Tajima
Art direction and cover design by Michelle Ishay-Cohen

Artisan books are available at special discounts when purchased in bulk for
premiums and sales promotions as well as for fund-raising or educational
use. Special editions or book excerpts also can be created to specification.
For details, contact the Special Sales Director at the address below, or send
an e-mail to specialmarkets@workman.com.

For speaking engagements,
contact speakersbureau@workman.com.

Published by Artisan
A division of Workman Publishing Co., Inc.
225 Varick Street
New York, NY 10014-4381
artisanbooks.com

Artisan is a registered trademark of
Workman Publishing Co., Inc.

Published simultaneously in Canada
by Thomas Allen & Son, Limited

Printed in China

First printing, August 2019

1 3 5 7 9 10 8 6 4 2

Dedicated to my mother, Pamela,
and her unique connection
to the magic of the natural world.

And to my father, William,
and son, Ezra.

Contents

Introduction

Cooking with whole foods simply means choosing foods that are in their natural state or as close to it as possible. When it comes to finding the motivation to get into the kitchen and cook, what could be more inspiring than seasonal, fresh ingredients—from a bunch of newly picked deep green kale or a rich orange winter squash to savory seeds, grains, and beans in every shape and color? These beautiful foods don't need much preparation to turn them into a nourishing, flavorful meal. In a whole food diet, there is no room for ingredients that are highly refined or processed or that contain anything artificial. Real whole foods are brimming with flavor and vitality and the innate intelligence to improve your health. Choosing to cook with whole foods means you are getting the maximum nutrition intended by nature, and when the foods are properly prepared, their nutrient value can even increase. Whether you are a vegetarian, a vegan, or an omnivore, a whole food diet can help you achieve and maintain optimum health and wellness. And when you cook with whole foods, the ingredients that grow around you become both your muse and your guide.

One of the most exciting aspects of my work as a chef, teacher, and writer is inspiring other people to cook. It's a privilege to see students and readers overcome their trepidation or even reluctance about cooking and eating well, transforming their time in the kitchen into a pleasurable, gratifying, and nourishing experience. My approach to cooking is rooted, in part, in my belief that a desire to cook is in our DNA and that cooking is something for which we all have a natural ability.

This book is based on the premise that all chefs and experienced home cooks know: Successful meals come from good ingredients, reliable techniques, and a collection of go-to recipes that are so familiar they become second nature. Intuitive chefs and cooks can adapt methods and basic recipes to suit the season, the occasion, and the needs and desires of the people they're feeding, as well as their own cravings. The key to successful whole food cooking lies in this same principle: Mastering a handful of techniques and basic recipes that can be applied to produce and other ingredients you have on hand, no matter the season, will nurture your inherent ability to cook.

Following complicated recipes when you are under any kind of pressure can be frustrating and time-consuming, so this collection is organized into accessible base recipes with multiple variations. Learning some key base recipes—whether for a chia Bircher bowl, salad dressing, nut milk, or soup—will not only enable you to prepare healthy meals and get the most out of your whole food ingredients but also help you become a better and more confident cook. The base recipes included in this book are the building blocks of my cooking routine. This collection has been endlessly adapted to meet the needs of my own evolving diet and those of my clients. I teach these recipes to both beginner cooks and professional chefs who want to incorporate vegan and whole food meals into their diets and menus.

These recipes are also integral to the meal prep plans you'll find at the back of this book (see pages 374–382). Prepping meals ahead in batches is an economical solution to our time-starved lifestyles, and a guaranteed way to ensure a steady flow of healthy food options no matter what your daily demands are.

Spending time in the kitchen may not be something you want to do every day, but mastering some simple cooking techniques will make a significant impact on your overall well-being. Once you've stocked your pantry with basic whole food ingredients and some seasonal vegetables, you'll be ready to create healthful and sustaining meals (usually in less time than it takes to order in). Getting in the swing of mixing and matching different recipes from a variety of chapters in this book will make eating well easy, fun, and absolutely delicious.

Cooking with ingredients straight from nature does much more than just feed us: it connects us to our environment and the seasons; gives us a regular opportunity to be creative with flavors, colors, and textures; helps us fine-tune our intuition; and draws friends and families together. I have been both delighted and honored to have the opportunity to touch people's lives by rekindling their natural ability to nourish themselves through cooking. I hope this book does just that for you.

How to Use This Book

The recipes in this book are divided into twenty chapters. All the chapters except the one devoted to vegetables include at least one base recipe and many variations. The introduction to the recipes in each chapter includes information on texture, flavor, and suggested add-ins and garnishes, as well as guidelines for storing and freezing. These introductory sections are intended to help you view the base recipes as blueprints. The variations that stem from each base recipe will demonstrate how you can adapt recipes to suit your own needs, use what you have on hand, and ultimately create your own arsenal of reliable dishes.

The vegetable chapter is organized around basic techniques for preparing all sorts of produce year-round. You'll learn how to steam, roast, sauté, quick-pickle, and ferment vegetables from the land, as well as how to toast or soak and simmer vegetables from the sea—that is, seaweeds. The recipes will get you started, but these techniques will take you far beyond that. You'll also find charts for steaming and roasting seasonal vegetables.

What is perhaps the most valuable aspect of this approach is that you can make any recipe (or use any technique) with what's available and not have to bookmark a recipe for a future season. Take the dressings (beginning on page 214), for example. Each is made with a base of blended vegetables. One base recipe uses sweet corn, but when corn is not in season, simply choose a base recipe that calls for zucchini, carrots, or jarred artichoke hearts,

among other options. All of the base recipes are made with readily available ingredients, while in the variations, you'll find not only suggestions for other seasonal additions but also options for flavoring a dish with intriguing ingredients such as matcha, cacao, turmeric, and other herbs and spices. Adding these to the base recipe is the secret to elevating everyday food and keeping your meals interesting.

Meal prep is a large part of what I do for my clients and for myself weekly. Most of the recipes in this book are designed to be served over the course of a week, but there are also pantry staples that will keep for weeks or longer, and plenty of dishes that store well in the freezer. Prepping meals ahead is the only way to stick to healthy eating on a busy schedule, and you'll find an in-depth look at my approach and how to get organized beginning on page 370.

A Few Notes About Special Diets

Grain-free or restricted-grain diets are often recommended for people with autoimmune issues and inflammation, among other health concerns. Restricting or cutting out grains is more challenging for vegans and vegetarians, who usually rely on these nutritious and satisfying foods as the base of most meals. Grain dishes are also comforting, and many people miss them dearly, especially when first embarking on a limited-grain diet. But cutting back on or removing these ingredients from your diet can motivate you to find other healthy ways to satisfy your hunger. You may discover that you eat many more vegetables after lessening your grain consumption. If you keep foods like steamed squash, roasted sweet potatoes, and lots of prepped greens in the fridge, along with vegetables for the Steamed Vegetable Salads (page 173) and cooked beans of various types, you will have plenty of convenient options to choose from. However, grains (whole, not refined) play a really important role in a healthy diet and a sustainable food system, so I don't suggest omitting them from your diet unless a health problem requires that you do.

For many people, a good approach might be eating one meal a day that is centered around whole grains. What that meal is will change depending on the season. In winter, for example, whole-grain porridges make a warming breakfast, but in the summer, you might prefer to eat a brown rice bowl for lunch. An all-vegetable dinner of a simple soup, a generous bowl of steamed vegetables, or a big crunchy salad with chickpeas or another creamy bean has always been my choice for my evening meal. When I eliminated grains from my own diet for a time, I created the Grain-Free Chia Bircher Bowl (page 22) and the Grain-Free Porridge (page 46). You'll also find grain-free variations in the Seeded Crackers, Muffins, Seeded Bars, and Granola chapters.

OPPOSITE: Beet–Fennel Seed Bread (page 53) topped with Beet and Cashew Butter Bean Pâté (page 155) (top); Black Rice–Black Sesame Bread (page 53) spread with avocado (bottom)

Eating Gluten-Free

The recipes in this book are gluten-free. I developed them because there is a real need for healthy gluten-free recipes, both vegan and dairy-free. Many commercial food products that are labeled gluten-free are a far worse choice than the ones that contain gluten (unless of course you have celiac disease; even then, you are still better off avoiding such products). A commercial gluten-free flour blend is never going to be as healthful as sprouted whole-grain wheat, rye, or spelt flour, unless it contains only whole grains. The gluten-free recipes in this book use oat, buckwheat, millet, almond, brown rice, and coconut flours, which are now available in most well-stocked markets. If you can find these flours made from sprouted grains, then by all means use them. Sprouting removes phytic acid (see page 66) and increases digestibility and nutrient absorption. Oats are used in some recipes in this book; if you are allergic to gluten, be sure to purchase certified gluten-free oats.

Eating Sugar-Free

When I talk about sugar-free recipes, I'm referring to those that are free of concentrated sweeteners like maple syrup, brown rice syrup, coconut sugar, and honey. These sweeteners are all healthier alternatives to refined sugar; however, they can still elevate blood sugar and affect your health over time, and they can be pretty addictive. But since sugar is a flavor enhancer, you don't always end up with a delicious result when you cut it out of a recipe. For this reason, I like to add sweet spices, citrus, berries, cacao, and vanilla, all of which impart a lot of flavor and a nod toward sweetness while eliminating the need for a concentrated sweetener—plus you get to really taste the other ingredients because they are not masked by too much sugar.

For baked goods like muffins, the recipes do include small amounts of maple syrup. To make those recipes sugar-free, or very low in sugar, I replace the maple syrup with orange juice, which allows the flavor of other ingredients like almonds, coconut oil, vanilla, and berries to really shine. This way, a muffin becomes a nutritious snack rather than a sweet treat but still satisfies the urge for a comforting baked good. That said, eating sugar-free does take getting used to. But once your taste buds adjust to a diet low in sugar (it takes less time than you think), you'll find that flavorful food simply doesn't need added sugar. Keeping it out of your everyday meals and snacks means it's easier to keep track of your daily intake if you do choose to eat a sugary treat.

A FEW THINGS TO KEEP IN MIND

Before choosing what to make, think about what is in season where you live. Food made with ingredients at their peak is not only better for us (because it contains higher amounts of nutrients due to less time in transit) and the environment (fewer food miles) but also tastes best.

Read through the entire base recipe and then the variation, if you have chosen one, before you start. If the base recipe or variation includes ingredients that you haven't used before, be sure to consult the Texture and Flavor sections in the chapter's opening text, which will help you understand what to expect and what to aim for.

For best results with any of the baking recipes, use a digital scale. Volume measures can vary greatly depending on the method—your cup of oats, for example, may be very different from mine, and the same goes for any flour. A digital scale guarantees precision. That said, if you don't have a scale, spoon any dry ingredients into the cup measure—don't pack them in—and level them off with the flat edge of a knife.

OPPOSITE: Roasted vegetables (see pages 178–179) with Pine Nut Chickpea Pâté with Rosemary (page 157)

Chia Bircher Bowls

—

Chia Oat Bircher Bowl
(BASE RECIPE) 20

Grain-Free Chia Bircher Bowl
(BASE RECIPE) 22

Matcha Chia Bircher Bowl · 23

Peach or Nectarine Chia Bircher Bowl · 23

Cacao and Maca Chia Bircher Bowl · 23

Apple-Citrus Chia Bircher Bowl · 25

Golden Milk Chia Bircher Bowl · 25

If you're new to whole food cooking, start with these recipes for chia Bircher bowls. The few moments of advance planning and the 10 minutes you'll spend assembling any of these will reward you with a delicious, energy-boosting breakfast for days. (And if you don't have time to make a batch ahead, you can still whip one up in less than 30 minutes.) Combining oats (or soaked seeds and coconut) with chia seeds, hemp seeds, and ground flax and an almond-milk base gives them a creamy consistency. You can portion them out into individual jars so you have a nourishing breakfast at the ready every morning. And you can feel good starting the day with any of the recipes here, as they're high in protein and contain so many nutrient-dense foods. These breakfast bowls are all customizable, and the base recipes are the ideal blank canvas for showcasing summer fruit and berries or a Simple Compote (pages 96–105). Not only are these chia Bircher bowls easier to make than your average morning smoothie, they are also more satisfying and sustaining.

Here you will find two base recipes: one made with oats, and a grain-free version based on soaked seeds and coconut. You can use either base for any of the variations that follow. If you eat grains, start with the Chia Oat Bircher Bowl; it's a true crowd-pleaser (if you are allergic to gluten, be sure to purchase gluten-free oats). Note that with either of these bases, you'll need to soak the almonds (and, if making the grain-free version, the seeds) overnight.

These bowls are best at room temperature, so remove that morning's portion from the fridge about half an hour before you plan to eat it (if you're taking it to work, this is no problem). Top it with fresh fruit or berries or one of the compotes and a splash of plain or flavored nut milk (see pages 71–77); on cooler days, you can warm up the nut milk. For added crunch, sprinkle with toasted seeds, nuts, or flaked coconut, or just top with ground flax seeds, hemp seeds, or maca powder.

Notes

TEXTURE

These breakfast puddings will thicken quite quickly and be ready to eat in under 30 minutes, but they will also thicken further overnight in the fridge. You can easily adjust the consistency by adding nut milk or water if the pudding is too thick; or stir in a little more chia and flax if it's too runny.

FLAVOR

You can flavor these puddings in a hundred different ways—be as adventurous as you like. Scan your tea and spice cabinets for inspiration. Either of the base recipes will hit the spot, especially with the garnishes suggested opposite, but if you want to change up the flavors, the variations make this nutritious breakfast all the more interesting.

BLENDING

Although these recipes are best made with a high-powered blender, you can use a regular upright blender. Just be sure to blend the ingredients until smooth and creamy. When adding fresh turmeric or ginger to either of the bases, finely chop it first.

ADD-INS

Many of your favorite superfood ingredients can be incorporated into these bowls. If you choose one with a pungent flavor, like mushroom powder, ashwagandha, or maca, start with less than the suggested dose, as the taste can intensify when the pudding sits overnight. If you're going nut-free, replace the nuts with raw sunflower or pumpkin seeds (these will need to be soaked first). If you're looking for something a little sweeter, stir in dried mulberries, as in the Golden Milk Chia Bowl. Or blend in a couple of dates with the almonds and water in any variation, or simply drizzle the sweetener of your choice over the chia bowl. Adding coconut butter to a blended base (as in the Golden Milk Chia Bowl) is a nice way to enrich it; be sure to use store-bought coconut butter, which has a finer texture than homemade.

GARNISHES

If you want to dress up these bowls beyond the toppings suggested on page 26 (edible flowers, ground freeze-dried berries, grated citrus zest, and bee pollen), it can be fun to match the bowls with a nut milk of the same color (see pages 71–77) and then garnish them with toppings in the same tone as well.

STORING AND FREEZING

Stored in clean glass jars in the fridge, most of these chia puddings will keep well for up to 4 days. Those containing fresh fruit, though, are best eaten within 3 days. The bowls based on oats can be portioned out into individual servings and frozen for up to 3 months. Defrost each portion in the fridge overnight and stir well before serving.

Chia Oat Bircher Bowl

MAKES ABOUT 4 CUPS | 960 ML | SERVES 4

½ cup (1¾ ounces | 50 g) rolled oats

¼ cup (1¼ ounces | 40 g) chia seeds

¼ cup (1 ounce | 30 g) hemp seeds

2 tablespoons (¼ ounce | 8 g) ground flax seeds

½ cup (2½ ounces | 70 g) whole raw almonds, soaked overnight in 2 cups (480 ml) filtered water

2¾ cups (660 ml) filtered water

1 tablespoon vanilla extract

2 teaspoons ground cinnamon

Pinch of fine sea salt

Combine the oats and the chia, hemp, and flax seeds in a medium bowl; set aside. Drain and rinse the almonds and transfer them to an upright blender. Add the 2¾ cups (660 ml) water, vanilla, cinnamon, and salt and blend until completely smooth, then pour into the oat mixture. Stir well to combine and set aside for 25 to 30 minutes, until thick and creamy. This can be eaten immediately, with any of the toppings suggested on page 26, or stored in an airtight container in the fridge for up to 4 days. It will thicken further in the fridge.

OPPOSITE: Chia Oat Bircher Bowl with Spiced Plum-Ginger Compote (page 101), toasted walnuts, and Rose Almond Milk (page 72)

Grain-Free Chia Bircher Bowl

MAKES 5 CUPS | 1.2 L | SERVES 4 TO 6

½ cup (2½ ounces | 70 g) raw pumpkin seeds, soaked overnight in 2 cups (480 ml) filtered water

½ cup (2¼ ounces | 65 g) raw sunflower seeds, soaked overnight in 2 cups (480 ml) filtered water

¼ cup (1¼ ounces | 40 g) chia seeds

¼ cup (1 ounce | 30 g) hemp seeds

2 tablespoons (¼ ounce | 8 g) ground flax seeds

½ cup (2½ ounces | 70 g) whole raw almonds, soaked overnight in 2 cups (480 ml) filtered water

3 cups (720 ml) filtered water

2 tablespoons (⅓ ounce | 10 g) coconut flour

1 tablespoon vanilla extract

2 teaspoons ground cinnamon

Pinch of fine sea salt

½ cup (1 ounce | 25 g) unsweetened flaked dried coconut (see Note)

Drain the pumpkin seeds and sunflower seeds in a strainer, rinse under cold water, and set the strainer over a bowl to drain thoroughly. Combine the chia, hemp, and flax seeds in a medium bowl; set aside. Drain and rinse the almonds and transfer them to an upright blender. Add the 3 cups (720 ml) water, coconut flour, vanilla, cinnamon, and salt and blend until completely smooth, then add the dried coconut and drained seeds and briefly blend or pulse until the seeds are roughly chopped. Pour into the chia mixture, stir well to combine, and set aside for 25 to 30 minutes, until thick and creamy. This can be eaten immediately, with any of the toppings suggested on page 26, or stored in an airtight container in the fridge for up to 4 days. It will thicken further in the fridge.

NOTE: Flaked dried coconut adds texture to this grain-free bowl. If you can only get shredded coconut, just stir it in at the end rather than blending it.

Matcha Chia Bircher Bowl

MAKES ABOUT 4 CUPS | 960 ML | SERVES 4

___

1 recipe Chia Oat Bircher Bowl or Grain-Free Chia Bircher Bowl, omitting the cinnamon

4 teaspoons (8 g) ceremonial-grade matcha tea powder (see Resources, page 392)

1 teaspoon ground cardamom

1 Medjool date, pitted (optional)

Make the chia bowl following the instructions for the base recipe, adding the matcha, cardamom, and date, if using, to the blender along with the almonds and omitting the cinnamon. **Pictured on page 26**

Peach or Nectarine Chia Bircher Bowl

MAKES ABOUT 4 CUPS | 960 ML | SERVES 4

___

1 recipe Chia Oat Bircher Bowl or Grain-Free Chia Bircher Bowl, using 1½ cups (360 ml) water and ½ teaspoon cinnamon

2 medium-large (12 ounces | 340 g) ripe peaches or nectarines, halved, pitted, and chopped, plus more for serving

Make the chia bowl following the instructions for the base recipe, adding the peaches or nectarines to the blender along with the almonds and blending until completely smooth. Serve garnished with additional sliced peaches or nectarines and/or any of the toppings suggested on page 26. Because of the raw fruit, this bowl should be stored for no longer than 2 to 3 days. **Pictured on page 26**

Cacao and Maca Chia Bircher Bowl

MAKES ABOUT 4 CUPS | 960 ML | SERVES 4

___

1 recipe Chia Oat Bircher Bowl or Grain-Free Chia Bircher Bowl

¼ cup (½ ounce | 16 g) cacao powder (see the sidebar on page 297)

2 tablespoons (½ ounce | 14 g) mesquite powder (see the sidebar)

4 teaspoons (½ ounce | 16 g) gelatinized maca powder (see Resources, page 393)

1 tablespoon coconut butter

Make the chia bowl following the instructions for the base recipe, adding the cacao, mesquite, maca, and coconut butter to the blender along with the almonds and blending until smooth. Serve with any of the toppings suggested on page 26; this bowl tastes particularly good with Cherry Vanilla Compote (page 101) and Rose Almond Milk (page 72). **Pictured on page 26**

MESQUITE POWDER

Part of the legume family, the mesquite tree produces bean pods, which can be dried and ground into a powder. Mildly sweet, the powder has a rich, earthy flavor with smoky, caramel-like notes that complement cacao perfectly, simultaneously enriching it and sweetening and balancing its bitterness. Mesquite is a traditional Native American food, and the pods are rich in protein, iron, calcium, and magnesium. It's also high in fiber and has a low glycemic index, which makes it helpful in stabilizing blood sugar levels. Mesquite is a sustainable crop as it comes from drought-resistant trees that don't require irrigation (or chemical fertilizers).

Apple-Citrus Chia Bircher Bowl

MAKES ABOUT 4 CUPS | 960 ML | SERVES 4

1 recipe Chia Oat Bircher Bowl or Grain-Free Chia Bircher Bowl, using 1½ cups (360 ml) water and 1 teaspoon cinnamon

¾ cup (180 ml) freshly squeezed orange juice

¾ cup (6½ ounces | 185 g) thick coconut yogurt or whole-milk yogurt

1 medium-large (8 ounces | 230 g) apple, grated (1½ cups)

1 teaspoon grated orange zest

¼ cup (1¼ ounces | 35 g) golden raisins (optional)

Make the chia bowl following the instructions for the base recipe, adding the orange juice and yogurt to the blender along with the almonds and blending until smooth. Continue as directed, then mix in the apple, orange zest, and raisins, if using. Because of the raw apple, this should be stored for no longer than 2 to 3 days. **Pictured on page 26**

Golden Milk Chia Bircher Bowl

MAKES ABOUT 4 CUPS | 960 ML | SERVES 4

1 recipe Chia Oat Bircher Bowl or Grain-Free Chia Bircher Bowl

½ cup (1¼ ounces | 35 g) unsweetened shredded dried coconut

One 4-inch (10 cm) piece (1 ounce | 30 g) fresh turmeric, peeled and chopped (finely chopped if using a regular blender), or 2 teaspoons ground turmeric

1 tablespoon coconut butter

2 teaspoons ground cardamom

Pinch of freshly ground black pepper

⅓ cup (1½ ounces | 42 g) dried golden mulberries or golden raisins

Make the chia bowl following the instructions for the base recipe, adding the coconut, turmeric, coconut butter, cardamom, and pepper to the blender along with the almonds and blending until smooth. Then continue as directed, stirring in the mulberries once the dry and wet mixtures are combined. **Pictured on page 26**

GOLDEN MILK

Golden milk is a delicious drink made with milk, ground turmeric, ginger, and other warming spices. Black pepper and some type of fat are added to boost the absorption of curcumin, the anti-inflammatory compound in turmeric.

OPPOSITE: Ingredients for Apple-Citrus Chia Bircher Bowl

CHIA BIRCHER BOWL TOPPINGS

Since these bowls are best suited to the warmer months, they work brilliantly topped with fresh fruit and berries. The Simple Compotes (pages 96–105) offer endless options for flavor pairings. Homemade nut and seed milks (see pages 71–77) are an important component for enriching and enhancing the flavors of any of these bowls as well. For winning combinations, try these options (pictured clockwise from top left):

- Chia Oat Bircher Bowl (page 20) with raspberries (fresh and dried)

- Golden Milk Chia Bircher Bowl (page 25) with bee pollen

- Cacao and Maca Chia Bircher Bowl (page 23) with Cherry Vanilla Compote (page 101) and orange zest

- Peach Chia Bircher Bowl (page 23) with almond milk (see page 71) and hemp seeds

- Apple-Citrus Chia Bircher Bowl (page 25) with blueberries, almond milk (see page 71), and edible flowers

- Golden Milk Chia Bircher Bowl (page 25) with Golden Milk (page 88) and bee pollen

- Matcha Chia Bircher Bowl (page 23) with Matcha Almond Milk (page 72) and strawberries

Genius Whole-Grain Porridges

—

When an autumnal chill has set in and the mornings are brisk, there is almost no better way to start the day than with a comforting porridge—warming, nourishing, and delicious. Although porridge can be made with any grain, I prefer whole grains for their great texture and more complex flavor—as well as their abundance of concentrated nutrients. Here you'll find recipes using millet, whole oats, buckwheat, and black rice, but you can use the same technique for quinoa, wheat, rye, or spelt berries (heartier grains will take a bit longer to cook). All of these must be presoaked. Soaking whole grains overnight removes phytic acid (see page 66) and sparks the sprouting process, which awakens the nutrients in the grains and makes them more easily digestible.

I call these recipes "genius" porridges because I had two revelations while developing them. The first was that ground grains will cook up into porridge much faster than grains that are whole. The problem with grinding raw grains in a mill or spice grinder is that they can't be soaked first. However, you can blend presoaked whole grains with fresh water to get the same textural results as a ground grain while getting all the nutritional benefits of a soaked grain. My second revelation was that you can blend nuts, seeds, or coconut into the water called for in the recipe (before adding the grains) to make a creamy base for cooking the whole grains. Even a small amount of nuts or seeds will change the flavor and texture while boosting the protein content. Discovering these two techniques opened up a whole world of delicious and nutritionally enhanced porridges with the most luscious and satisfying textures.

This chapter also includes a base recipe and two variations for a grain-free porridge. When developing the grain-free porridge base recipe, I wanted the same warming and creamy texture whole-grain porridges have. To achieve that, the recipe uses a combination of soaked nuts and seeds, along with some coconut flour. Once this base is warmed through, flax and chia seeds are added to thicken the mixture. Since chia and flax don't need to be cooked, those porridges come together rather quickly.

On page 45, you'll find suggestions for how to customize your porridges—both sweet and savory. I hope you'll agree: they're genius!

Notes

TEXTURE

The great thing about these whole-grain recipes is that you can grind the grains as fine or as coarse as you like. The recipe instructions in this chapter result in cracked grains, so the porridges have some texture. If you like the idea of a silky-smooth porridge (which will cook much faster), blend the soaked grains with the water until completely smooth, then pour into the pot. Bring to a boil, whisking constantly until thickened, then cover the pot, reduce the heat to low, and simmer for 4 to 6 minutes, stirring frequently with a wooden spoon. The exact time will vary depending on the grain you use, but once the raw taste has gone, the porridge is ready. If you want to add sliced pear or grated apple to one of these smoother porridges, wait until the porridge is cooked before stirring in the fruit. (Note that it is easier to reheat porridge made with more coarsely ground grains, as the smoother ones have a tendency to clump; however, with the help of a whisk and a bit of attention, it can be done.)

FLAVOR

Adding coconut, nuts, seeds, or spices to any of the grain-based porridges makes them more flavorful and interesting. Just as with grains, soaking the nuts or seeds is important for enhancing nutrients and making them more absorbable and digestible. It's easy to remember to do this if you soak them at the same time as the grains (in separate containers).

To change up the flavor, you can use brewed tea instead of water when grinding the soaked grains (see Buckwheat Chai Porridge). Since you're most likely eating the porridge for breakfast, you can use teas that have caffeine, such as a robust chai or Chinese Pu-erh—both of these are warming and add a great depth of flavor. For herbal teas, like ginger, fennel, nettle, dandelion, or turmeric, steep them overnight to get the most of their medicinal benefits.

If you want a savory breakfast, use any of the grain base recipes, omitting any spices, and stir in miso at the end (as in the Savory Millet-Sesame Porridge with Miso) or top your bowl with sliced avocado, scallions, toasted sesame or sunflower seeds, ground flax seeds, tamari, and flax oil or olive oil. You can also treat the porridge like a congee and top it with minced ginger, turmeric, chile, fermented vegetables (homemade or store-bought), toasted nori, and/or a poached or boiled egg.

Adding some oil or another fat to any of the whole-grain porridges will enrich and enhance its flavor. Because you need some fat to get all the anti-inflammatory benefits of turmeric, you'll find coconut butter (or coconut oil) in the recipe for the Golden Milk Millet Porridge; you could use ghee instead or stir in melted butter or olive oil at the end.

ADD-INS

You can add fresh or frozen berries, grated apple, or sliced ripe pear or stone fruits once your porridge is cooked, allowing a few minutes for the fruit to cook or heat through before serving. Dried fruit can be added at the beginning of cooking.

Before you drizzle your breakfast porridge with maple syrup or honey, taste it without any added sweetener; you might find that you really don't need it, especially if you top the porridge with berries. Avoiding sugar in the morning will give you sharper mental focus and a sustained energy throughout the day (and omitting it helps break a sugar addiction). For variations like the Buckwheat-Cacao Porridge with Walnut and Rose, you have the option of blending in dates to balance the bitterness of the cacao.

GARNISHES

Sometimes a plain porridge topped simply with a nut or seed milk is just what you need in the morning. But these recipes provide a great opportunity for finishing the porridge with a nutrient-dense garnish and toppings; see the following page for suggestions.

STORING AND FREEZING

Stored in the fridge in airtight containers, these porridges will keep for 4 to 5 days. Pour leftover cooked porridge into a widemouthed glass jar or container and allow to cool before covering and placing in the fridge. These porridges can also be frozen (leave at least 1 inch | 2.5 cm of headspace in each container). Defrost in the fridge overnight; see the directions for reheating.

REHEATING

To reheat leftover porridge, spoon about 1 cup (240 ml) cooked porridge per serving into a small saucepan, add 2 to 3 tablespoons (30 to 45 ml) water or nut milk per serving, and bring to a simmer over high heat, stirring frequently. Cover the pan, reduce the heat to low, and simmer for a minute or so longer, until the porridge is heated through. Stir once more and serve.

PORRIDGE TOPPINGS AND GARNISHES

As with any simple grain dish, toppings play a key role in adding flavor, texture, and extra nutrients. Here the toppings also decide in which direction you want to take your porridge—sweet or savory. Both options make for a satisfying breakfast or meal anytime.

When going a sweeter route, think about the flavors of the porridge you've chosen and select a compote to match—if you're making one of the base recipes, any flavor compote will work, and the same goes for flavored nut milks (see pages 71–77). See page 38 for my favorite combinations.

To make any of these porridges savory, make the base recipes plain with no cinnamon or cardamom, or make the Savory Millet-Sesame Porridge with Miso or the Whole Oat Porridge with Winter Squash and Ginger.

Sweet Porridge Toppings

o Homemade nut or seed milk (see pages 71–77)
o Fresh berries
o Sliced fresh fruit
o A Simple Compote (pages 96–105)
o Toasted seeds, nuts, or coconut (see page 390)
o Ground flax seeds
o Raw hemp seeds
o Citrus zest
o Freeze-dried berries
o Bee pollen

Savory Porridge Toppings

o Thinly sliced scallions or chives
o Toasted seeds and nuts (see page 390)
o Sliced avocado
o Ground flax seeds
o Cold-pressed flax or extra-virgin olive oil
o Fermented vegetables (see pages 192–195)
o Magic Mineral Dust (page 202)
o Crumbled toasted nori (see page 202)
o Tamari
o Steamed greens, squash, or broccoli
o Grated ginger
o Chopped parsley

OPPOSITE: Buckwheat Chai Porridge with Blueberry Compote with Cardamom and Orange(page 97) (top) and with Apricot-Fennel Compote (page 101) and almond milk (see page 71) (bottom)

Millet Porridge

MAKES 4 CUPS | 960 ML | SERVES 4

1 cup (6½ ounces | 185 g) millet, soaked overnight in 2 cups (480 ml) filtered water

4 cups (960 ml) filtered water

Pinch of fine sea salt

Drain and thoroughly rinse the millet (see the sidebar). Transfer it to an upright blender, add the 4 cups (960 ml) water and the salt, and pulse until the grains are coarsely ground. Pour the mixture into a medium pot and bring to a boil over high heat, whisking frequently. Cover the pot, reduce the heat to low, and simmer for 18 to 20 minutes, stirring occasionally with a wooden spoon to prevent sticking, until the porridge is thick and creamy and no longer has a raw taste. (Tasting the mixture is especially important when making millet porridge, as it will taste raw and slightly bitter until it's properly cooked.) Serve hot, with any of the toppings suggested on page 32. Pour leftover porridge into a widemouthed glass jar or other container and allow to cool, then cover tightly and store in the fridge for up to 5 days. To reheat, see page 32.

WASHING MILLET

Millet needs to be washed especially well to remove saponin, a natural bitter coating that acts to protect millet from bugs and other wildlife. (Quinoa has the same coating.) Put the millet in a bowl (or the pot you'll cook it in), fill it with water, and thoroughly swish the millet around with your fingers; drain in a strainer and repeat. This can be done before or after soaking.

Millet-Coconut Porridge with Pear and Cardamom

MAKES ABOUT 4½ CUPS | 1.1 L | SERVES 4

1 recipe Millet Porridge

½ cup (1¼ ounces | 35 g) unsweetened shredded dried coconut

1 teaspoon ground cardamom

1 firm but ripe medium-large pear (8 ounces | 230 g), peeled, cored, and sliced into ½-inch (1.25 cm) slices, plus more for serving

2 teaspoons grated orange zest or lemon zest (optional)

Make the porridge following the instructions for the base recipe, adding the coconut and cardamom to the water from the base recipe and blending until smooth, then adding the drained millet and continuing as directed. Add the pears about 5 minutes before the porridge is done and cook until soft and juicy, then stir in the citrus zest, if using. Serve with sliced pears, as well as any of the sweet toppings suggested on page 32.

Golden Milk Millet Porridge

MAKES ABOUT 5 CUPS | 1.2 L | SERVES 6

½ cup (2½ ounces | 70 g) whole raw almonds, soaked overnight in 2 cups (480 ml) filtered water

One 4-inch (10 cm) piece (1 ounce | 30 g) fresh turmeric, peeled and chopped (finely chopped if using a regular blender), or 1 tablespoon ground turmeric

One 2-inch (5 cm) piece (1 ounce | 30 g) fresh ginger, peeled and chopped (finely chopped if using a regular blender), or 2 teaspoons ground dry ginger

1 teaspoon ground cardamom

1 teaspoon ground cinnamon

½ teaspoon freshly grated nutmeg (see the sidebar on page 43)

⅛ teaspoon freshly ground black pepper

1 tablespoon extra-virgin coconut oil or coconut butter

1 recipe Millet Porridge

Drain and rinse the almonds and transfer them to an upright blender. Add the turmeric, ginger, cardamom, cinnamon, nutmeg, pepper, and coconut oil or butter, along with the water and salt from the base recipe, and blend until smooth. Add the millet and continue as directed, adding an extra 1 cup (240 ml) water when bringing the porridge to a boil. Serve with any of the sweet toppings suggested on page 32.

Savory Millet-Sesame Porridge with Miso

MAKES 4 CUPS | 960 ML | SERVES 4

½ cup (2½ ounces | 70 g) raw unhulled sesame seeds, soaked overnight in 1 cup (240 ml) filtered water

1 recipe Millet Porridge

2 tablespoons (1 ounce | 30 g) unpasteurized mellow white miso, chickpea miso, or sweet white miso, or more to taste

Drain and rinse the sesame seeds and transfer them to an upright blender. Add the water and salt from the base recipe and blend until smooth, then add the drained millet and continue as directed. Once the porridge is cooked, put the miso in a small bowl, add about ¼ cup (60 ml) of the porridge, and stir until a smooth paste forms, then stir into the porridge. Add more miso to taste. Mix well and remove from the heat (don't let it boil, as too much heat will damage the enzymes in miso). Serve with any of the savory toppings suggested on page 32.

Pictured on page 38

Buckwheat Porridge

MAKES ABOUT 4 CUPS | 960 ML | SERVES 4

1 cup (5½ ounces | 160 g) raw buckwheat groats, soaked overnight in 2 cups (480 ml) filtered water

4 cups (960 ml) filtered water

1 teaspoon ground cinnamon or cardamom

Pinch of fine sea salt

Drain the buckwheat in a strainer and rinse thoroughly under running water until it's no longer slimy; drain well. Transfer it to an upright blender, add the 4 cups (960 ml) water, cinnamon, and salt, and pulse until the grains are cracked. Pour into a medium pot and bring to a boil over high heat, whisking frequently. Cover the pot, reduce the heat to low, and simmer for about 15 minutes, stirring occasionally to prevent sticking, until the grains are soft and the porridge is creamy. Serve hot, with any of the toppings suggested on page 32. Pour leftover porridge into a widemouthed glass jar or other container and allow to cool, then cover tightly and store in the fridge for up to 5 days. To reheat, see page 32.

Buckwheat Chai Porridge

MAKES 5 CUPS | 1.2 L | SERVES 4 TO 6

¼ cup (½ ounce | 14 g) loose chai tea or 4 chai tea bags (see Note)

1 recipe Buckwheat Porridge

Filtered water

½ cup (2½ ounces | 70 g) whole raw almonds, soaked overnight in 2 cups (480 ml) filtered water

½ cup (1¼ ounces | 35 g) unsweetened shredded dried coconut

Place the tea in a saucepan. Bring the 4 cups (960 ml) water from the base recipe to a boil and pour over the tea. Brew for 10 minutes, or until nice and strong. Strain the tea into an upright blender (compost the tea leaves or tea bags). You will have slightly less than 4 cups liquid, so add more water to make up the difference. Drain and rinse the almonds and add them to the blender, along with the coconut and the spices and salt from the base recipe. Blend until smooth, then add the drained buckwheat, pulse, and continue with the recipe as directed. If the porridge becomes too thick, add water as necessary. Serve with any of the sweet toppings suggested on page 32. **Pictured on page 33**

NOTE: You can use the chai tea recipe on page 86 here instead of brewing the tea; just add water as needed to get 4 cups (960 ml).

Buckwheat-Cacao Porridge with Walnut and Rose

MAKES 5 CUPS | 1.2 L | SERVES 4 TO 6

½ cup (1¾ ounces | 50 g) raw walnuts, soaked overnight in 2 cups (480 ml) filtered water

1 recipe Buckwheat Porridge, using cinnamon

¼ cup (½ ounce | 16 g) cacao powder (see the sidebar on page 297)

3 tablespoons (¾ ounce | 22 g) mesquite powder (see the sidebar on page 23) or 4 Medjool dates, pitted

1 tablespoon coconut butter or extra-virgin coconut oil

1 tablespoon organic rose water (see the sidebar)

Fresh or dried organic rose petals for garnish (optional; see the sidebar on page 301)

Drain and rinse the walnuts and transfer them to an upright blender. Add the water, cinnamon, and salt from the base recipe, along with the cacao, mesquite or dates, and coconut butter, and blend until smooth. Add the drained buckwheat, pulse, and continue as directed. When the porridge is cooked, stir in the rose water. Serve topped with rose petals, if desired, and any of the sweet toppings suggested on page 32.

ROSE WATER

The rose water found in most grocery stores contains preservatives and flavorings that make it quite strong tasting (although you'll rarely see these ingredients listed). You will need to reduce the amount called for in these recipes by half if you're using one of these rose waters. See Resources (page 392) for my favorite organic Bulgarian rose water.

SWEET AND SAVORY PORRIDGES

Porridges are ideal winter foods. They're warming, soothing, and hearty and can be made sweet or savory. Pictured here, from left to right:

○ Beet-Macadamia Black Rice Porridge with Coconut and Ginger (page 41), topped with toasted coconut, dried raspberries, and Almond-Coconut Milk (page 76)

○ Savory Millet-Sesame Porridge with Miso (page 35), topped with avocado, parsley, and Magic Mineral Dust (page 202)

○ Strawberry-Cardamom Grain-Free Porridge (page 47) with almond milk (see page 71) and Strawberry Goji Compote (page 97)

Black Rice Porridge

MAKES ABOUT 4 CUPS | 960 ML | SERVES 4

¾ cup (4¾ ounces | 135 g)
forbidden black rice, soaked
overnight in 3 cups (720 ml)
filtered water

4 cups (960 ml) filtered water

Pinch of fine sea salt

Drain and rinse the rice and transfer it to an upright blender. Add the
4 cups (960 ml) water and the salt and pulse until the rice is coarsely
ground. Pour into a medium pot and bring to a boil over high heat,
whisking frequently. Cover the pot, reduce the heat to low, and simmer
for 25 to 30 minutes, stirring occasionally to prevent sticking, until the rice
is tender and the porridge is creamy. Remove from the heat and let stand,
covered, for a few minutes; this rest will release any rice that is stuck to
the bottom of the pot. Stir once more and serve with any of the toppings
suggested on page 32. Pour leftover porridge into a widemouthed glass jar
or other container and allow to cool, then cover tightly and store in the
fridge for up to 5 days. To reheat, see page 32.

Beet-Macadamia Black Rice Porridge with Coconut and Ginger

MAKES 5 CUPS | 1.2 L | SERVES 4 TO 6

1 small-medium (4 ounces | 110 g) red beet, peeled and grated

1 cup (3 ounces | 85 g) unsweetened shredded dried coconut

½ cup (2½ ounces | 70 g) raw macadamia nuts (see Note)

One 2-inch (5 cm) piece (1 ounce | 30 g) fresh ginger, peeled and chopped (finely chopped if using a regular blender)

1 recipe Black Rice Porridge

Combine the beet, coconut, macadamia, and ginger in an upright blender, add the water and salt from the base recipe, and blend until smooth. Add the rice and continue as directed. Serve with any of the sweet toppings suggested on page 32.

Pictured on page 38

NOTE: You can substitute cashews for the macadamias if you like.

BLENDING NUTS OR GRAINS WITH WATER

When blending nuts or grains with water, use the measuring marks on your blender to measure the water before adding the nuts or grains; that way, you don't need to use a liquid measuring cup.

Black Rice–Almond Porridge with Golden Raisins, Fennel, and Orange

MAKES 5 CUPS | 1.2 L | SERVES 4 TO 6

½ cup (2½ ounces | 70 g) whole raw almonds, soaked overnight in 2 cups (480 ml) filtered water

2 teaspoons fennel seeds

1 teaspoon ground cardamom

1 recipe Black Rice Porridge

¼ cup (1¼ ounces | 35 g) golden raisins

1 tablespoon grated orange zest

Drain and rinse the almonds and transfer them to an upright blender. Add the fennel seeds, the cardamom, and the water and salt from the base recipe and blend until smooth, then add the rice and continue as directed, adding the golden raisins to the pot along with the rice mixture. When the porridge is cooked, stir in the orange zest. Serve with any of the sweet toppings suggested on page 32.

Whole Oat Porridge

MAKES 4 CUPS | 960 ML | SERVES 4

1 cup (5½ ounces | 160 g) whole oat groats, soaked overnight in 3 cups (720 ml) filtered water

4 cups (960 ml) filtered water

1 teaspoon ground cinnamon

Pinch of fine sea salt

Drain and rinse the oat groats and transfer them to an upright blender. Add the 4 cups (960 ml) water, cinnamon, and salt and pulse until the grains are coarsely ground. Pour into a medium pot and bring to a boil over high heat, whisking frequently. Cover the pot, reduce the heat to low, and simmer for about 20 minutes, stirring occasionally to prevent sticking, until the grains are soft and the porridge is creamy. Serve hot, with any of the toppings suggested on page 32. Pour leftover porridge into a widemouthed glass jar or other container and allow to cool, then cover tightly and store in the fridge for up to 5 days. To reheat, see page 32.

Whole Oat–Apple Porridge with Almonds and Nutmeg

MAKES ABOUT 5 CUPS | 1.2 L | SERVES 4 TO 6

½ cup (2½ ounces | 70 g) whole raw almonds, soaked overnight in 2 cups (480 ml) filtered water

2 teaspoons freshly grated nutmeg (see the sidebar)

1 recipe Whole Oat Porridge

1 medium-large (8 ounces | 230 g) apple, grated (1½ cups)

Drain and rinse the almonds and transfer them to an upright blender. Add the nutmeg, along with the water, cinnamon, and salt from the base recipe, and blend until smooth, then add the drained oats and continue as directed. When the porridge is cooked, stir in the grated apple and cook for 5 minutes more, or until the apple has softened. Serve with any of the sweet toppings suggested on page 32.

NUTMEG

Buy nutmeg whole and grate it as needed. You'll find that the flavor is much less harsh when nutmeg is freshly grated. Although you can purchase a special grater for nutmeg, you can simply use a Microplane zester.

Whole Oat Porridge with Winter Squash and Ginger

MAKES ABOUT 6 CUPS | 1.4 L | SERVES 4 TO 6

One 2-inch (5 cm) piece (1 ounce | 30 g) fresh ginger, peeled and chopped (finely chopped if using a regular blender)

1 recipe Whole Oat Porridge, omitting the cinnamon

3½ cups (1 pound | 455 g) cubed peeled winter squash (¾-inch | 2 cm cubes)

2 teaspoons tamari, or more to taste

Put the ginger in an upright blender, along with the water and salt from the base recipe, and blend until smooth. Add the drained oats and continue as directed. Add the squash to the pot along with the oat mixture and cook as directed until the porridge is creamy and the squash is soft. Add the tamari and adjust the seasoning to taste. Serve with any of the savory toppings suggested on page 32. **Pictured on the following page**

PORRIDGES—HOW TO CUSTOMIZE

Grain	Sweet Porridge	Savory Porridge
Black Rice	Black Rice–Almond Porridge with Golden Raisins, Fennel, and Orange (page 41) + Apricot-Fennel Compote (page 101) + Toasted seeds (see page 390) + Almond milk (see page 71)	Black Rice Porridge (page 40) + Avocado + Lacto-Fermented Radishes (page 195) + Cilantro leaves + Extra-virgin olive oil or flax oil
Buckwheat	Buckwheat-Cacao Porridge with Walnut and Rose (page 37) + Raspberries (fresh or Compote, page 96) + Rose Almond Milk (page 72)	Buckwheat Porridge (page 36, prepared without cinnamon or cardamom) + Steamed broccoli and peas (see pages 170 and 171) + Poached egg (see page 383) + Scallions + Sliced chili or hot sauce + Crumbled feta (optional)
Grain-Free	Cacao-Orange Grain-Free Porridge (page 47) + Spiced Plum-Ginger Compote (page 101) + Orange zest + Rosemary Macadamia and Pumpkin Seed Milk (page 77)	Because of the coconut, this porridge is best served sweet.
Millet	Millet-Coconut Porridge with Pear and Cardamom (page 35) + Sliced pear + Lemon zest + Brazil Nut Milk with Star Anise and Vanilla Bean (page 76)	Savory Millet-Sesame Porridge with Miso (page 35) + Sliced avocado + Sliced scallions or chives + Fermented Carrots with Turmeric and Ginger (page 192) + Magic Mineral Dust (page 202) + Flax oil or olive oil
Whole Oats	Whole Oat–Apple Porridge with Almonds and Nutmeg (page 43) + Cherry Vanilla Compote (page 101) + Cashew milk (see page 71)	Whole Oat Porridge with Winter Squash and Ginger (page 43) + Tamari + Sliced scallions or chives + Chopped parsley + Toasted seeds (see page 390)

OPPOSITE: Whole Oat Porridge with Winter Squash and Ginger

Grain-Free Porridge

MAKES ABOUT 3½ CUPS | 840 ML | SERVES 4

½ cup (2½ ounces | 70 g) whole raw almonds, soaked overnight in 2 cups (480 ml) filtered water

3 cups (720 ml) filtered water

¼ cup (⅔ ounce | 20 g) coconut flour

Pinch of fine sea salt

½ cup (2¼ ounces | 65 g) raw sunflower seeds, soaked overnight in 2 cups (480 ml) filtered water

½ cup (1 ounce | 30 g) unsweetened flaked dried coconut

3 tablespoons (1 ounce | 30 g) whole flax seeds

2 tablespoons (⅔ ounce | 20 g) chia seeds

Drain and rinse the almonds and transfer them to an upright blender. Add the 3 cups (720 ml) water, coconut flour, and salt, and blend until smooth. Drain and rinse the sunflower seeds and add them to the blender, along with the coconut. Pulse until the seeds and coconut are coarsely ground. Pour into a medium pot and bring to a boil over high heat, whisking frequently. Remove from the heat and whisk in the flax and chia seeds until thoroughly combined. Cover the porridge and set aside for 5 minutes to thicken. Whisk the porridge once more and serve with any of the sweet toppings suggested on page 32. Pour leftover porridge into a widemouthed glass jar or other container and allow to cool, then cover tightly and store in the fridge for up to 4 days. To reheat, see page 32.

Strawberry-Cardamom Grain-Free Porridge

MAKES 4 CUPS | 960 ML | SERVES 4 TO 6

1 recipe Grain-Free Porridge, using 2 cups (480 ml) water

2 cups (8 ounces | 230 g) hulled fresh or frozen strawberries

1½ teaspoons ground cardamom

1 teaspoon vanilla extract

Make the porridge following the instructions for the base recipe, adding the strawberries and cardamom to the blender along with the almonds and blending until smooth, then continue as directed. Once the chia and flax seeds have thickened, whisk in the vanilla. Serve with any of the sweet toppings suggested on page 32. **Pictured on page 39**

Cacao-Orange Grain-Free Porridge

MAKES ABOUT 3½ CUPS | 840 ML | SERVES 4

1 recipe Grain-Free Porridge

¼ cup (½ ounce | 16 g) cacao powder (see the sidebar on page 297)

½ teaspoon ground cinnamon

1 tablespoon grated orange zest, plus more for garnish

Make the porridge following the instructions for the base recipe, adding the cacao and cinnamon to the blender along with the almonds and blending until smooth. Continue as directed, whisking in the orange zest with the flax and chia seeds. Serve garnished with orange zest and any of the sweet toppings suggested on page 32.

Gluten-Free Breads

——

Finding healthful commercially made gluten-free bread is nearly impossible. But the flavorful and versatile recipes in this chapter, made with activated grains and seeds and completely flour-free, are breads you can feel good about eating. All of these taste delicious toasted and spread with avocado or nut butter (see pages 112–114) or topped with poached eggs or any of the bean pâtés (see pages 152–157). These loaves keep well, and they can also be sliced and frozen, ready to be toasted for breakfast or a snack.

I made my first version of this type of bread a few years ago after one of my clients discovered a recipe by a talented blogger named Sophie Mackenzie. Her "Unbelievable Bread" is made with soaked quinoa and millet. Since then, I've experimented with recipes using my favorite grains and adding soaked seeds for more protein and texture. In this chapter, you'll find breads made with imaginative combinations like beets and fennel, nori and pumpkin seeds, and carrots and turmeric. Have fun mixing and matching these vibrant loaves with your favorite toppings; see page 60 for suggestions.

Notes

TEXTURE

When avoiding gluten, eggs, and refined starches, it can be a challenge to make whole-grain bread with a good texture. The secret to the moist, satisfying texture of the breads in this chapter is the combination of soaked seeds and grains, rolled oats, and psyllium husks. Psyllium comes from the seeds of an herb called *Plantago ovata* that is mostly grown in India. Containing both soluble and insoluble fiber, it is used medicinally for supporting the gastrointestinal system. When water is added to psyllium husks, they form a thick gel that helps bind the dough in these recipes. Although many people say psyllium has no flavor, it actually can be overpowering when too much is used, so these recipes use a minimal amount. Be sure to buy psyllium husks, not psyllium powder, which usually has an unpleasant taste. You can find psyllium husks in the vitamin section of your local health food store.

Keep in mind that you'll need to soak the seeds and/or grains overnight before making any of these breads.

FLAVOR

The two base recipes, for Seeded Rice Bread and Buckwheat Millet Bread, are the most neutral in flavor and go well with any sweet or savory topping. The recipes are extremely versatile; if you don't have one of the nuts or seeds called for, simply substitute whatever you do have on hand. Once you've made a couple of these recipes, you can use the variations as guides for creating your own custom breads.

ADD-INS

All of these breads are good with olives, nuts, seeds, or dried fruit stirred into the batter. Chopped rehydrated or toasted seaweed can also be stirred in just before baking. If you want to add herbs or spices, it's best to incorporate them when you are blending the grains to ensure even distribution. If you're experimenting with adding vegetables, be careful using ones with a high moisture content as they can make the batter too wet. Grated root vegetables like carrots, beets, sweet potatoes, and parsnips work best.

GARNISHES

Garnishes and toppings like sliced avocado, spreadable cashew or goat cheese, bean pâtés (see pages 152–157), and nut or seed butters (see pages 112–114) with a Simple Compote (pages 96–105) all look striking on the Black Rice–Black Sesame Bread, the Carrot-Turmeric Bread, and the Pumpkin Seed Bread with Greens and Nori. Sprinkling the toppings with Dulse Rose Za'atar (page 201), chopped scallions or parsley, or flaky salt will make them even more attractive.

STORING AND FREEZING

These breads keep incredibly well, and the Seeded Rice Bread and its variations actually improve after a day. In cooler temperatures, you can store these loaves in airtight containers at room temperature for up to 3 days. Well wrapped, they will keep for up to a week in the fridge. The sliced bread freezes perfectly and can then be defrosted in the toaster as needed. Although the loaves containing grated vegetables stay quite moist, these breads are generally best toasted.

Seeded Rice Bread

MAKES ONE 4½ x 8½-INCH | 11.5 x 21 CM LOAF

1½ cups (9¾ ounces | 280 g) short-grain brown rice, soaked overnight in 4 cups (960 ml) filtered water

½ cup raw unhulled sesame, pumpkin, or sunflower seeds (weight depends on the seeds used), soaked overnight with the rice (above)

1 cup (240 ml) filtered water

1 cup (3½ ounces | 100 g) rolled oats

2 tablespoons (¼ ounce | 8 g) psyllium husks

1 tablespoon aluminum-free baking powder

3 tablespoons (45 ml) extra-virgin coconut or olive oil

1 teaspoon fine sea salt

Raw black sesame, sunflower, or pumpkin seeds for sprinkling over loaf

Preheat the oven to 350°F (180°C). Line a 4½ x 8½-inch (11.5 x 21 cm) loaf pan with parchment paper, leaving at least a 1-inch (2.5 cm) overhang on each long side. Set aside. Pour the soaked rice and seeds into a large strainer and rinse well under cold running water. Place the strainer over a bowl and set aside to drain thoroughly.

Transfer the drained rice and seeds to a food processor, add the 1 cup (240 ml) water, oats, psyllium husks, baking powder, oil, and salt, and process until well combined and the grains have broken down but the mixture still has some texture. Scrape the sides and process again. Transfer the batter to the prepared pan, making sure to spread it into the corners. Sprinkle the top with the raw seeds and bake for 40 minutes.

Rotate the pan and bake for another 40 minutes, or until the edges of the bread are golden and have pulled away from the sides of the pan. Use the parchment paper overhang to lift the loaf out of the pan and onto a wire rack to cool. Be sure to cool the bread completely before slicing, or it will still be sticky inside. On the day it is baked, this bread has a very hard crust, but it softens after a day. Store the loaf in an

CONTINUED

airtight container at cool room temperature for up to 3 days or in the fridge for 1 week. You can freeze the sliced bread in an airtight container for up to 3 months. The bread is best eaten lightly toasted.

Black Rice–Black Sesame Bread

MAKES ONE 4½ x 8½-INCH | 11.5 x 21 CM LOAF

1 recipe Seeded Rice Bread, replacing ½ cup (3¼ ounces | 95 g) of the brown rice with the same amount of forbidden black rice and using raw black sesame seeds

Make the bread following the instructions for the base recipe. Top the loaf with black sesame seeds and bake as directed. **Pictured on page 59**

Beet–Fennel Seed Bread

MAKES ONE 4½ x 8½-INCH | 11.5 x 21 CM LOAF

1 recipe Seeded Rice Bread, using sunflower seeds, ¾ cup (180 ml) water, and 1¼ teaspoons salt

1 medium-large (8 ounces | 230 g) red beet, grated (2½ cups)

4 teaspoons (⅙ ounce | 5 g) fennel seeds

Make the bread following the instructions for the base recipe, adding half the grated beet and half the fennel seeds to the food processor along with the rice and sunflower seeds. Process as directed, then transfer the batter to a bowl and stir in the remaining beets and fennel seeds. Bake as directed. **Pictured on page 61**

Pumpkin Seed Bread with Greens and Nori

MAKES ONE 4½ x 8½-INCH | 11.5 x 21 CM LOAF

1 recipe Seeded Rice Bread, using pumpkin seeds, ¾ cup (180 ml) water, and 1¼ teaspoons salt

1 cup (¾ ounce | 22 g) finely chopped kale

2 sheets nori, toasted and crushed (see the sidebar on page 202)

½ cup (2½ ounces | 70 g) raw pumpkin seeds, soaked overnight in 1 cup (240 ml) filtered water

Make the bread following the instructions for the base recipe, adding the kale when processing the rice and seed mixture; transfer the batter to a bowl. Drain and rinse the additional ½ cup pumpkin seeds and stir them into the batter along with the nori. Sprinkle the top of the batter with pumpkin seeds and bake as directed. **Pictured on page 61**

ABOVE AND OPPOSITE: Making Pumpkin Seed Bread with Greens and Nori

Buckwheat Millet Bread

MAKES ONE 4½ x 8½-INCH | 11.5 x 21 CM LOAF

1 cup (5½ ounces | 160 g) raw buckwheat groats, soaked overnight in 4 cups (960 ml) filtered water

½ cup (3¼ ounces | 90 g) millet, soaked with the buckwheat (above)

1 cup (3½ ounces | 100 g) rolled oats

1 cup (240 ml) filtered water

2 tablespoons (¼ ounce | 8 g) psyllium husks

1 tablespoon aluminum-free baking powder

3 tablespoons (45 ml) extra-virgin coconut or olive oil

1¼ teaspoons fine sea salt

Raw seeds for sprinkling

Preheat the oven to 350°F (180°C). Line a 4½ x 8½-inch (11.5 x 21 cm) loaf pan with parchment paper, leaving at least a 1-inch (2.5 cm) overhang on each long side. Set aside. Pour the buckwheat and millet into a large strainer and rinse until the buckwheat is no longer slimy. Set aside to drain thoroughly.

Transfer the soaked grains to a food processor and add the oats, 1 cup (240 ml) water, psyllium husks, baking powder, oil, and salt. Process until combined and the grains have broken down but the mixture still has texture. Scrape the sides and process again. Transfer the batter to the prepared pan, spreading it out well. Sprinkle the top with the seeds and bake for 1 hour and 20 minutes.

The bread is ready when the edges of the loaf are golden and have pulled away from the sides. Use the parchment to lift the loaf out of the pan and onto a wire rack. Be sure to cool the bread completely before slicing, or it will still be sticky inside. Store the loaf in an airtight container at cool room temperature for up to 3 days or in the fridge for 1 week. You can freeze the sliced bread in an airtight container for up to 3 months.

Sunflower–Poppy Seed Bread

MAKES ONE 4½ x 8½-INCH | 11.5 x 21 CM LOAF

1 recipe Buckwheat Millet Bread, replacing the millet with ½ cup (2¼ ounces | 65 g) raw sunflower seeds, soaked overnight with the buckwheat groats

1 cup (4½ ounces | 130 g) raw sunflower seeds, soaked overnight in 1 cup (240 ml) filtered water

2 tablespoons (½ ounce | 15 g) poppy seeds, plus more for sprinkling

Raw sunflower seeds for sprinkling

Make the bread following the instructions for the base recipe, then transfer the batter to a bowl. Drain and rinse the additional sunflower seeds and stir them into the batter along with the poppy seeds. Transfer the batter to the prepared pan, making sure to spread it into the corners, top with poppy and sunflower seeds, and bake as directed. **Pictured on page 61**

Fruit and Nut Bread

MAKES ONE 4½ x 8½-INCH | 11.5 x 21 CM LOAF

½ cup (2½ ounces | 75 g) golden raisins

½ cup (2½ ounces | 70 g) raw pumpkin seeds, soaked overnight in 2 cups (480 ml) filtered water

½ cup (2¼ ounces | 65 g) raw sunflower seeds, soaked overnight with the pumpkin seeds (above)

1 cup (5 ounces | 140 g) whole raw almonds or hazelnuts, soaked overnight in 2 cups (480 ml) filtered water

1 recipe Buckwheat Millet Bread

2 teaspoons ground cinnamon

Put the raisins in a bowl, cover with boiling water, and soak for 5 minutes; drain and set aside. Drain and rinse the seeds. Drain, rinse, and roughly chop the almonds. Make the bread following the instructions for the base recipe, adding the cinnamon when blending the grains. Transfer the batter to a bowl and stir in the drained seeds, chopped nuts, and raisins. Spread into the prepared pan, making sure to spread it into the corners. Bake as directed. **Pictured on the following page**

Carrot-Turmeric Bread

MAKES ONE 4½ x 8½-INCH | 11.5 x 21 CM LOAF

1 recipe Buckwheat Millet Bread

2 teaspoons ground turmeric

2 medium (6 ounces | 115 g) carrots, grated (2½ cups)

Golden flax seeds for sprinkling

Make the bread following the instructions for the base recipe, adding the turmeric when processing the batter. Add half the grated carrots and pulse until just combined, then add the remaining carrots and pulse to incorporate. Transfer the batter to the prepared pan, making sure to spread it into the corners, sprinkle with flax seeds, and bake as directed. **Pictured on page 61**

ABOVE: Fruit and Nut Bread; OPPOSITE: Black Rice-Black Sesame Bread

BREADS—HOW TO CUSTOMIZE

Bread	Toppings
Black Rice–Black Sesame Bread (page 53)	Avocado + Boiled egg (see page 383) + Freshly ground pepper ————————— Roasted tomatoes (see page 179) + Feta or cashew cheese + Chopped parsley
Beet-Fennel Seed Bread (page 53)	Beet and Cashew Butter Bean Pâté (page 155) + Radish microgreens + Flaky sea salt ————————— Fresh goat cheese or cashew cheese + Fennel and Green Cabbage Kraut (page 194)
Pumpkin Seed Bread with Greens and Nori (page 53)	Avocado + Poached egg (see page 383) + Scallions ————————— Herbed Butter Bean Pâté with Leeks and Spinach (page 155) + Capers

Bread	Toppings
Sunflower-Poppy Seed Bread (page 57)	Almond and Sunflower Butter with Coconut (page 113) + Blueberry Compote with Cardamom and Orange (page 97) ————————— Pine Nut Chickpea Pâté with Rosemary (page 157) + Sliced scallions
Fruit and Nut Bread (page 57)	Cacao-Hazelnut Butter with Warm Spices (page 113) + Flaky sea salt ————————— Fresh goat cheese or cashew cheese + Sliced fresh pears + Flaky sea salt + Extra-virgin olive oil
Carrot-Turmeric Bread (page 57)	Cashew Chickpea Pâté with Turmeric, Chili, and Lime (page 157) + Extra-virgin olive oil + Freshly ground pepper ————————— Sliced avocado + Fermented Carrots with Turmeric and Ginger (page 192)

OPPOSITE, CLOCKWISE FROM TOP RIGHT: Sunflower–Poppy Seed Bread; Black Rice–Black Sesame Bread topped with avocado and boiled egg; Sunflower–Poppy Seed Bread topped with Pine Nut Chickpea Pâté with Rosemary; Beet–Fennel Seed Bread topped with Beet and Cashew Butter Bean Pâté; Carrot-Turmeric Bread topped with Cashew Chickpea Pâté with Turmeric, Chili, and Lime; Pumpkin Seed Bread with Greens and Nori topped with Herbed Butter Bean Pâté with Leeks and Spinach

Nut and Seed Milks and Drinks

——

Filled with flavor and natural goodness, homemade nut and seed milks are a world away from the store-bought versions. The flavor of most commercial almond milks is almost unrecognizable (and after you take another look at the ingredients lists, you probably won't want to consume them again either—nut milks have some of the longest ingredients lists of all packaged milk alternatives). Once you learn the basic formula for making your own nut and seed milks, you will be privy to a world of elevated breakfasts, delectable drinks or snacks, and sublime flavors.

These milks can be used in an endless variety of delicious ways, from transforming your morning bowl of oatmeal to providing a refreshing or warming pick-me-up in the afternoon. Make a batch of plain almond milk (see page 71) once or twice a week to use in all kinds of lattes, from matcha or turmeric to dandelion and beet hot chocolate (all recipes included in this chapter). In the summer months, the nut milks can be added to iced teas and blend beautifully with floral waters, like rose and orange blossom.

When you know you'll be eating porridge or granola or making smoothies during the week, prepare an extra batch of plain nut or seed milk to use for these, but don't strain it; the pulp provides sustenance and fiber. Or liven up your breakfast routine with one of the flavored nut milks. There are infinite opportunities to be creative with the recipes in this chapter—while boosting your daily nutritional intake at the same time.

Notes

TEXTURE

There are two ways to enjoy nut or seed milk: unstrained, with the fiber from the whole nuts or seeds, which is best suited to eating with porridge or granola or making smoothies, and strained, which has a silky-smooth texture that is optimal for drinking. For the best results with the strained milks, you may want to invest in a nut-milk bag (see Resources, page 393). However, you can also use a thin kitchen towel (sometimes called a grain sack) or several layers of fine cheesecloth for straining the milk. Almonds have the most pulp after straining, and you can save it for making grain-free crackers (see pages 282–284). Other nuts, like cashews, pistachios, walnuts, and macadamias, almost completely dissolve when you blend them with water, so you'll be left with very little pulp, but if you plan to sip these milks, do strain them.

There are a couple of ways you can adjust the consistency of strained nut milks. One is to foam them in a milk frother. Not all milks foam well; almond milks are the most reliable. I find that milks made with certified raw almonds (usually from Spain or Italy) that have not been pasteurized do not foam as well as those made with almonds from California (these almonds are labeled as raw but are required by law to be pasteurized—unless you're buying directly from the almond grower). The foam, perhaps along with a compote (see pages 96–105), will make your breakfast seem like an indulgent treat. Another way to change the consistency is to blend the nut milk in an upright blender until frothy. If you add a little coconut butter or coconut oil, the foam will be richer and thicker. Adding cacao, mesquite, or another superfood powder will also thicken the milk. After it is chilled, the Superfood Chocolate Milk has a delicious mousse-like layer on top.

Although I recommend a 1:4 ratio of nuts to water for all these nut and seed milk recipes, you can increase the amount of nuts or seeds if you want a richer milk. You might want to try that for finishing soups or when you are making a vegan béchamel or dessert cream. On the other hand, because high-quality organic raw nuts are expensive, these milks can be stretched by adding an extra cup (240 ml) of water (but the almond milks won't foam in that case).

MILK FOAMING

Homemade almond milk foams quite well in an electric milk frother (see Resources, page 393) and is perfect for making any of the lattes in this chapter. Not all frothers can hold a full cup (240 ml) of milk, so if that is the case, you can halve these recipes or simply use the blender method.

FLAVOR

Flavoring these strained nut milk bases is excellent fun. You can create a custom flavor each time you blend a batch. If you want to flavor the whole batch of milk, you can add any fibrous roots, like fresh ginger or turmeric, when blending the nuts and water, then strain it all at once. Beware when using turmeric, though; it will stain your nut-milk bag bright yellow, so add the turmeric after straining (it will break down enough in a high-powered blender). Powders like matcha tea, cacao, and maca; ground spices; vanilla bean seeds; and freeze-dried fruits can all be added to strained nut milk and simply blended to combine.

If you do not want to include sweeteners in your everyday meals, here are a few tricks to subtly add sweetness without using dates, honey, maple syrup, or other concentrated sweeteners.

- Add a large handful of shredded dried coconut to the nuts when blending.
- Blend a spoonful of coconut butter into the strained milk.

- Replace 1 cup (240 ml) or more of the water with raw coconut water.
- Add a generous dash of vanilla extract to the strained nut milk.
- Add a pinch of cinnamon (if it will complement the other flavors).

If you want to flavor a nut milk but are undecided about how to do so, first taste it plain and think about what it is you're craving. Perhaps you'd like a splash of rose water in your walnut milk, or maybe a pinch of freshly grated nutmeg along with some vanilla extract. A tablespoon of raw cacao with a spoonful of coconut butter and the seeds of half a vanilla bean will add a special touch to your nut milk without making it overly chocolaty. Taste as you go, and keep adding until you are happy with the flavor.

You can also add subtle and unusual flavor notes to a nut milk by replacing the water with brewed tea, which will infuse it with a whole new taste and step up your everyday breakfasts. Try chai, Earl Grey, sencha, mint, rose, nettle, fennel, or ginger tea for your next batch.

Another way to enrich the flavor of a simple nut milk is to toast the nuts before blending. This results in a more luxurious milk with a more pronounced flavor, but keep in mind that toasted nuts cannot be activated to remove the phytic acid (see the sidebar below). For a delicious "toasted" flavor and a highly nutritious drink, use activated nuts (soaked, drained, and dehydrated nuts, also called sprouted nuts) in place of the soaked nuts; these are also convenient to have on hand when you've forgotten to soak your nuts. You would need a dehydrator to make your own, but activated or sprouted nuts can be purchased ready to use (see Resources, page 393).

ADD-INS

There are a couple of tricks you might want to try to add color to nut milks. If you are making a rose milk by using rose tea as the base or adding rose water to the strained nut milk (see Rose Almond Milk), you will not achieve a soft rosy color without some help. Blending in a little freeze-dried beet juice powder will give the milk a lovely pink tinge. When making pistachio or pumpkin seed milk, you might want to boost the green color by adding a dash of matcha tea powder. You can create almost any color nut milk you like using freeze-dried fruits, vegetables, or fresh or powdered turmeric.

Adaptogens like ashwagandha and mushroom powders can all be blended directly into your nut milk. Because some have strong flavors, start with less than the recommended dose given on the package. Most mushroom powders go well with cacao, and it will also help tame some of the more bitter adaptogen powders. See the Adaptogen Latte Mix for an easy way to add adaptogens and superfoods to your milks.

Steamed vegetables like carrots, sweet potato, or squash (see pages 170–171) can be added to strained

PHYTIC ACID

Phytic acid is an enzyme inhibitor that is present in the skin of whole grains, beans, nuts, and seeds; it also protects these ingredients from sprouting until they are exposed to water. The aforementioned foods are some of the most nutrient-dense ingredients available, but if the phytic acid is not deactivated, the nutrients can't be released or properly absorbed. Presoaking whole grains, beans, nuts, and seeds breaks down the phytic acid, thereby activating the nutrients and making them easier to digest. You can further reduce the presence of phytic acid by adding an acidic medium like unpasteurized vinegar, lemon juice, or whey along with the salt to the soaking water.

nut milk for a lovely creamy texture and naturally sweet flavor; add them to nut milks after straining. All these vegetables go well with warm spices such as cinnamon, nutmeg, and ginger. They create a thick and delicious milk to fold into your morning oats in the colder months.

Another easy way to increase the nutrient value is to whisk a tablespoon or two of chia seeds into the strained milk. This helps give the milk more body while boosting the protein and omega-3 content. Whisk well when adding them to prevent clumping, and then again before drinking. If you incorporate chia seeds into a thicker milk like the Superfood Chocolate Milk, they will be suspended and not sink to the bottom, creating a pudding.

Don't flavor nut milks with fresh fruit unless you will drink the milk within a day. If you're tempted to add fresh fruit, try the Strawberry Almond Milk when local strawberries arrive.

GARNISHES

Nut and seed milks really don't need any garnishes, but it can be fun to float an edible flower or rose petal on top, or to add a sprig of mint, rosemary, or lavender if the milk is infused with one of these. For thicker milks, you can dust the top with a colorful powder such as turmeric, rose, cacao, or matcha, or freeze-dried berry dust.

STORING AND FREEZING

Stored in tightly sealed glass jars or bottles in the fridge, these nut and seed milks keep well for 5 days. If you're using just a little of the milk at a time, it's a good idea to divide it among a few jars so the whole batch is not continually exposed to air when you open the container. Nut and seed milks can be frozen for up to 3 months; depending on the fat content of the nuts, or if you added coconut butter or oil, the milk may need to be blended again once defrosted. When freezing, be sure to leave a good 1½ inches (3.75 cm) headspace above the milk.

If you'd like to have a stash of soaked nuts on hand for making these milks on the spur of the moment, you can freeze soaked and drained nuts and seeds in an airtight container for up to 3 months.

NUT AND SEED SOAKING TIMES

Soak in 2 cups (480 ml) filtered water. Any nuts and seeds called for in the recipes that don't appear in the chart below do not need to be soaked. Soaked nuts and seeds can be drained, rinsed, and frozen for up to 3 months.

1 Cup Nuts/Seeds	Weight	Time
Almonds	5 ounces (140 g)	10 to 12 hours
Brazil Nuts	4½ ounces (130 g)	10 to 12 hours
Hazelnuts	4½ ounces (130 g)	10 to 12 hours
Pecans	3½ ounces (100 g)	6 to 8 hours
Pistachios	4½ ounces (130 g)	6 to 8 hours
Pumpkin Seeds	5 ounces (140 g)	10 to 12 hours
Sesame Seeds (Black or Unhulled)	4½ ounces (130 g)	10 to 12 hours
Sunflower Seeds	4½ ounces (130 g)	10 to 12 hours
Walnuts	3½ ounces (100 g)	6 to 8 hours

USING NUT AND SEED MILKS

Nut and seed milks are endlessly useful for adding richness, flavor, and color to breakfasts of all kinds. They also make a great snack and are an ideal healthy afternoon pick-me-up. Plain nut or seed milk can be used to enrich soups, sauces, and other savory dishes. Pictured here from left to right:

BACK ROW

○ Rosemary Macadamia and Pumpkin Seed Milk (page 77)

○ Brazil Nut Milk with Star Anise and Vanilla Bean (page 76)

○ Cardamom–Pumpkin Seed Milk (page 72)

MIDDLE ROW

○ Carob Vanilla Milk with Mint (page 77)

○ Strawberry Almond Milk (page 72)

○ Superfood Chocolate Milk (page 91)

○ Matcha Almond Milk (page 72)

○ Maca-Cinnamon Hazelnut Milk (page 73)

○ Pumpkin-Nutmeg Almond Milk (page 73)

○ Cacao-Mesquite Walnut Milk (page 73)

○ Golden Milk (page 88)

FRONT ROW

○ Black Sesame Milk (page 76)

○ Rose Almond Milk (page 72)

Nut or Seed Milk

MAKES 4 CUPS | 960 ML | SERVES 4 TO 8

1 cup whole raw nuts or seeds
(weights will vary; see Nut and
Seed Soaking Times on page 67),
soaked overnight in 2 cups
(480 ml) filtered water

4 cups (960 ml) filtered water

Pinch of fine sea salt

Set a strainer over a medium bowl and line it with a nut-milk bag, several layers of cheesecloth, or a thin kitchen towel (sometimes called a "grain sack"); set aside. Drain and rinse the nuts or seeds and transfer them to an upright blender. Add the 4 cups (960 ml) water and the salt and blend on high speed until completely smooth, about 45 seconds. Pour the milk into the lined strainer, gather the edges of the bag or cloth together, and gently squeeze the milk into the bowl until as much of the liquid as possible is extracted and you are left with dry pulp. (You can reserve almond pulp to make crackers [see pages 282–284]; it can be kept in the fridge for up to 5 days or frozen for up to 3 months.) The milk is ready to serve immediately. To store, pour the strained milk into a glass jar, seal, and store in the fridge for up to 5 days. Shake well before using.

INSTANT NUT MILK

You can still make a nut milk even if you've forgotten to soak nuts or seeds overnight. Simply follow the recipe above, but use raw cashews, macadamia nuts, hemp seeds, or a combination, as these nuts and seeds don't require soaking. Be sure to blend until completely smooth, and follow the directions above for straining and storing. One-half cup nut butter can also be used in place of the soaked nuts or seeds.

Strawberry Almond Milk

MAKES 2 CUPS | 480 ML | SERVES 2 TO 4

2 cups (480 ml) almond milk, made using the Nut or Seed Milk base recipe

1 cup (5 ounces | 140 g) fresh strawberries, hulled

1 teaspoon vanilla extract

Combine the almond milk, strawberries, and vanilla in an upright blender and blend until smooth. Serve immediately, or refrigerate and serve chilled. The strawberry milk can be stored for 1 day in the fridge. **Pictured on page 68**

Rose Almond Milk

MAKES 2 CUPS | 480 ML | SERVES 4

2 cups (480 ml) almond milk, made using the Nut or Seed Milk base recipe

2 teaspoons organic rose water (see the sidebar on page 37), plus more to taste, or 1 drop pure rose oil

1 teaspoon coconut butter

1 teaspoon vanilla extract

⅛ teaspoon beet juice powder (see Resources, page 392), plus more as needed for desired color

Fresh or dried organic rose petals for garnish (optional; see the sidebar on page 301)

Combine the almond milk, rose water, coconut butter, vanilla, and beet juice powder in an upright blender and blend until smooth. Add more beet juice powder and rose powder to get the desired color and taste. Serve the milk chilled or warmed, garnished with dried rose petals, if desired. **Pictured on page 62**

Cardamom–Pumpkin Seed Milk

MAKES 2 CUPS | 480 ML | SERVES 2 TO 4

2 cups (480 ml) pumpkin seed milk, made using the Nut or Seed Milk base recipe

¼ teaspoon ground cardamom

2 teaspoons coconut butter

¼ teaspoon ceremonial-grade matcha tea powder (see Resources, page 392)

½ teaspoon vanilla extract

Combine the pumpkin seed milk, cardamom, coconut butter, matcha, and vanilla in an upright blender and blend until smooth. Serve immediately, or refrigerate for up to 5 days. **Pictured on page 69**

Matcha Almond Milk

MAKES 2 CUPS | 480 ML | SERVES 2 TO 4

2 cups (480 ml) almond milk, made using the Nut or Seed Milk base recipe

2 teaspoons ceremonial-grade matcha tea powder (see Resources, page 392)

1 teaspoon coconut butter

½ teaspoon vanilla extract

Combine the almond milk, matcha, coconut butter, and vanilla in an upright blender and blend until smooth. Serve immediately, or refrigerate for up to 5 days. **Pictured on page 69**

Pumpkin-Nutmeg Almond Milk

MAKES 2 CUPS | 480 ML | SERVES 4

1½ cups (360 ml) almond milk, made using the Nut or Seed Milk base recipe

½ cup (3¾ ounces | 105 g) mashed squash (recipe follows)

1 teaspoon vanilla extract

½ teaspoon freshly grated nutmeg (see the sidebar on page 43)

¼ teaspoon ground cinnamon

Combine the almond milk, mashed squash, vanilla, nutmeg, and cinnamon in an upright blender and blend until completely smooth. Serve immediately, or refrigerate for up to 3 days. **Pictured on page 69**

NOTE: This milk is fantastic stirred into plain oatmeal or porridge.

Mashed Squash

MAKES 2 CUPS | 15 OUNCES | 425 G

½ medium winter squash, such as kabocha, Red Kuri, or buttercup (1¼ pounds | 565 g), seeded, peeled, and cut into 1-inch (2.5 cm) dice (about 4 cups)

Set up a steamer following the instructions on page 170. Steam the squash for 10 to 15 minutes, or until soft. Transfer to a bowl and thoroughly mash with a fork. Store the squash in an airtight container in the fridge for up to 4 days.

Maca-Cinnamon Hazelnut Milk

MAKES 2 CUPS | 480 ML | SERVES 4

2 cups (480 ml) hazelnut milk, made using the Nut or Seed Milk base recipe

1 teaspoon ground cinnamon

2 teaspoons gelatinized maca powder (see Resources, page 393)

1 teaspoon vanilla extract

Combine the hazelnut milk, cinnamon, maca, and vanilla in an upright blender and blend until completely smooth. Serve immediately, or refrigerate for up to 5 days. **Pictured on page 69**

Cacao-Mesquite Walnut Milk

MAKES 2 CUPS | 480 ML | SERVES 4

2 cups (480 ml) walnut milk, made using the Nut or Seed Milk base recipe

3 tablespoons (⅖ ounce | 12 g) cacao powder (see the sidebar on page 297)

2 tablespoons (½ ounce | 15 g) mesquite powder (see the sidebar on page 23)

1 tablespoon coconut butter

2 teaspoons vanilla extract

2 Medjool dates, pitted

Combine the walnut milk, cacao, mesquite, coconut butter, vanilla, and dates in an upright blender and blend until completely smooth. Serve immediately, or refrigerate for up to 4 days. **Pictured on page 69**

NUT MILKS—HOW TO CUSTOMIZE

Nut or Seed	Flavorings
Almond	Matcha, rose water, cacao, carob, turmeric, vanilla, dried berries (such as goji, raspberry, blueberry, or strawberry), cardamom, nutmeg, steamed squash; Earl Grey, mint, or sencha tea in place of water; coffee or dandelion coffee in place of half the water
Brazil Nut	Vanilla, coconut butter, dates, allspice, star anise, ginger
Cashew	Turmeric, matcha, vanilla, cinnamon, coconut butter, cacao, cardamom, rose water, chai tea in place of water, spirulina, dried berries (goji, raspberry, strawberry, or blueberry)
Hazelnut	Cacao, maca, mesquite, cinnamon, dates, orange blossom water
Hemp Seed	Coconut butter, macadamia, vanilla, cardamom, rose water, dried berries (goji, raspberry, strawberry, or blueberry), spirulina
Macadamia	Rose water, matcha, vanilla, cacao, cinnamon, ginger, carob, turmeric, dried berries (goji, raspberry, strawberry, or blueberry); rosemary, mint, or fennel tea in place of water
Pecan	Mesquite, cacao, ginger, cinnamon, dates, maca, nutmeg, coffee or dandelion coffee in place of half the water
Pistachio	Matcha, vanilla, peppermint oil or mint tea in place of water
Pumpkin Seed	Matcha, cardamom, vanilla, rosemary tea in place of water
Sesame Seed	Dates, ginger, vanilla, cinnamon, ginger, rose water, dried berries (raspberry or strawberry)
Sunflower Seed	Vanilla, coconut butter, rose water
Walnut	Cacao, dates, cinnamon, maca, nutmeg, rose water, orange blossom water, mesquite

Almond-Coconut Milk

MAKES 4 CUPS | 960 ML | SERVES 4 TO 8

1 cup (5 ounces | 140 g) whole raw almonds, soaked overnight in 2 cups (480 ml) filtered water

1 cup (3 ounces | 85 g) unsweetened shredded dried coconut

4 cups (960 ml) filtered water

Pinch of fine sea salt

Set a strainer over a bowl and line it with a nut-milk bag, layers of cheesecloth, or a thin kitchen towel; set aside. Drain and rinse the almonds and transfer them to an upright blender. Add the coconut, 4 cups (960 ml) water, and salt and blend until smooth. Pour into the lined strainer, gather the edges of the bag or cloth together, and gently squeeze the milk into the bowl until you've extracted as much liquid as possible. (Compost the pulp.) Serve immediately, or pour into a glass jar, seal, and refrigerate for up to 5 days. Shake well before using.

Black Sesame Milk

MAKES 2 CUPS | 480 ML | SERVES 4

¼ cup (1¼ ounces | 35 g) raw black sesame seeds, soaked overnight in 1 cup (240 ml) filtered water

¼ cup (1¼ ounces | 35 g) whole raw almonds, soaked overnight in 1 cup (240 ml) filtered water

2 cups (480 ml) filtered water

Pinch of fine sea salt

2 Medjool dates, pitted (optional)

1 teaspoon vanilla extract

1 teaspoon coconut butter

Set a strainer over a bowl and line it with a nut-milk bag, layers of cheesecloth, or a thin kitchen towel; set

aside. Drain and rinse the sesame seeds and almonds and transfer them to an upright blender. Add the 2 cups (480 ml) water and the salt and blend until smooth, then pour into the lined strainer. Gather the edges of the bag or cloth together and gently squeeze the milk into the bowl until you've extracted as much liquid as possible. (Compost the pulp.) Rinse the blender, then add the strained milk, the dates, if using, the vanilla, and the coconut butter and blend until smooth. Serve immediately, or pour into a glass jar, seal, and refrigerate for up to 4 days. Shake well before serving. **Pictured on page 68**

Brazil Nut Milk with Star Anise and Vanilla Bean

MAKES 2 CUPS | 480 ML | SERVES 2 TO 4

2 cups (480 ml) filtered water

8 whole star anise

¼ cup (2¼ ounces | 65 g) raw Brazil nuts, soaked overnight in ½ cup (240 ml) unfiltered water

Pinch of fine sea salt

1 Medjool date, pitted

½ teaspoon vanilla extract

¼ vanilla bean, split, seeds scraped out and reserved, pod reserved for another use

Put the water and star anise in a small pot and bring to a boil over high heat. Cover, reduce the heat to low, and simmer for 1 minute. Remove from the heat, remove the lid, and set aside to steep for at least 10 minutes.

Set a strainer over a bowl and line it with a nut-milk bag, layers of cheesecloth, or a thin kitchen towel; set aside. Strain the star anise tea into an upright blender. Drain and rinse the Brazil nuts and add them to the blender along with the salt. Blend until smooth. Pour into the lined strainer, gather the edges of the bag or cloth together, and gently squeeze the milk into the bowl until you've extracted as much liquid as possible. (Compost the pulp.) Rinse the blender, then add the Brazil nut–star anise milk, date, vanilla extract, and vanilla seeds and blend until smooth. Serve immediately, or pour into a glass jar, seal, and refrigerate for up to 4 days. Shake well before serving. **Pictured on page 69**

Carob Vanilla Milk with Mint

MAKES 2 CUPS | 480 ML | SERVES 2 TO 4

6 large sprigs (½ ounce | 15 g) fresh mint

2 cups (480 ml) boiling filtered water

½ cup (2½ ounces | 70 g) whole raw almonds, soaked overnight in 1 cup (240 ml) filtered water

Pinch of fine sea salt

5 tablespoons (1 ounce | 30 g) carob powder

1 tablespoon coconut butter

2 teaspoons vanilla extract

Put the mint in a large jar. Place a metal spoon in the jar (this will prevent it from cracking), pour in the boiling water, push the mint down into the water, and steep for 10 minutes.

Set a strainer over a bowl and line it with a nut-milk bag, layers of cheesecloth, or a thin kitchen towel; set aside. Strain the mint tea into an upright blender. Drain and rinse the almonds and add them to the blender along with the salt. Blend until smooth. Pour into the lined strainer, gather the edges of the bag or cloth together, and gently squeeze the milk into the bowl until you've extracted as much liquid as possible. (Compost the pulp.) Rinse the blender, add the mint-almond milk, carob, coconut butter, and vanilla, and blend until smooth. Serve immediately, or pour into a glass jar, seal, and refrigerate for up to 4 days. Shake well before serving. **Pictured on page 68**

Rosemary Macadamia and Pumpkin Seed Milk

MAKES 2 CUPS | 480 ML | SERVES 2 TO 4

5 large sprigs (½ ounce | 15 g) rosemary, roughly chopped

2 cups (480 ml) boiling filtered water

¼ cup (1¼ ounces | 35 g) raw pumpkin seeds, preferably Austrian (see Resources, page 393), soaked overnight in ½ cup (120 ml) filtered water

¼ cup (1¼ ounces | 35 g) raw macadamia nuts

Pinch of fine sea salt

½ teaspoon vanilla extract

1 teaspoon raw honey (optional)

Put the rosemary in a large jar. Place a metal spoon in the jar (this will prevent it from cracking), pour in the boiling water, push the rosemary down into the water, and steep for 10 minutes.

Set a strainer over a bowl and line it with a nut-milk bag, layers of cheesecloth, or a thin kitchen towel; set aside. Strain the rosemary tea into an upright blender. Drain and rinse the pumpkin seeds and add them to the blender along with the macadamia nuts and salt and blend until smooth. Pour into the lined strainer, gather the edges of the bag or cloth together, and gently squeeze the milk into the bowl until you've extracted as much liquid as possible. (Compost the pulp.) Stir the vanilla into the milk. If using the honey, rinse the blender, add the strained milk and honey, and blend until well combined. Serve immediately, or pour into a glass jar, seal, and refrigerate for up to 5 days. Shake well before serving. **Pictured on page 68**

NUT MILK LATTES

Matcha Latte

MAKES ABOUT ¾ CUP | 180 ML | SERVES 1

1 teaspoon ceremonial-grade matcha tea powder (see Resources, page 392)

½ cup (120 ml) almond milk, made using the Nut or Seed Milk base recipe

¼ cup (60 ml) boiled and slightly cooled filtered water (170°F | 77°C)

Sift the matcha into a wide cup or a small bowl. Heat the almond milk in a milk frother (see Note). As it heats, pour the hot water over the matcha and whisk vigorously until frothy. Pour in the foamed milk and serve immediately. **Pictured on the following page**

NOTE: If you don't have a milk frother, warm the almond milk in a small saucepan over medium heat; remove from the heat just before it simmers and pour into an upright blender. Add the matcha and hot water and blend until foamy. This latte can also be made with a full cup (240 ml) of almond milk and no water.

Pink Chai Latte

MAKES ABOUT 1 CUP | 240 ML | SERVES 1

1 cup (240 ml) almond milk, made using the Nut or Seed Milk base recipe

1 tablespoon Pink Chai Latte Mix (recipe follows)

Foam the almond milk and latte mix in a milk frother. Pour into a cup and serve hot. **Pictured on page 81**

OPPOSITE: Matcha tea powder; RIGHT: Pink Chai Latte Mix

NOTE: If you don't have a milk frother, or if yours is not large enough to hold a cup of milk, warm the almond milk in a small saucepan over medium heat; once it is simmering, pour into an upright blender, add the latte mix, and blend until frothy. Serve immediately.

Pink Chai Latte Mix

MAKES ABOUT ⅓ CUP | 1½ OUNCES | 45 G, ENOUGH FOR 5 SERVINGS

¼ cup (1¼ ounces | 35 g) beet juice powder (see Resources, page 392)

2 tablespoons (¼ ounce | 8 g) ground ginger

1 teaspoon ground cinnamon

1 teaspoon ground cardamom

¼ teaspoon ground allspice

Combine the beet juice powder, ginger, cinnamon, cardamom, and allspice in a small jar or bowl and stir well. Store in an airtight jar for up to 2 months.

FROM LEFT TO RIGHT: Adaptogen Dandelion Latte, Matcha Lattes, Beet Hot Chocolate, Turmeric Latte, Iced Earl Grey Tea with Almond Milk and Rose Water, almond milk, Pink Chai Latte, Turmeric Latte Mix

Dandelion Chai Latte

MAKES 1 CUP | 240 ML | SERVES 1

½ cup (120 ml) Dandelion Chai Latte Mix
(recipe follows)

½ cup (120 ml) almond milk, made using the Nut or
Seed Milk base recipe

Heat the dandelion chai mix in a small saucepan over
high heat until simmering and pour into a mug. Foam
the almond milk in a milk frother, add to the mug,
and serve immediately.

NOTE: If you don't have a milk frother,
combine the chai mix and almond milk in a
small saucepan and bring to a simmer over
high heat. Pour into an upright blender and
blend until frothy. Serve immediately. If using
this method, you can add coconut butter, as
in the Dandelion Latte, if you like.

Dandelion Chai Latte Mix

MAKES ABOUT 5 CUPS | 1.2 L, ENOUGH FOR
10 SERVINGS

6 cups (1.4 l) filtered water

One 2-inch (5 cm) piece (1 ounce | 30 g)
fresh ginger, peeled and roughly chopped
(about 2 tablespoons)

2 tablespoons (⅓ ounce | 10 g) cardamom pods

2 cinnamon sticks, broken up

8 whole star anise

10 whole cloves

½ teaspoon black peppercorns

3 tablespoons (¾ ounce | 22 g) roasted dandelion
root granules (see Resources, page 392)

Combine the water, ginger, cardamom, cinnamon,
star anise, cloves, and peppercorns in a medium pot

and bring to a boil over high heat. Cover, reduce the
heat, and simmer for 10 minutes. Add the dandelion
root granules and simmer for another 10 minutes.
Remove from the heat and allow to cool. Strain into
glass jars, seal tightly, and store in the fridge for up
to 2 weeks.

Dandelion Latte

MAKES 1 CUP | 240 ML | SERVES 1

½ cup (120 ml) Dandelion Coffee (recipe follows)

½ cup (120 ml) almond milk, made using the Nut or
Seed Milk base recipe

1 to 2 teaspoons coconut butter (see Note)

Combine the dandelion coffee and almond milk in
a small saucepan and bring to a simmer over medium-
high heat. Pour into an upright blender, add the
coconut butter, and blend until frothy. Pour into a
cup and serve immediately.

NOTE: Store-bought coconut butter has a
finer texture than homemade coconut butter
and works better here.

Dandelion Coffee

MAKES ABOUT 5½ CUPS | 1.3 L | SERVES 6 TO 10

6 cups (1.4 l) filtered water

3 tablespoons (¾ ounce | 22 g) roasted dandelion
root granules (see Resources, page 392)

Combine the water and dandelion root granules in a
medium pot and bring to a boil over high heat. Cover,
reduce the heat to low, and simmer for 10 minutes.
Strain and serve, or let cool and store in tightly sealed
glass jars in the fridge for up to 2 weeks. Reheat
before serving.

Mocha Dandelion Latte

MAKES 1 CUP | 240 ML | SERVES 1

½ cup (120 ml) Dandelion Coffee (opposite)

½ cup (120 ml) almond milk, made using the Nut or Seed Milk base recipe

1 teaspoon chopped cacao butter (see Resources, page 393)

1 teaspoon high-quality cacao powder, plus more for dusting (see the sidebar on page 297)

Heat the dandelion coffee and almond milk in a small saucepan over high heat until the mixture simmers. Pour into an upright blender, add the cacao butter and cacao powder, and blend until frothy. Pour into a mug, dust the top with cacao powder, and serve immediately.

NOTE: If you have a milk frother, you can use it to foam the almond milk. While it foams, bring the dandelion coffee to a simmer in a small saucepan, then pour into a mug and stir in the cacao butter and cacao powder until dissolved. Top with the foamed milk and serve dusted with cacao powder.

Adaptogen Dandelion Latte

MAKES 1 CUP | 240 ML | SERVES 1

½ cup (120 ml) almond milk, made using the Nut or Seed Milk base recipe

½ cup (120 ml) Dandelion Coffee (opposite; see Note)

1 scant tablespoon (⅕ ounce | 6 g) Adaptogen Latte Mix (recipe follows)

1 teaspoon coconut butter

¼ teaspoon vanilla extract

Bring the almond milk and dandelion coffee to a simmer in a small saucepan over high heat. Meanwhile, put the adaptogen latte mix, coconut butter, and vanilla in an upright blender. Pour in the simmering milk mixture and blend until foamy. Pour into a mug and serve immediately. **Pictured on page 80**

NOTE: If you don't have brewed dandelion coffee, you can replace it with additional almond milk and 1 tablespoon high-quality raw cacao powder.

Adaptogen Latte Mix

MAKES 1½ CUPS | 5¼ OUNCES | 150 G, ENOUGH FOR 24 SERVINGS

½ cup (3 ounces | 85 g) gelatinized maca powder (see Resources, page 393)

¼ cup (⅔ ounce | 20 g) ashwagandha powder (see Resources, page 392)

¼ cup (¾ ounce | 22 g) reishi mushroom powder (see Resources, page 392)

¼ cup (½ ounce | 15 g) chaga mushroom powder (see Resources, page 392)

2 tablespoons (⅕ ounce | 6 g) ground cinnamon

2 tablespoons (⅛ ounce | 4 g) freshly grated nutmeg (see the sidebar on page 43)

Combine the maca, ashwagandha, reishi, chaga, cinnamon, and nutmeg in a small bowl and stir well to combine. Store in an airtight jar in a cool place for up to 6 months. **Pictured on page 85**

ADAPTOGENS

An adaptogen is an herb, a plant, or a mushroom that enhances the body's adaptive response to stress by helping to restore balance and support normal immune function. Some examples of adaptogens are ashwagandha, chaga mushrooms, ginseng, maca, reishi mushrooms, rhodiola, and tulsi. The ones used in the book are explained here.

Ashwagandha

Ashwagandha is a perennial herb native to India that is used in Ayurvedic medicine. The root is dried and ground into a powder that can be infused as a tea or added to drinks or meals. Ashwagandha has a deep, earthy flavor that pairs well with warming spices.

Chaga Mushrooms

Recognized as a king of medicinal mushrooms, chaga mushrooms have long been used in traditional medicine for stimulating the immune system and reducing inflammation. They are high in B vitamins and have one of the highest concentrations of antioxidants of any food. Chaga mushrooms can be purchased granulated, which is best for brewing tea, or as a fine powder, which can be added directly to drinks.

Maca Powder

Maca is a root vegetable that is native to South America. Classified as an adaptogen, maca is also used to balance hormones and boost fertility. It has a delicious malty, caramel-like flavor that makes it a great addition to drinks and porridges. Maca is available in powders that are raw or gelatinized—gelatinized maca is easier to digest and absorb.

Reishi Mushrooms

Reishi mushrooms are known in traditional Chinese medicine to promote radiant health and a long life by helping to harmonize the functions of the body, mind, and spirit. This potent adaptogenic mushroom supports immune function and mental clarity, promotes restful sleep, and is known to be calming and strengthening for the nervous system.

OPPOSITE: (First row) cacao powder, Turmeric Latte Mix, ground turmeric; (second row) chaga mushroom powder, ground ginger, reishi mushroom powder; (third row) beet juice powder, Pink Chai Latte Mix, Beet Hot Chocolate Mix; (fourth row) ashwagandha root, Adaptogen Latte Mix, ashwagandha powder, whole nutmeg

Black Tea Chai Latte

MAKES 1¼ CUPS | 300 ML | SERVES 1

¾ cup (180 ml) Brewed Chai (recipe follows)

½ cup (120 ml) almond milk, made using the Nut or Seed Milk base recipe, or Almond-Coconut Milk (page 76)

1 teaspoon coconut butter

Combine the chai and almond milk in a small saucepan and bring to a simmer over high heat. Pour into an upright blender, add the coconut butter, and blend until foamy. Pour into a mug and serve immediately.

Brewed Chai

MAKES ABOUT 3¼ CUPS | 780 ML,
ENOUGH FOR 4 SERVINGS

4 cups (960 ml) filtered water

8 whole star anise

2 tablespoons (⅓ ounce | 10 g) cardamom pods

2 cinnamon sticks, broken into pieces

1 tablespoon fennel seeds

1 teaspoon whole cloves

1 teaspoon black peppercorns

One 4-inch (10 cm) piece (1 ounce | 30 g) fresh turmeric, peeled and chopped (optional)

One 2-inch (5 cm) piece (1 ounce | 30 g) fresh ginger, peeled and chopped

6 tablespoons (¾ ounce | 22 g) black tea

Combine the water, star anise, cardamom, cinnamon, fennel, cloves, peppercorns, turmeric, if using, and ginger in a small pot and bring to a boil over high heat. Cover, reduce the heat to low, and simmer for 10 minutes. Remove from the heat, add the tea, cover again, and set aside for 10 minutes to steep. Strain into a jar, pressing on the solids to extract as much liquid as possible. Use in the Black Tea Chai Latte, or drink hot with milk, sweetened to taste, if desired. Allow the chai to cool before storing in the fridge for up to 2 weeks.

Turmeric Latte

MAKES 1 CUP | 240 ML | SERVES 1

1 cup (240 ml) almond milk, made using the Nut or Seed Milk base recipe

2 teaspoons Turmeric Latte Mix (recipe follows)

½ teaspoon extra-virgin coconut oil (optional)

Foam the almond milk and latte mix in a milk frother. Pour into a cup, stir in the coconut oil, if using, and serve immediately. **Pictured on page 81**

NOTE: If you don't have a milk frother, or if yours is not large enough to hold a cup of milk, put the latte mix and oil in a blender. Bring the almond milk to a simmer in a small saucepan over high heat. Pour into the blender and blend until frothy, then pour into a cup and serve immediately.

Turmeric Latte Mix

MAKES ABOUT ½ CUP | 1¾ OUNCES | 50 G,
ENOUGH FOR 12 SERVINGS

¼ cup (1 ounce | 30 g) ground turmeric

2 tablespoons (¼ ounce | 8 g) ground ginger

1 tablespoon rosemary powder (see the sidebar)

1 tablespoon ground cardamom

1 tablespoon ground fennel seeds

1 teaspoon ground cinnamon

¼ teaspoon freshly ground black pepper

Combine the turmeric, ginger, rosemary powder, cardamom, fennel, cinnamon, and pepper in a small jar or bowl and stir well. Store in an airtight jar for up to 3 months. **Pictured on page 81**

ROSEMARY POWDER

Rosemary powder is a great alternative in many recipes where the fresh herb cannot be used. Put 3 tablespoons (¼ ounce | 8 g) dried rosemary in an electric spice grinder and grind until fine; it will take a couple of minutes to get it to a powdery consistency. Store in a small jar for up to 3 months.

Beet Hot Chocolate

MAKES 1 CUP | 240 ML | SERVES 1

1 cup (240 ml) almond milk, made using the Nut or Seed Milk base recipe

2 tablespoons (½ ounce | 14 g) Beet Hot Chocolate Mix (recipe follows)

Bring the almond milk to a simmer in a small saucepan over high heat. Pour into an upright blender, add the beet hot chocolate mix, and blend until foamy. Pour into a mug and serve immediately. **Pictured on page 80**

NOTES: For a beet rose hot chocolate, stir in 1 teaspoon organic rose water (see the sidebar on page 37) before serving.

If you have a milk frother that holds 1 cup of liquid, you can add the milk and beet hot chocolate mix to it and heat together.

Beet Hot Chocolate Mix

MAKES 1 CUP | 3¾ OUNCES | 105 G, ENOUGH FOR 8 SERVINGS

½ cup (1 ounce | 32 g) high-quality cacao powder (see the sidebar on page 297)

½ cup (2½ ounces | 70 g) beet juice powder (see Resources, page 392)

Combine the cacao and beet juice powder in a small jar or bowl and stir to combine. Store in a glass jar for up to 3 months. **Pictured on page 85**

OTHER NUT MILK DRINKS

Golden Milk

MAKES ABOUT 4 CUPS | 960 ML | SERVES 4 TO 6

1 recipe Almond-Coconut Milk (page 76) or almond milk, made using the Nut or Seed Milk base recipe

One 6-inch (15 cm) piece (1½ ounces | 45 g) fresh turmeric, peeled and chopped (finely chopped if using a regular blender), or 1 tablespoon ground turmeric

One 3-inch (7.5 cm) piece (1½ ounces | 45 g) fresh ginger, peeled (and finely chopped if using a regular blender), or 2 teaspoons ground ginger

1 tablespoon coconut butter or extra-virgin coconut oil

½ teaspoon ground cinnamon

½ teaspoon ground cardamom

Large pinch of freshly ground black pepper

Combine the almond-coconut milk, turmeric, ginger, coconut butter, cinnamon, cardamom, and pepper in an upright blender and blend on high speed until completely smooth and frothy. Serve the milk at room temperature, chilled, or warm. To warm the milk, heat it in a small pot over medium heat; remove from the heat just before the milk simmers. If you want a foamy consistency, blend the milk again in an upright blender. Alternatively, you can warm the milk in a milk frother; it won't foam much, but this is an easy way to warm the milk and give it a lovely texture. The milk can be stored in a tightly sealed glass jar in the fridge for up to 5 days. **Pictured on page 69**

Iced Sencha with Almond Milk and Orange Blossom Water

MAKES ABOUT ¾ CUP | 180 ML | SERVES 1

⅔ cup (160 ml) strong brewed sencha tea (see Resources, page 392), chilled

2 tablespoons (30 ml) almond milk, made using the Nut or Seed Milk base recipe, chilled

¼ teaspoon orange blossom water, or to taste

Combine the tea, milk, and orange blossom water in a glass and stir well. Add ice, if desired, and serve.

Iced Earl Grey Tea with Almond Milk and Rose Water

MAKES 1 CUP | 240 ML | SERVES 1

⅔ cup (160 ml) brewed Earl Grey tea, chilled

⅓ cup (80 ml) almond milk, made using the Nut or Seed Milk base recipe, chilled

½ teaspoon organic rose water (see the sidebar on page 37), plus more to taste

A dried organic rosebud or fresh organic rose petal for garnish

Combine the tea, milk, and rose water in a glass and stir well. Add ice, if desired, garnish with the rosebud or petal, and serve immediately.

OPPOSITE: Iced Sencha with Almond Milk and Orange Blossom Water (left) and Iced Earl Grey Tea with Almond Milk and Rose Water (right)

Superfood Chocolate Milk

MAKES ABOUT 4 CUPS | 960 ML | SERVES 8

1 recipe Almond-Coconut Milk (page 76) or almond milk, made using the Nut or Seed Milk base recipe

¾ cup (1½ ounces | 45 g) high-quality cacao powder (see Note)

¼ cup (¾ ounce | 22 g) mesquite powder (see the sidebar on page 23)

2 tablespoons (1 ounce | 30 g) coconut butter

2 tablespoons (30 ml) extra-virgin coconut oil

1 tablespoon gelatinized maca powder (see Resources, page 393)

1 tablespoon vanilla extract

1 teaspoon ground cinnamon

Pinch of fine sea salt

Pour the almond-coconut milk into an upright blender, add the cacao, mesquite, coconut butter, coconut oil, maca, vanilla, cinnamon, and salt, and blend until smooth and frothy. Pour into a glass jar, cover tightly, and refrigerate until chilled. Once the milk is chilled, you can scoop off and eat the luxurious mousse-like topping that will have formed, then shake the chocolate milk before serving it cold. Or, to serve warm, shake well and heat in a small pot over medium heat; remove from the heat just before the hot chocolate simmers. If you want a foamy consistency, blend again in an upright blender. Alternatively, you can use a milk frother to warm it up; it won't foam much, but this is an easy way to warm the milk, and it gives the drink a lovely texture. The milk can be stored in a tightly sealed glass jar in the fridge for up to 5 days.

NOTE: This intense chocolate drink provides the uplifting and satisfying properties of cacao without the usual sugar. For best results, use top-quality cacao powder (see Resources, page 393).

OPPOSITE: Superfood Chocolate Milk

Simple Compotes

—

Richly colored fruit compotes have the ability to transform a plain porridge into a sublime breakfast or, when folded into thick yogurt, make an instant healthy dessert or refreshing afternoon snack. A nearly effortless compote of stewed apple or peaches can even be the basis for a breakfast bowl when topped with toasted seeds, nuts, berries, ground flax, and yogurt or nut milk. If you take the time to whip up one of these compotes at the beginning of the week, it will provide you with many enjoyable meals and excellent snacks.

Making a double batch of a compote gives you the option of blending half into a chia pudding (see pages 296–305) or turning some of it into a quick sugar-free chia jam. Although some of these compotes rely on seasonal fruit, many of them can be made at any time of the year using stored apples from the farmers' market or frozen berries or cherries. Since berries are naturally low in sugars and high in antioxidants and flavor, I tend to make berry compotes most often, and I find that they taste just as good made with frozen berries as with fresh.

All of these compotes are really easy to make, but don't underestimate how delicious they are or how many variations you can create using these base recipes as starting points. Just a dash of freshly ground cardamom, a pinch of saffron, or a scattering of grated turmeric can turn a simple compote into something striking and memorable.

Notes

TEXTURE

The beauty of a compote is in the way the flesh of the fruit melts as it cooks, creating a loose jam-like texture that varies depending on the fruit you choose. If you have really juicy fruit, you may want to reduce the juice or water in these recipes slightly. You don't want to dilute the flavor or turn the fruit into a sauce—and you can always stir in a little more liquid later. You need to add arrowroot or kuzu (see the following page) to most of these compotes to thicken the juices just enough to coat the fruit. But you won't need it with plums or apples, as their flesh breaks down and thickens the juices without any outside help.

FLAVOR

Cooking fruit into a compote is a great way to improve less-than-perfect fruit, as it intensifies and concentrates the flavor. You can use orange juice to provide sweetness and bright, slightly tart notes, or you can substitute apple or pear juice for a sweeter compote, or simply replace it with water. If you'd like to highlight the orange flavor, zest the orange before juicing and stir in zest to taste after the compote is cooked. Vanilla also enhances the natural sweetness of berries or fruit, and it tastes good with every variation.

A couple of teaspoons of rose or orange blossom water are an unexpected way to elevate the flavors; stir these in after the fruit or berries have cooked. You can also flavor a compote with tea by adding a tea bag to the simmering fruit. This is best with longer-cooking fruits, as the tea needs time to steep.

ADD-INS

Adding a spice to your compote means you can make a different flavor every time. If you're experimenting with more exotic spices or particularly pungent ones, add just a pinch to start and then increase to taste.

Grated fresh ginger or turmeric will give a simple compote an assertive flavor; these taste best when cooked with the fruit rather than added at the end. Turmeric, which will also give your compote an eye-catching color, works particularly well with peaches, apricots, and pears.

Whole or chopped dried fruit like raisins or apricots can also be added at the beginning of cooking. And don't forget fresh herbs like rosemary, thyme, and basil, which can be simmered with the fruit for an interesting twist.

GARNISHES

Since these compotes are essentially used as garnishes, you don't really need much else. However, for a pretty look, top the Blueberry Compote with Cardamom and Orange with a scattering of fresh blueberries or a peach compote with fresh black currants when they are in season. Fresh or dried edible flowers are also lovely additions. Look to your farmers' market or your own garden for seasonal inspiration.

STORING AND FREEZING

These compotes all keep well in the fridge for up to 5 days. They can also be frozen for up to 3 months, although some will be a little more liquid when defrosted—you can always drain them a bit if you want them thicker. Be sure to freeze them with at least 1½ inches (3.75 cm) of headspace above the top of the compote to allow for expansion.

Berry Compote

MAKES 2 CUPS | 480 ML

3 to 4 cups fresh or frozen berries (weight depends on the berries used; see the variations for measures); halve or quarter strawberries into ½-inch | 1.25 cm pieces

½ cup (120 ml) freshly squeezed orange juice

1 teaspoon vanilla extract

Tiny pinch of fine sea salt

2 teaspoons arrowroot powder (see the sidebar)

1 tablespoon filtered water

Combine the berries, orange juice, vanilla, and salt in a medium pot and bring to a boil over high heat. Cover the pan, reduce the heat to low, and simmer for 5 minutes, or until the berries have softened and released their juice. Dissolve the arrowroot in the water in a small cup, then slowly drizzle into the simmering berries, stirring constantly. Once the compote has returned to a simmer and thickened, remove from the heat. Serve warm or at room temperature. Store the cooled compote in a sealed jar in the fridge for up to 5 days.

ARROWROOT AND KUZU

My compote thickeners of choice are arrowroot and kuzu; both are flavorless and have a long shelf life. Arrowroot, a white powdery starch that comes from a West Indian plant, is easily found in supermarkets and is inexpensive. Kuzu, a white starch that comes from a wild Japanese mountain root, is used medicinally in Japan and in macrobiotic cooking; it is known for its soothing effect on the stomach and for its immune-boosting properties. It is much more expensive than arrowroot, and it comes in white lumps that must be crushed before measuring; you will need about a third less kuzu than arrowroot in any recipe. Although it's not absolutely necessary to thicken every compote you make, especially one you plan on spooning over breakfast porridge—where the extra juice is welcome— adding arrowroot or kuzu does result in a nicer presentation, as the fruit takes on a lovely sheen.

Blueberry Compote with Cardamom and Orange

MAKES 2½ CUPS | 600 ML

1 recipe Berry Compote, using 4 cups
(1 pound | 455 g) blueberries

¼ teaspoon ground cardamom

1 teaspoon grated orange zest

Make the compote following the instructions for the base recipe, adding the cardamom to the pot along with the blueberries. Once the compote is cooked, stir in the orange zest. **Pictured on page 92 (top left)**

Berry–Rose Petal Compote

MAKES 2½ CUPS | 600 ML

1 recipe Berry Compote, using 2 cups (8 ounces | 230 g) strawberries, hulled and cut into ½-inch (1.25 cm) pieces, and 2 cups (6 ounces | 170 g) raspberries

1 cup (½ ounce | 15 g) organic fresh rose petals (see the sidebar on page 301)

2 teaspoons organic rose water (see the sidebar on page 37; optional)

Make the compote following the instructions for the base recipe, adding the rose petals to the pot along with the berries. When the compote is cooked, remove from the heat and stir in the rose water, if using.

Strawberry Goji Compote

MAKES ABOUT 2½ CUPS | 600 ML

1 recipe Berry Compote, using 4 cups
(1 pound | 455 g) strawberries

6 tablespoons (1½ ounces | 40 g) dried goji berries

Make the compote following the instructions for the base recipe, adding the goji berries to the pot along with the strawberries. **Pictured on page 92 (center)**

NEED A QUICK (SUGAR-FREE) BERRY JAM?

Chia seeds can be stirred into crushed raw or cooked berries to give them a jam-like consistency. Though most chia jam recipes include added sweeteners, if you use orange juice and vanilla as a base, you won't need one. To make a jammy topping for toast, pancakes, or waffles, make one of the berry compotes, omitting the arrowroot. Once it's cooked, stir in ¼ cup (1⅓ ounces | 40 g) chia seeds; when the compote has stopped steaming, chill in the fridge until thickened. Using chia seeds is also a nice way to add protein and omega-3s to your compote.

COMPOTES—HOW TO CUSTOMIZE

Compote	Pairings
Blueberry Compote with Cardamom and Orange (page 97)	As a topping for oatmeal
	On toast with nut butter (see pages 112–114)
Berry–Rose Petal Compote (page 97)	As a topping for halved and toasted grain-free muffins (see pages 313–318)
	With cookies and labneh or whipped cream
Strawberry Goji Compote (page 97)	As a topping for Strawberry-Cardamom Grain-Free Porridge (page 47) with almond milk (see page 71)
	As a topping for Rose Sesame Waffles (page 369) with yogurt
Cherry Vanilla Compote (page 101)	As a topping for Cacao and Maca Chia Bircher Bowl (page 23) with Rose Almond Milk (page 72)
	As a topping for Matcha Cardamom Waffles (page 365) with yogurt
Spiced Plum-Ginger Compote (page 101)	Warmed and served over vanilla ice cream with toasted walnuts (see page 390)
	As a topping for Orange Blossom Waffles (page 365) with yogurt
Apricot-Fennel Compote (page 101)	As a topping for yogurt
	As a topping for Buckwheat Chai Porridge (page 37) with almond milk (see page 71)

Compote	Pairings
Apple-Hibiscus Compote (page 104)	As a topping for oatmeal or a Genius Whole-Grain Porridge (pages 34–47) with almond milk (see page 71)
	As a topping for yogurt and berries
Apple-Rosemary Compote with Blackberries (page 104)	With foamed almond milk (see page 71) and toasted hazelnuts (see page 390)
	As a topping for Sugar-Free Granola with Berries and Mesquite (page 353) with cashew milk (see page 71)
Saffron Apple Compote with Cardamom and Lime (page 105)	Topped with toasted pistachios (see page 390)
	As a topping for Millet Porridge (page 34) with Almond-Coconut Milk (page 76)
Quince–Star Anise Compote with Vanilla Bean (page 105)	Warmed and served with Brazil Nut Milk with Star Anise and Vanilla Bean (page 76)
	Topped with toasted almonds or walnuts (see page 390)
Pear Turmeric Compote with Citrus (page 105)	Swirled into coconut yogurt
	As a topping for Chia Oat Bircher Bowl (page 20) with almond milk (see page 71)

OPPOSITE: Apricot-Fennel Compote with coconut yogurt

Stone Fruit Compote

MAKES ABOUT 2½ CUPS | 600 ML

1½ pounds (680 g) ripe peaches, plums, apricots, or cherries (see Note)

½ cup (120 ml) freshly squeezed orange juice or filtered water

Tiny pinch of fine sea salt

1 teaspoon arrowroot powder

2 teaspoons filtered water

½ teaspoon vanilla extract

If using peaches, plums, or apricots, halve and pit them. Cut each half into ½-inch (1.25 cm) wedges and slice the wedges in half crosswise. If using cherries, pit them. Put the fruit in a medium pot, add the orange juice and salt, and bring to a simmer over high heat. Cover the pot, reduce the heat to low, and simmer for 8 to 10 minutes, until the fruit is soft. Dissolve the arrowroot in the water in a small cup, then drizzle it into the pot, stirring constantly. Once the compote has returned to a simmer and thickened, remove from the heat and stir in the vanilla. Serve warm or at room temperature. Store the cooled compote in a sealed jar in the fridge for up to 5 days.

NOTE: If using plums, omit the arrowroot powder.

Cherry Vanilla Compote

MAKES 2¼ CUPS | 540 ML

1 recipe Stone Fruit Compote, using cherries, pitted (about 4 cups), ¾ cup (180 ml) orange juice, and 1 teaspoon vanilla extract

½ vanilla bean, split, seeds scraped out, seeds and pod reserved

½ teaspoon ground cinnamon

Make the compote following the instructions for the base recipe, adding the vanilla seeds and pod and the cinnamon to the pot along with the cherries. Increase the cooking time to 25 to 30 minutes, depending on the type of cherries you're using; sour cherries will cook more quickly than sweet ones. When the cherries are soft and beginning to collapse, drizzle in the dissolved arrowroot, stirring constantly, and continue as directed. Store the compote with the vanilla pod, but remove it before serving; use it to garnish the compote, if you like. **Pictured on page 92 (bottom left)**

NOTE: You can also make this recipe using frozen cherries; you'll need 4 cups (about two 10-ounce | 283 g) bags. Reduce the orange juice or water to ¼ cup (60 ml) and simmer the cherries for only 5 minutes before adding the dissolved arrowroot.

Spiced Plum-Ginger Compote

MAKES ABOUT 2¾ CUPS | 660 ML

1 recipe Stone Fruit Compote, using plums (about 8 medium) and omitting the arrowroot

2 teaspoons grated peeled fresh ginger or ½ teaspoon ground ginger

½ teaspoon ground cinnamon

½ teaspoon ground cardamom

Make the compote following the instructions for the base recipe, adding the ginger, cinnamon, and cardamom to the pot along with the plums. Firmer plums will take a bit longer to cook. **Pictured on the following page**

Apricot-Fennel Compote

MAKES 2½ CUPS | 600 ML

1 recipe Stone Fruit Compote, using apricots (about 16 medium)

1 teaspoon ground fennel seeds, plus more to taste

Make the compote following the instructions for the base recipe, adding the fennel to the pot along with the apricots and juice. Continue as directed, adding more fennel to taste to the finished compote. **Pictured on page 99**

ABOVE: Spiced Plum-Ginger Compote; OPPOSITE: Ingredients for Apple-Rosemary Compote with Blackberries

Fall Fruit Compote

MAKES ABOUT 2½ CUPS | 600 ML

1½ pounds (680 g) apples, pears, or quinces

½ cup (120 ml) filtered water

Pinch of fine sea salt

1 teaspoon vanilla extract

Peel, quarter, and core the fruit. Cut apples into ½-inch (1.25 cm) slices, pears into ¾-inch (2 cm) dice, and quinces into ¼-inch (6 mm) slices. Put the fruit in a medium pot, add the water, salt, and vanilla, and bring to a boil over high heat. Cover the pot, reduce the heat to low, and simmer for 10 to 15 minutes, until the fruit is cooked through; stir the fruit halfway through to ensure even cooking. Serve warm or at room temperature. Store the cooled compote in a sealed jar in the fridge for up to 5 days.

Apple-Hibiscus Compote

MAKES ABOUT 2½ CUPS | 600 ML

1 tablespoon dried organic hibiscus flowers or 1 hibiscus tea bag

1 recipe Fall Fruit Compote, using apples (about 3 medium-large)

If using loose hibiscus flowers, tie them up in a piece of cheesecloth. Make the compote following the instructions for the base recipe, adding the hibiscus to the pot along with the apples. Remove the hibiscus flowers or tea bag before serving or storing.

Apple-Rosemary Compote with Blackberries

MAKES ABOUT 2¾ CUPS | 660 ML

1 recipe Fall Fruit Compote, using apples (about 3 medium-large)

2 teaspoons minced fresh rosemary

1 cup (4 ounces | 115 g) fresh or frozen blackberries

Make the compote following the instructions for the base recipe, adding the rosemary to the pot along with the apples. When the apples are tender, stir in the blackberries and simmer for 1 to 2 minutes, until they have softened. Remove from the heat.
Pictured on page 92 (bottom right)

Saffron Apple Compote with Cardamom and Lime

MAKES ABOUT 2½ CUPS | 600 ML

1 recipe Fall Fruit Compote, using apples (about 3 medium-large)

½ teaspoon ground cardamom

¾ teaspoon saffron threads

1 teaspoon freshly squeezed lime juice, or more to taste

Make the compote following the instructions for the base recipe, adding the cardamom and saffron to the pot along with the apples. When the compote is cooked, remove from the heat and stir in the lime juice.

Quince–Star Anise Compote with Vanilla Bean

MAKES ABOUT 2½ CUPS | 600 ML

1 recipe Fall Fruit Compote, using quinces (about 2 medium-large)

6 whole star anise

1 vanilla bean, split, seeds scraped out, seeds and pod reserved

Make the compote following the instructions for the base recipe, adding the star anise and vanilla pod and seeds to the pot along with the quinces. Remove the vanilla pod and star anise before serving, or use them as a garnish for the compote.

Pear Turmeric Compote with Citrus

MAKES ABOUT 2½ CUPS | 600 ML

1 recipe Fall Fruit Compote, using pears (about 3 medium) and replacing the water with freshly squeezed orange juice

1 tablespoon finely grated peeled fresh turmeric (use a Microplane)

1 teaspoon arrowroot powder

2 teaspoons filtered water

Make the compote following the instructions for the base recipe, adding the turmeric to the pot along with the pears. In a small cup, dissolve the arrowroot in the water and set aside. When the compote is cooked, stir the arrowroot mixture, drizzle it into the pot, and stir gently until the compote has returned to a simmer and thickened, then remove from the heat. **Pictured on page 92 (center right)**

Nut, Seed, and Coconut Butters

—

Nut butters—rich, toasty, thick, and creamy, with a delicate crunch of flaky sea salt—are endlessly useful. (I'm so passionate about them that I usually tuck a jar into my luggage when I travel. Then, no matter where I am, I can treat myself to a generous smear of these butters on a cracker or a slice of ripe fruit, or even eat them straight out of the jar.) It's difficult to find good nut or seed butters that are organic, sugar-free, and made with freshly toasted nuts or seeds. Most commercial nut butters taste rancid because of long exposure to heat or light. Nothing beats butters made with nuts or seeds freshly toasted in your own kitchen. And you can tweak and flavor them by adding spices and/or vanilla bean seeds, cacao, or fruit and berry powders. For a savory use, the nut and seed base recipes can also be substituted for tahini in Quick Tahini Sauces (pages 246–247).

Homemade coconut butter is even quicker and easier to make than homemade nut and seed butters, because there's no need to toast the coconut. You simply grind dried coconut in the food processor until it becomes smooth and creamy. Coconut butter can be spread on toast as you would butter, melted for a sugar-free sauce for waffles or pancakes, or added to smoothies for extra protein. While good-quality coconut butter is commercially available, what you'll rarely find in stores are interesting flavors like the ones in this chapter.

Nut and seed butters can become savory spreads with the addition of herbs or spices, olive oil, and sea salt. These make tasty toppings for toast or crackers, of course, but you can also try spreading one of these savory butters on a plate and topping with salad. They will add richness and intrigue to the simplest meals. The Black Sesame–Nori Butter was inspired by a healthy Vegemite alternative called Mighty Spread, made by the Broken Head Company in New South Wales, Australia. The combination of nutritional yeast and toasted nori gives it a delicious umami flavor. And, just like my beloved Vegemite, it tastes great smeared on toast with avocado.

Cashew butter is the only nut butter that also works well when made with raw nuts. Butter made with raw cashews is a perfect neutral base for sauces and dressings and is used in the Lemony Roasted Cauliflower with Coriander (page 182). It is one of the only nut butters that I consistently purchase (see Resources, page 393).

Notes

TEXTURE

A soft, spreadable texture is the hallmark of a successful nut or seed butter, and that comes from being patient when grinding the toasted nuts in a food processor. The butter will become glossy and quite liquid once it is ready, so even though it may look smooth, you want to keep processing until you reach that point. Once you're there, add any flavorings you like and blend to combine. If you add ingredients like cacao, matcha, or a large amount of spices before the butter is liquid, it will seize up and never become smooth and shiny. For a nut butter with a crunchy texture, see the method used in the Cacao-Hazelnut Butter with Warm Spices.

Although dried coconut is soft, it will probably take longer than you expect to get to a buttery consistency, and it usually won't be as smooth as commercial coconut butter. The fresher and richer in oil your dried coconut is, the more easily it can be blended into butter. Look for it in the bulk bins of your local health food store, where it's usually fresher than the packaged variety. You can use either shredded or flaked coconut, but be sure to weigh it rather than use a cup measure, as the volume measure will vary depending on the type. Never use reduced-fat coconut.

FLAVOR

This is the fun part! Have a good look through your spice drawer before deciding what you might want to add to your nut butter. But if you taste the butter before thinking about what to incorporate, you might be tempted to leave it as is—it's hard to improve on freshly toasted nuts kissed with good sea salt! Don't limit yourself to sweet spices or superfood powders, as some of these butters, such as the Black Sesame–Nori Butter and the Salted Almond Butter with Sumac and Chili, can stand firmly on the savory side. The Pecan-Rosemary Butter works in both savory and sweet combinations. Because they are light in color and delicate in flavor, the coconut butters are a fantastic canvas for dried berry powders. Kids especially love drizzling these pretty butters over toast, pancakes, or porridge.

ADD-INS

Spices, herbs, salts, and superfood powders are probably the easiest add-ins for nut or seed butters. If you'd like to add vanilla, avoid the extract, which will make the butter pasty; opt for the seeds from a vanilla bean instead. Pure organic essential oils are the top option for adding flavors like rose, orange, and lemon. Be sure to add these only a drop at a time, as they are superstrong. Citrus zest can also be added.

GARNISHES

It may seem odd to think of garnishing a humble spread, but nut and seed butters are easy to dress up if you want a pretty snack or a breakfast to serve guests. Once you've spread one of these butters on bread, crackers, or sliced apples, pears, or peaches, or added it to porridge, scatter whole berries, crushed freeze-dried berries, chopped nuts, fresh or dried organic rose petals, edible flowers, or flaky black or white sea salt over it.

STORING AND FREEZING

Nut, seed, and coconut butters keep well stored in sealed glass jars or airtight containers at room temperature for up to 1 month (after that, their flavor will be less fresh). You can store them in the fridge for longer, but coconut butter will become brittle. To scoop and spread a refrigerated nut or coconut butter easily, or to soften it for drizzling, place the sealed jar in a bowl of boiling-hot water for a few minutes and stir the butter a few times, until smooth and spreadable. Leave it in the water longer for a runnier consistency.

NUT BUTTER FLAVORINGS

Nut or seed butters can be colored and flavored with fresh herbs, like rosemary or thyme; dried spices, like ginger, chile, and sumac; powdered fruit or berries; cacao; mesquite; and matcha. Try some of these options (pictured from left to right):

TOP ROW

○ Raspberry Coconut Butter (page 116)

○ Mango-Vanilla Coconut Butter (page 116)

○ Toasted Coconut Butter (page 115)

○ Salted Almond Butter with Sumac and Chili (page 114)

MIDDLE ROW

○ Raspberry-Cacao Coconut Butter with Orange (page 116)

○ Spiced Walnut Mesquite Butter (page 114)

○ Strawberry Coconut Butter (page 116)

○ Pistachio Coconut Butter with Matcha (page 116)

BOTTOM ROW

○ Black Sesame–Nori Butter (page 114)

○ Gold Butter (page 114)

○ Almond and Sunflower Butter with Coconut (page 113)

○ Cacao-Hazelnut Butter with Warm Spices (page 113)

○ Pecan-Rosemary Butter (page 113)

Nut or Seed Butter

MAKES 1 CUP | 240 ML

---

2 cups raw whole nuts or seeds (weight depends on the nuts or seeds used; see the variations for measures), toasted (see page 390)

1 teaspoon flaky sea salt, or to taste

Put the nuts or seeds in a food processor and process for 2 minutes, or until they form a ball. Break up the ball, scrape down the sides of the processor, and blend until the butter is completely smooth and liquid, 3 to 4 minutes longer. Scrape the sides of the processor again, add the flaky salt, and pulse to combine. Store in a sealed glass jar or an airtight container at room temperature for up to 1 month (in hot weather, store in the fridge).

Pecan-Rosemary Butter

MAKES ABOUT ¾ CUP | 180 ML

1 recipe Nut or Seed Butter, using 1 cup (3½ ounces | 100 g) raw pecans, toasted (see page 390), and 1 cup (4½ ounces | 130 g) raw cashews, toasted (see page 390)

1¼ teaspoons finely minced fresh rosemary

Make the nut butter following the instructions for the base recipe. Once the butter is completely smooth and liquid, add the rosemary and blend well. Add the salt from the base recipe and pulse to combine. **Pictured on page 111**

Almond and Sunflower Butter with Coconut

MAKES 1 CUP | 240 ML

1 recipe Nut or Seed Butter, using 1 cup (5 ounces | 140 g) whole raw almonds, toasted (see page 390), and 1 cup (4½ ounces | 130 g) raw sunflower seeds, toasted (see page 390)

1 cup (3 ounces | 85 g) unsweetened shredded dried coconut, toasted (see page 390)

Make the nut butter following the instructions for the base recipe, adding the coconut to the food processor along with the almonds and sunflower seeds. Once the butter is smooth and liquid, add the salt from the base recipe and pulse to combine. **Pictured on page 111**

Cacao-Hazelnut Butter with Warm Spices

MAKES ¾ CUP | 180 ML

1 recipe Nut or Seed Butter, using 2 cups (9 ounces | 260 g) raw hazelnuts, toasted (see page 390) and skinned

2 tablespoons (¼ ounce | 8 g) cacao powder (see the sidebar on page 297)

1 teaspoon ground cinnamon

1 teaspoon ground ginger

½ teaspoon ground cardamom

½ teaspoon freshly grated nutmeg (see the sidebar on page 43)

Put ½ cup (2¼ ounces | 65 g) of the hazelnuts in a food processor and pulse until the pieces are about the size of a red lentil. Remove the chopped nuts from the processor and set aside. Add the remaining nuts to the processor and make the nut butter following the instructions for the base recipe. Once the butter is completely smooth and liquid, add the cacao and spices, and the salt from the base recipe, and process to combine. Add the reserved chopped hazelnuts and pulse to combine. **Pictured on page 111**

Salted Almond Butter with Sumac and Chili

MAKES 1 CUP | 240 ML

1 recipe Nut or Seed Butter, using 2 cups (10 ounces | 280 g) whole raw almonds, toasted (see page 390)

4 teaspoons (¼ ounce | 8 g) ground sumac, or to taste

1 teaspoon red chili pepper flakes

Pinch of cayenne pepper, or more to taste

Make the nut butter following the instructions for the base recipe. Once the butter is completely smooth and liquid, add the sumac, red chili pepper flakes, and cayenne, and the salt from the base recipe, and process to combine. Add more cayenne to taste and blend again. **Pictured on page 111**

Spiced Walnut Mesquite Butter

MAKES ⅔ CUP | 160 ML

1 recipe Nut or Seed Butter, using 2 cups (7 ounces | 200 g) raw walnuts, toasted (see page 390)

1 tablespoon mesquite powder (see the sidebar on page 23)

½ teaspoon ground ginger

¼ teaspoon ground cinnamon

Make the nut butter following the instructions for the base recipe. Once the butter is completely smooth and liquid, add the mesquite, ginger, and cinnamon, and the salt from the base recipe, and process to combine. **Pictured on page 111**

Gold Butter

MAKES ABOUT 1 CUP | 240 ML

1 recipe Nut or Seed Butter, using 1 cup (4½ ounces | 130 g) raw cashews, toasted (see page 390), and 1 cup (4½ ounces | 130 g) raw macadamia nuts, toasted (see page 390)

1½ teaspoons Turmeric Latte Mix (page 87) or ¼ teaspoon ground turmeric plus a pinch each of ground ginger, cinnamon, cardamom, and black pepper, or more to taste

Make the nut butter following the instructions for the base recipe. Once the butter is completely smooth and liquid, add the latte mix (or the spices) and process to blend. Taste and add more seasoning, if desired. Add the salt from the base recipe and pulse to combine. **Pictured on page 110**

Black Sesame–Nori Butter

MAKES ABOUT 1 CUP | 240 ML

1 recipe Nut or Seed Butter, using 2 cups (10 ounces | 280 g) raw black sesame seeds, toasted (see page 390)

3 tablespoons (45 ml) extra-virgin olive oil

2 tablespoons (⅓ ounce | 10 g) nutritional yeast

1 sheet nori, toasted and crumbled (see the sidebar on page 202)

2 teaspoons tamari

½ teaspoon brown rice vinegar

Make the seed butter following the instructions for the base recipe, adding the olive oil when the sesame seeds have broken down and become pasty. Once the butter is smooth (it won't become as liquid as a nut butter), add the yeast, nori, tamari, and vinegar and process until smooth. Add the salt from the base recipe and pulse to combine. **Pictured on page 110**

Coconut Butter

MAKES 1 CUP | 240 ML

**4 cups (12 ounces | 340 g) unsweetened shredded dried coconut
or 7 cups (12 ounces | 340 g) unsweetened flaked dried coconut**

Put the coconut in a food processor and process for 10 to 15 minutes, scraping down the sides every couple of minutes, until the butter is completely smooth and quite liquid. Store in a tightly sealed glass jar at room temperature for up to 1 month.

NOTES: Coconut butter will be runny the day it's made and then will firm up in cool weather. In warm weather, it will stay soft and separate a little; stir well before using. It will become hard if stored in the fridge. You can soften the butter easily by placing the sealed jar in a bowl of boiling-hot water for a few minutes, then stirring it to blend.

For a lovely rich flavor and golden color, make this with toasted coconut (see page 390). Pulse in a large pinch of flaky sea salt for this version. **Pictured on page 111**

Mango-Vanilla Coconut Butter

MAKES 1 CUP | 240 ML

1 recipe Coconut Butter

¼ cup (1 ounce | 30 g) mango powder

½ vanilla bean, split, seeds scraped out and reserved, pod reserved for another use

Pinch of fine sea salt

Make the coconut butter following the instructions for the base recipe. Once the butter is smooth and liquid, add the mango powder, vanilla seeds, and salt and blend until combined. **Pictured on page 111**

Pistachio Coconut Butter with Matcha

MAKES 1 CUP | 240 ML

1 recipe Coconut Butter, reducing the shredded dried coconut to 2 cups (6 ounces | 170 g)

1 cup (4½ ounces | 130 g) shelled raw pistachios

2 teaspoons ceremonial-grade matcha tea powder (see Resources, page 392)

Pinch of fine sea salt

Make the coconut butter following the instructions for the base recipe, adding the pistachios to the processor along with the coconut. Once the butter is smooth and liquid, add the matcha and salt and blend until combined. **Pictured on page 111**

Raspberry-Cacao Coconut Butter with Orange

MAKES 1 CUP | 240 ML

1 recipe Coconut Butter

5 tablespoons (½ ounce | 17 g) raspberry powder

2 tablespoons (¼ ounce | 8 g) cacao powder (see the sidebar on page 297)

⅛ teaspoon fine sea salt

4 to 6 drops pure orange oil

Make the coconut butter following the instructions for the base recipe. Once the butter is smooth and liquid, add the raspberry powder, cacao, salt, and orange oil and blend until combined. **Pictured on page 110**

Strawberry or Raspberry Coconut Butter

MAKES 1 CUP | 240 ML

1 recipe Coconut Butter

3 tablespoons (⅓ ounce | 10 g) strawberry or raspberry powder, or more to taste

½ vanilla bean, split, seeds scraped out and reserved, pod reserved for another use

Pinch of fine sea salt

Make the coconut butter following the instructions for the base recipe. Once the butter is smooth and liquid, add the strawberry or raspberry powder, vanilla seeds, and salt and blend until combined. Add more strawberry or raspberry powder to taste and blend again. **Raspberry Coconut Butter pictured on page 110**

OPPOSITE: Making Strawberry Coconut Butter

ON   OFF-PULSE

NUT BUTTERS—HOW TO CUSTOMIZE

Nut Butter	Pairings
Pecan-Rosemary Butter (page 113)	With steamed carrots (see page 171) as a dip
	On crackers with fresh sliced pears
Almond and Sunflower Butter with Coconut (page 113)	On toasted Sunflower–Poppy Seed Bread (page 57) with Blueberry Compote with Cardamom and Orange (page 97)
	Spread over Oat Pecan Crackers with Rosemary and Raisins (page 289)
Cacao-Hazelnut Butter with Warm Spices (page 113)	Served with sliced plums, apples, and berries
	By the spoonful when a chocolate craving strikes
Salted Almond Butter with Sumac and Chile (page 114)	In a sandwich with grated carrots, scallions, cucumber, avocado, kraut, and a generous drizzle of olive oil
	As a dip for Pickled Carrots with Coriander and Chile (page 194)
Gold Butter (page 114)	On toasted Carrot-Turmeric Bread (page 57)
	Drizzled over a tropical fruit salad
Black Sesame–Nori Butter (page 114)	On toast with avocado
	Smeared over a plate and topped with a fresh vegetable salad or Steamed Vegetable Salad (page 173)
Toasted Coconut Butter (page 115)	Spread over toast and topped with Berry Chia Jam (see page 97), sliced banana, and cinnamon
	Blended into almond milk (see page 71)
Mango-Vanilla Coconut Butter (page 116)	Warmed slightly and used as a frosting for cupcakes or cookies
	Swirled into plain oatmeal or any Genius Whole-Grain Porridge (pages 34–47) with Berry Compote (page 96)
Pistachio Coconut Butter with Matcha (page 116)	Blended into a green smoothie
	On toast with sliced banana
Raspberry-Cacao Coconut Butter with Orange (page 116)	Rolled into balls and frozen for a sweet chocolaty treat. (Be sure the mixture is firm at cool room temperature before rolling; if not, refrigerate until firm.)
	Smeared over Beet-Millet Crackers with Dill Seeds (page 289)
Strawberry or Raspberry Coconut Butter (page 116)	Warmed and drizzled over Orange Blossom Waffles (page 365)
	Blended into berry smoothies

OPPOSITE, CLOCKWISE FROM TOP: Gold Butter on Carrot-Turmeric Bread; Raspberry-Cacao Coconut Butter with Orange on Beet-Millet Crackers with Dill Seeds; Pecan-Rosemary Butter on Oat Pecan Crackers with Rosemary and Raisins

Simple and Healing Soups

—

Having a jar of one of these healing and comforting vegetable soups in the fridge is like having money in the bank. Keep a few jars of different flavors on hand and you'll feel like a millionaire. These simple soups are a convenient way to eat healthily while maintaining a demanding schedule, and they're one of the best ways to easily increase your daily vegetable intake.

Not only are these soups quick to prepare, using just about any vegetable you may have on hand, but they can also be effortlessly transformed into a complete meal just by adding ingredients such as leftover cooked beans, grains, or greens (or all three) and topping them with toasted nuts and seeds, sprouts, or herbs. Or just serve them with some toasted hearty bread or seeded crackers (see pages 282–289).

All of these soups are easy to digest, so they're great for a quick meal any time of day or night as they won't weigh you down. The simplest variations are superclean and healthy but still soothing and satisfying. In fact, the recipes are perfect for a cleanse, and a terrific alternative in the colder months to a juice fast. If you want to do a soup cleanse, stock several different versions in your fridge— the simpler the better, with a focus on greens. This will give you the option of alternating them throughout the day. See the Meal Prep section for a Soup and Broth Cleanse (page 381).

As in other chapters, the base recipes here can be springboards for your own creations. There are infinite pathways you can take; use the Notes opposite to guide you. These soups are particularly quick to make because they are based on water instead of stock (I prefer filtered water over a commercially made stock any day). But if you make your own stock and have some on hand, by all means use it.

Most of these recipes make 6 to 8 servings, but if that's more than you need at the moment, no worries; they freeze well.

Notes

TEXTURE

Soups made with zucchini, cauliflower, broccoli, and other faster-cooking vegetables usually need less water than you might expect to get the proper creamy consistency. When experimenting with your own variations, it may be tempting to add "just a little more" water to cover the vegetables, but don't! Once the vegetables start cooking, they will release liquid, and if you've added extra liquid, it can water down the flavor. If you find that your soup is too liquid after blending the first batch, strain out a cup (240 ml) or more of the cooking liquid before blending the second batch. On the other hand, if your soup is too thick, which can happen with beets, carrots, and other very starchy vegetables, you can add a little more water to thin it out when blending.

FLAVOR

As simple as these base recipe soups are, sometimes it's nice to change things up and add a squeeze of lemon juice, or season them with miso instead of sea salt and tamari, or enrich them with coconut, seeds, or nuts. When you have vibrant, flavorful fresh vegetables from the farmers' market, there's no need for any such additions. But here are some ideas for when your vegetables are a bit lackluster or you just want a change.

Replacing 1½ to 2 cups (360 to 480 ml) of the water with coconut milk adds flavor and richness. Alternatively, adding a couple of tablespoons (½ oz | 30 g) of coconut butter when blending the soup will give it a subtle coconut flavor and a silky texture. If your soup needs brightening up or the flavor combination you chose seems muddled, add some fresh lemon juice while blending, or squeeze a lemon wedge over each portion just before serving. Lemon is especially good with any of the broccoli soups.

Adding whole nuts or seeds when you're blending is like making a nut milk right in the soup itself. You could also reduce the water a little and add a nut or seed milk (see page 71) at the end, or use one to thin

the soup slightly, as with the Sweet Potato Soup with Coriander, Chili, and Ginger.

Traditionally made unpasteurized miso, which is packed with live active enzymes and probiotics, can be added to any of these soups to enhance their flavor and nutritional value. Just be sure that you do not boil it, or the delicate enzymes will be destroyed; stir in the miso right before removing the soup from the heat. When reheating soups containing miso, be careful to bring them just to a light simmer. Also keep in mind that since miso is salty, you will need to reduce or even eliminate the salt in the recipe. The darker the miso and the longer it is aged, the stronger tasting it will be.

If you want to add fresh herbs like dill, cilantro, tarragon, or basil, stir some in at the beginning of cooking and the rest once the soup is cooked. If you want a more pronounced flavor, pulse in more chopped herbs after seasoning the soup. You can also use fresh herbs as a garnish. For sturdier herbs like thyme, rosemary, and sage, it's best to add them to the pan along with the garlic, as cooking helps mellow their flavor.

To give the soup an anti-inflammatory boost and a gorgeous golden glow, stir in 2 to 3 tablespoons (½ to ⅔ ounce | 15 to 20 g) peeled and chopped fresh turmeric along with the garlic for any of the recipes except the broccoli-based ones. If you want to add ginger, go with a similar amount. Dry spices or spice blends are best added after the garlic (and/or ginger and turmeric, if using) has cooked, as these will absorb moisture and make the garlic more likely to stick to the pan.

These soups call for extra-virgin coconut oil because it has a high smoke point and is better for high-heat cooking, but you can substitute extra-virgin olive oil or unrefined sesame oil. Or, if you want to add a rich, deep flavor, use ghee—it's especially good in soups seasoned with curry powder or warming spices. Finally, you won't really notice the flavor of the oil unless you add extra when blending the soup, which is a lovely way to enrich soups in the colder months.

ADD-INS

Spinach or other greens are a great addition to these soups. Toss a handful of baby spinach into the bottom of your bowl and pour the hot soup over it; by the time it gets to the table, the greens will be cooked. If you want to use very sturdy greens, steam or blanch them first.

GARNISHES

Any of these soups can be finished with a drizzle of good olive oil, some coarsely ground black pepper, and a sprinkle of chopped parsley, dill, or cilantro, depending on the other flavors in the soup. Bright, peppery micro greens make a great garnish, and a sprinkling of a flavored salt can be nice too. For a bit of crunch, sprinkle toasted sunflower, pumpkin, or sesame seeds; chopped toasted nuts; or Hazelnut Dukkah (page 153) over the soup.

STORING AND FREEZING

These vegetable soups keep well for 4 to 5 days in the fridge. Pour the soup into jars or other containers and allow to cool to room temperature before covering tightly and refrigerating. They can also be frozen for up to 3 months. The starchier soups, such as those containing squash or root vegetables, freeze particularly well; other frozen soups are greatly improved with a quick blast in the blender once they're defrosted. (If you freeze a couple of portions each time you make soup, you'll end up with a nice selection of flavors to choose from.) Freeze them in 1- or 2-portion containers and leave 1½ inches (3.5 cm) of headspace to allow for expansion.

TO PEEL OR NOT TO PEEL?

Since all the nutrients are just under the skin of vegetables, it's usually best to leave the skin on. In general, peel only winter squashes (you can leave the skin on Red Kuri squash and, if you don't mind a slight greenish tinge, green kabocha too). However, if your root vegetables look old—especially winter storage vegetables, like parsnips—peel them to avoid the possibility of a bitter taste.

Cauliflower Soup

MAKES 3 QUARTS | 2.8 L | SERVES 6 TO 8

2 tablespoons (30 ml) extra-virgin coconut oil

1 medium (8 ounces | 230 g) yellow onion, diced

3 large garlic cloves, finely chopped

2 teaspoons fine sea salt, plus more to taste

2 small-medium (4 pounds | 1.8 kg) cauliflower, cut into 1-inch (2.5 cm) florets (about 14 cups)

6 cups (1.4 l) filtered water

Freshly ground black pepper

Tamari (optional)

Warm the oil in a large pot over medium-high heat. Add the onion and cook for 6 to 8 minutes, until beginning to brown. Stir in the garlic and salt and cook for 3 to 4 minutes, until the garlic is golden and fragrant. Add the cauliflower and water, raise the heat, and bring to a boil. Press the cauliflower down to submerge it as much as possible. It won't all be submerged, and that's okay. Cover the pot, reduce the heat to low, and simmer for 12 to 14 minutes, until the cauliflower is tender, pressing it down into the simmering liquid again halfway through cooking. Test the cauliflower by inserting a sharp knife into a floret; it should glide in easily. Remove from the heat, scoop out 1 cup (240 ml) of the liquid, and set aside. Stir in pepper to taste and allow the soup to cool slightly.

Working in batches, scoop the soup into an upright blender (filling it no more than two-thirds full) and puree on high speed until smooth and velvety, adding some of the reserved cooking liquid if necessary to reach the desired consistency, then pour into a large bowl or another large pot. Season to taste with more salt and pepper, and with tamari, if using, and serve warm. Store leftover soup in jars in the fridge for up to 5 days, or freeze for up to 3 months.

Cauliflower Soup with Greens and Dill

MAKES ABOUT 3½ QUARTS | 3.3 L | SERVES 6 TO 8

1 recipe Cauliflower Soup, using 7 cups
(1.7 l) water

1 cup (1 ounce | 30 g) chopped fresh dill,
plus sprigs for garnish

1 medium bunch kale or collard greens
(10 ounces | 285 g), chopped (10 cups)

Make the soup following the instructions for the
base recipe, adding half the dill along with the
cauliflower. When the cauliflower is cooked, stir
in the greens, raise the heat to bring the soup back
to a simmer, and cook for 2 to 3 minutes, until the
greens are tender but still bright green. Remove
from the heat, add the remaining dill, and continue
as directed. Serve the soup garnished with dill
sprigs. **Pictured on page 130**

Curried Cauliflower Soup

MAKES ABOUT 3 QUARTS | 2.8 L | SERVES 6 TO 8

1 recipe Cauliflower Soup

One 4-inch (10 cm) piece (1 ounce | 30 g)
fresh turmeric, peeled and chopped
(about ¼ cup; optional)

One 2-inch (5 cm) piece (1 ounce | 30 g)
fresh ginger, peeled and chopped (about ¼ cup)

4 teaspoons (¼ ounce | 7 g) curry powder
(recipe follows)

3 tablespoons (1½ ounces | 45 g) coconut butter
(optional)

Make the soup following the instructions for the
base recipe, adding the turmeric, if using, and ginger
along with the garlic. Cook for 5 minutes, then stir
in the curry powder. Add the cauliflower and water
and continue as directed, adding the coconut butter,
if using, when blending the soup (it will thicken the
soup a little). **Pictured on page 130**

Curry Powder

MAKES ABOUT ½ CUP | 2 OUNCES | 58 G

¼ cup (½ ounce | 15 g) coriander seeds

2 tablespoons (⅓ ounce | 10 g) cumin seeds

One 3-inch (7.5 cm) stick cinnamon, broken
into pieces

1 teaspoon whole cardamom pods

1 teaspoon black peppercorns

8 whole cloves

2 tablespoons (⅓ ounce | 10 g) ground turmeric

2 tablespoons (⅓ ounce | 10 g) ground ginger

¼ teaspoon cayenne pepper

Warm a skillet over medium heat and add the
coriander, cumin, cinnamon, cardamom, peppercorns,
and cloves. Toast for 2 to 3 minutes, or until fragrant.
Remove from the heat, transfer to an electric spice
grinder, and grind until fine. Place in a bowl and add
the turmeric, ginger, and cayenne; stir well. Store in a
tightly sealed jar for up to 3 months.

Broccoli Spinach Soup

MAKES 3 QUARTS | 2.8 L | SERVES 6 TO 8

2 tablespoons (30 ml) extra-virgin coconut oil

1 medium (8 ounces | 230 g) yellow onion, diced

3 large garlic cloves, finely chopped

2 teaspoons fine sea salt, plus more to taste

1 large (12 ounces | 340 g) leek (see Note), chopped (3 cups)

5 large heads (3½ pounds | 1.6 kg) broccoli, cut into 1-inch (2.5 cm) florets, stems peeled and cut into ½-inch (1.25 cm) dice (about 16 cups total)

6 cups (1.4 l) filtered water

12 cups (8 ounces | 230 g) regular or baby spinach, roughly chopped if using regular spinach

Freshly ground black pepper

Tamari (optional)

Warm the oil in a large pot over medium-high heat. Add the onion and cook for 6 to 8 minutes, until beginning to brown. Stir in the garlic and salt and cook for 3 to 4 minutes, until the garlic is golden and fragrant. Add the leek and cook for 3 minutes, or until softened. Add the broccoli and the water (the water should come to about 1 inch | 2.5 cm below the top of the vegetables) and bring to a boil over high heat. Cover the pot, reduce the heat to low, and simmer for 8 to 10 minutes, until the broccoli is tender, pressing it down into the liquid a couple of times during cooking to ensure that it cooks evenly. Test the broccoli by inserting a sharp knife into a stem; it should glide in easily.

Remove from the heat, scoop out 1 cup (240 ml) of the liquid, and set it aside. Stir in the spinach; it will cook in the residual heat. Add pepper to taste and let cool slightly before blending.

Working in batches, scoop the soup into an upright blender (filling it no more than two-thirds full) and puree on high speed until smooth and velvety, adding some of the reserved cooking liquid if necessary to reach the desired consistency, then pour into a large bowl or another large pot. Season to taste with more salt and pepper, and with tamari, if using, and serve warm. Store leftover soup in jars in the fridge for up to 4 days, or freeze for up to 3 months.

NOTE: To clean leeks, cut off the root and slit open lengthwise, leaving the layers attached at the root end. Rinse upside down under a stream of cold running water, fanning open the layers to wash away any grit.

VARIATION RECIPES

Broccoli Spinach Soup with Peas and Dill

MAKES ABOUT 3¾ QUARTS | 3.5 L | SERVES 6 TO 8

1 recipe Broccoli Spinach Soup, using 2½ pounds (1.13 kg) broccoli

1 cup (1 ounce | 30 g) chopped fresh dill

3 cups (1 pound | 455 g) frozen peas

Make the soup following the instructions for the base recipe, adding half the dill along with the broccoli. After the broccoli has cooked for 8 minutes, add the peas and bring back to a simmer, then remove from the heat, stir in the spinach and the remaining dill, and continue as directed. This soup has a thicker consistency than the other broccoli soups, so you will probably want to use all of the reserved cooking liquid. **Pictured on the following page**

Broccoli, Spinach, and Fennel Soup

MAKES ABOUT 3½ QUARTS | 3.3 L | SERVES 6 TO 8

1 recipe Broccoli Spinach Soup

4 teaspoons (⅙ ounce | 5 g) fennel seeds

1 medium (12 ounces | 340 g) fennel bulb, cored and cut into ½-inch (1.25 cm) dice (1½ cups)

Make the soup following the instructions for the base recipe, adding the fennel seeds along with the garlic and the diced fennel along with the leek.

FROM LEFT TO RIGHT: Broccoli Spinach Soup with Peas and Dill; Zucchini Soup with Cilantro and Jalapeño; Rosemary Butternut Squash Soup with Toasted-Hazelnut Milk; Curried Cauliflower Soup; Cauliflower Soup with Greens and Dill; Kabocha Squash Soup with Ginger, Turmeric, and Miso; Sweet Potato Soup with Coriander, Chili, and Ginger; Summer Squash and Sweet Corn Soup; Parsnip Miso Soup; Zucchini Soup with Cilantro and Jalapeño

Winter Squash Soup

MAKES ABOUT 2½ QUARTS | 2.4 L | SERVES 6

2 tablespoons (30 ml) extra-virgin coconut oil

1 medium (8 ounces | 230 g) yellow onion, diced

3 large garlic cloves, finely chopped

2 teaspoons fine sea salt, plus more to taste

1 large (4 pounds | 1.82 kg) kabocha, butternut, or other winter squash, halved, seeded, peeled, and cut into 1-inch (2.5 cm) cubes (about 10 cups)

5 cups (1.2 l) filtered water

Freshly ground black pepper

Tamari (optional)

Warm the oil in a large pot over medium-high heat. Add the onion and cook for 6 to 8 minutes, until beginning to brown. Stir in the garlic and salt and cook for 3 to 4 minutes, until the garlic is golden and fragrant. Add the squash and water (the water should come almost to the top of the chopped squash), raise the heat, and bring to a boil; then cover the pot, reduce the heat to low, and simmer for 12 to 15 minutes, until the squash is tender. Test by pressing a piece of squash against the side of the pot; it should crush easily with a little pressure. Remove from the heat, season with pepper to taste, and set aside to cool slightly.

Working in batches, scoop the soup into an upright blender (filling it no more than two-thirds full) and puree on high speed until smooth and velvety, then pour into a large bowl or another large pot. Season to taste with more salt and pepper, and with tamari, if using, and serve warm. Store leftover soup in jars in the fridge for up to 5 days, or freeze for up to 3 months.

Kabocha Squash Soup with Ginger, Turmeric, and Miso

MAKES ABOUT 3 QUARTS | 2.8 L | SERVES 6 TO 8

1 recipe Winter Squash Soup, using kabocha squash, 1 teaspoon salt, and 6 cups (1.4 l) water

One 4-inch (10 cm) piece (1 ounce | 30 g) fresh turmeric, peeled and chopped (about ¼ cup)

One 2-inch (5 cm) piece (1 ounce | 30 g) fresh ginger, peeled and chopped (about ¼ cup)

¼ cup (2 ounces | 60 g) unpasteurized sweet white miso, mellow white miso, or chickpea miso

Make the soup following the instructions for the base recipe, adding the turmeric and ginger along with the garlic and cooking for 5 minutes. Continue as directed, adding the miso when blending the soup. Season to taste with tamari, if using. **Pictured on page 131**

Rosemary Butternut Squash Soup with Toasted-Hazelnut Milk

MAKES ABOUT 3½ QUARTS | 3.3 L | SERVES 8

1 recipe Winter Squash Soup, using butternut squash

3 tablespoons (⅓ ounce | 10 g) chopped fresh rosemary

⅔ cup (3 ounces | 85 g) raw hazelnuts, toasted (see page 390) and skinned, plus more for garnish

2 cups (480 ml) filtered water

Freshly ground black pepper

Extra-virgin olive oil for drizzling

Make the soup following the instructions for the base recipe, adding the rosemary along with the garlic and continuing as directed. While the soup cooks, put the hazelnuts and water in an upright blender and blend until smooth; pour into a jar and set aside. Once the soup is blended, stir in the hazelnut milk and season to taste with more salt and pepper. Serve the soup topped with chopped hazelnuts, pepper, and a drizzle of olive oil.

OPPOSITE: Rosemary Butternut Squash Soup with Toasted-Hazelnut Milk

Root Vegetable Soup

MAKES ABOUT 3 QUARTS | 2.8 L | SERVES 6 TO 8

2 tablespoons (30 ml) extra-virgin coconut oil

1 medium (8 ounces | 230 g) yellow onion, diced

3 large garlic cloves, finely chopped

2 teaspoons fine sea salt, plus more to taste

4½ pounds (2 kg) parsnips, sweet potatoes, or other root vegetables, peeled and cut into 1-inch (2.5 cm) dice (about 15 cups)

6 bay leaves

6 cups (1.4 l) filtered water, or as needed

Freshly ground black pepper

Tamari (optional)

Warm the oil in a large pot over medium-high heat. Add the onion and cook for 6 to 8 minutes, until beginning to brown. Stir in the garlic and salt and cook for 3 to 4 minutes, until the garlic is golden and fragrant. Add the root vegetables, bay leaves, and water (the water should almost cover the vegetables), raise the heat, and bring to a boil; then cover the pot, reduce the heat to low, and simmer for 15 minutes, or until the vegetables are cooked through. Test by inserting a fork into a vegetable cube; it should glide in easily. Remove the bay leaves (compost them). Stir in pepper to taste and let the soup cool slightly.

Working in batches, scoop the soup into an upright blender (filling it no more than two-thirds full). Puree on high speed until smooth and velvety, adding water if necessary to get the desired consistency, then pour into a large bowl or another large pot. Season to taste with more salt and pepper, and with tamari, if using, and serve warm. Store leftover soup in jars in the fridge for up to 5 days, or freeze for up to 3 months.

Parsnip Miso Soup

MAKES ABOUT 3¾ QUARTS | 3.5 L | SERVES 8

1 recipe Root Vegetable Soup, using parsnips (about 10 medium-large; 14 cups chopped), 1 teaspoon salt, and 8 cups (1.9 l) water

5 tablespoons (2½ ounces | 75 g) unpasteurized chickpea miso, sweet white miso, or mellow white miso

Make the soup following the instructions for the base recipe, adding the miso when blending the soup. **Pictured on the following page**

Sweet Potato Soup with Coriander, Chili, and Ginger

MAKES 3 QUARTS | 2.8 L | SERVES 6 TO 8

1 recipe Root Vegetable Soup, using sweet potatoes (about 4 large; 15 cups chopped)

One 2-inch (5 cm) piece (1 ounce | 30 g) fresh ginger, peeled and chopped (about ¼ cup)

5 teaspoons (¼ ounce | 7 g) ground coriander

1½ teaspoons red chili pepper flakes, or more to taste

1½ cups (360 ml) almond milk (see page 71) for serving

Make the soup following the instructions for the base recipe, adding the ginger along with the garlic and cooking for 5 minutes. Stir in the coriander and red chili pepper flakes, then add the sweet potatoes and water and continue as directed. Blend in more red chili pepper flakes to taste. Just before serving, stir in the almond milk. (If you are not serving all the soup at once, add 2 tablespoons | 30 ml almond milk for every cup | 240 ml of heated soup.) **Pictured on page 131**

ABOVE: Parsnip Miso Soup; **CLOCKWISE FROM TOP RIGHT:** Sweet Potato Soup with Coriander, Chili, and Ginger; Zucchini Soup with Cilantro and Jalapeño; Broccoli Spinach Soup with Peas and Dill; Curried Cauliflower Soup; Summer Squash and Sweet Corn Soup; Parsnip Miso Soup; Kabocha Squash Soup with Ginger, Turmeric, and Miso; Cauliflower Soup with Greens and Dill

Zucchini Soup

MAKES ABOUT 2 QUARTS | 1.9 L | SERVES 4 TO 6

2 tablespoons (30 ml) extra-virgin coconut oil

1 medium (8 ounces | 230 g) yellow onion, diced

2 large garlic cloves, finely chopped

1½ teaspoons fine sea salt, plus more to taste

8 medium-large (4 pounds | 1.8 kg) zucchini, cut into 1-inch (2.5 cm) pieces (12 cups)

3¼ cups (840 ml) filtered water

Freshly ground black pepper

Tamari (optional)

Warm the oil in a large pot over medium-high heat. Add the onion and cook for 6 to 8 minutes, until beginning to brown. Stir in the garlic and salt and cook for 3 to 4 minutes, until the garlic is golden and fragrant. Add the zucchini and water, raise the heat, and bring a boil. Cover the pot, reduce the heat to low, and simmer for 8 to 10 minutes, until the zucchini is tender, pressing it down into the liquid a couple of times during cooking to ensure that it cooks evenly. Test by pressing a piece of zucchini against the side of the pot; it should crush easily. Remove from the heat and set aside to cool slightly.

Scoop out 2 cups (480 ml) of the liquid and set aside. Season the soup with pepper. Working in batches, scoop the soup into an upright blender (filling it no more than two-thirds full) and puree on high speed until smooth and velvety, adding some of the reserved cooking liquid if necessary to reach the desired consistency, then pour into a large bowl or another large pot. Season to taste with more salt and pepper, and with tamari, if using, and serve warm. Store leftover soup in jars in the fridge for up to 4 days or freeze for up to 3 months.

Zucchini Soup with Cilantro and Jalapeño

MAKES ABOUT 2 QUARTS | 1.9 L | SERVES 4 TO 6

1 large bunch cilantro

1 recipe Zucchini Soup

1 medium (1 ounce | 30 g) jalapeño, seeded and chopped (2 tablespoons)

Cayenne pepper (optional)

Trim the roots from the cilantro if necessary. Remove 1 cup (½ ounce | 15 g) cilantro leaves for the soup, plus additional leaves for garnish. Chop enough of the stems to make ½ cup (1½ ounces | 45 g). Make the soup following the instructions for the base recipe, adding the jalapeño and cilantro stems along with the garlic and then continuing as directed. When pureeing the soup, add the cilantro leaves to the blender after the soup is smooth and pulse until finely chopped. Season with cayenne if the soup is not spicy enough for your taste, and serve. **Pictured on page 130**

Summer Squash and Sweet Corn Soup

MAKES ABOUT 2¼ QUARTS | 2.1 L | SERVES 4 TO 6

1 recipe Zucchini Soup, using 2 pounds (910 g) yellow summer squash

3 large ears sweet corn, shucked and kernels cut off (about 3 cups | 13½ ounces | 385 g), 2 corncobs reserved

Make the soup following the instructions for the base recipe, adding the corn along with the squash. Break the 2 reserved cobs in half and add to the pot as well, then continue as directed, but increase the cooking time to 15 minutes, or until the corn is tender. Remove the cobs before blending the soup. **Pictured on page 131**

Beans

Marinated Beans
(BASE RECIPE) 148

Chickpeas with Chili and Parsley ∘ 148

Herbed Corona Beans ∘ 149

Adzuki Beans with Tamari, Scallions,
and Toasted Sesame Seeds ∘ 149

Heirloom Beans with Tomatoes
and Basil ∘ 149

Red Lentil Pâté
(BASE RECIPE) 152

Red Lentil Pâté with Dukkah ∘ 153

Red Lentil Pâté with Lemon
and Herbs ∘ 153

Butter Bean Pâté
(BASE RECIPE) 154

Beet and Cashew Butter Bean Pâté ∘ 155

Herbed Butter Bean Pâté with Leeks
and Spinach ∘ 155

Chickpea Pâté
(BASE RECIPE) 156

Chickpea Pâté with Almond,
Chili, and Sumac ∘ 157

Pine Nut Chickpea Pâté
with Rosemary ∘ 157

Cashew Chickpea Pâté with Turmeric,
Chili, and Lime ∘ 157

Quick Bean Sauce
(BASE RECIPE) 158

Pinto Bean Sauce with Tomatoes
and Oregano ∘ 159

Creamy White Bean Sauce
with Greens ∘ 159

Beans have always had a special place in my pantry. From shiny black beans to large plump Coronas and speckled Scarlet Runners, along with tiny French lentils, a good collection of beans will never leave you short on ideas of what to cook. Not only are beans an excellent source of protein, they also add a unique richness and texture that is unbeatable. And although they are often considered a side dish, there is no reason not to let beans take center stage.

This chapter focuses on three easy ways of preparing beans: marinated beans, bean pâtés, and bean sauces, with plenty of tasty variations. The marinated beans can be added to grain bowls and salads, used as a topper for good bread, or stirred into soups. The bean pâtés are great for smearing over toast and crackers, eating alongside a salad or in a lettuce cup, or serving with steamed or roasted vegetables, and they also make a tasty dip for crudités. The bean sauces turn simple vegetables or grains into complete meals. Serve the Pinto Bean Sauce with Tomatoes and Oregano with brown rice and sliced avocado or the Creamy White Bean Sauce with Greens over wedges of roasted squash in fall and winter or topped with ripe tomatoes, basil leaves, and a drizzle of olive oil in summer.

This chapter also includes a chart with cooking times for both pressure-cooking and simmering a large variety of beans. Plain cooked beans are a flexible base for any number of toppings and flavorings. Stir cooked greens into chickpeas and top with olive oil, avocado, and cilantro, and maybe some crumbled feta too. Stir them into soups, or make any of the recipes in this chapter.

It's essential to soak dried beans and cook them properly. Uniform cooking can be a challenge when using the simmering method, so I highly recommend a pressure cooker (see Resources, page 393) for creamy, perfectly cooked beans.

Although cooking beans from scratch is the best way to go, on occasion you may find yourself wanting a quick protein-based meal and have no soaked beans on hand. Red lentils are an easy option, as they don't require soaking and cook in under 20 minutes. Or make a bean sauce using canned beans, which is one of the best ways of masking their less than optimum flavor and texture. For other uses, follow the tips in Using Canned Beans on page 147.

Notes

TEXTURE

The creamy texture that makes beans so appealing comes from proper cooking, which starts with a good long overnight soak. If you want to plan ahead, you can soak beans, drain them, and keep them in the fridge for a couple of days until you're ready to cook them. Be sure to cook beans until they are completely soft inside, particularly because they tend to firm up a little as they cool; test a few when checking for doneness, to make sure they are evenly cooked. There is little risk of ruining beans by overcooking—even when they've begun to fall apart, they can still make a great sauce or pâté. And overcooked beans absorb the flavors of the marinade beautifully, even if the result can be a bit messy.

FLAVOR

The unique flavors of different beans can be enhanced by the aromatics you choose to incorporate. Well-cooked beans will enthusiastically soak up any flavor you add to them, but chickpeas, lentils, and white beans are particularly versatile, adapting well to any number of seasonings, from pungent spices to delicate herbs and an array of vinegars.

ADD-INS

When simmering or pressure-cooking dried beans, you can add whole garlic cloves, onion, bay leaves, chiles, or any aromatic herbs or spices. Once you are familiar with these base recipes and variations, you can play around with the ingredients you have on hand. Pantry ingredients like sun-dried tomatoes, artichoke hearts, capers, and olives are great additions to any of the base recipes.

GARNISHES

Any of the recipes here would benefit from a last-minute scattering of chopped fresh herbs, such as parsley, cilantro, dill, scallions, or chives. But don't be afraid to keep it simple—plain well-cooked beans taste amazing with just a glug of good olive oil and a sprinkling of flaky sea salt.

STORING AND FREEZING

All of the recipes in this chapter, as well as plain cooked beans, will keep well for up to 4 days stored (once cooled) in airtight containers in the fridge. You can also freeze drained cooked beans or any of the bean sauces in airtight containers for up to 3 months. Soaked and drained beans can also be frozen so they're ready to cook when you need them; no need to defrost them before cooking.

BEAN COOKING TIMES

The quantities in the chart below will give you enough beans for any of the recipes in this chapter plus a cup or so extra to store in the fridge or freezer for incorporating into soups or other dishes.

When simmering beans, the time can vary greatly, depending on the age of your beans, so the times in the chart are by necessity approximate—keep checking your beans until they are cooked through and creamy inside.

The pressure cooker times below are for cooking under high pressure. The natural release time is the time it takes for the pressure to release once the pot is off the heat; natural pressure release allows the pressure to come down on its own, eliminating the need for you to speed up the process by running the pot under cold water, and thereby allows the beans to continue to cook as the pressure drops. (Note that some beans cannot be pressure-cooked because their skins will come off, which can block the pressure valve.)

No matter which method you use, add a 2-inch (5 cm) piece of kombu to the pot. Kombu is high in minerals that help make beans more digestible, and it contains glutamic acid, which helps to tenderize the beans as well as bring out their flavor. Simply fish out the kombu once the beans are cooked (compost it). If you can't find kombu, you can use kelp or wakame, although its delicate texture will make it more difficult to remove after cooking. When using canned beans, seek out brands that include kombu (see Resources, page 392).

Beans (Use 1½ Cups)	Weight	Soaking Time (in 4 Cups | 960 ml Filtered Water)	Filtered Water for Cooking	Cooking Time	Yield
Adzuki Beans	10 ounces | 285 g	10 to 12 hours	6 cups (1.41 l)	40 to 50 minutes simmered; do not pressure-cook	4½ cups (1 pound, 8½ ounces | 695 g)
Black Beans	9½ ounces | 270 g	10 to 12 hours	6 cups (1.41 l) to simmer; 4 cups (960 ml) to pressure-cook	40 to 50 minutes simmered; 15 minutes in the pressure cooker plus 10 to 15 minutes natural pressure release	4¼ cups (1 pound, 6½ ounces | 640 g)
Butter Beans/ Baby Lima Beans	9½ ounces | 270 g	10 to 12 hours	4 cups (960 ml)	35 to 45 minutes simmered; do not pressure-cook	4 cups (1 pound, 5½ ounces | 610 g)
Cannellini Beans	9½ ounces | 270 g	10 to 12 hours	6 cups (1.41 l) to simmer; 4 cups (960 ml) to pressure-cook	40 to 90 minutes simmered; 15 minutes in the pressure cooker plus 10 to 15 minutes natural pressure release	4 cups (1 pound, 7 ounces | 655 g)
Chickpeas	9 ounces | 255 g	10 to 12 hours	6 cups (1.41 l) to simmer; 4 cups (960 ml) to pressure-cook	1 to 2 hours simmered; 20 minutes in the pressure cooker plus 10 to 15 minutes natural pressure release	4½ cups (1 pound, 7 ounces | 655 g)

Beans (Use 1½ Cups)	Weight	Soaking Time (in 4 Cups | 960 ml Filtered Water)	Filtered Water for Cooking	Cooking Time	Yield
French Lentils	9½ ounces | 270 g	10 to 12 hours	4 cups (960 ml)	35 to 40 minutes simmered; do not pressure-cook	4½ cups (1 pound, 8¼ ounces | 690 g)
Heirloom Beans, Extra Large (Scarlet Runner, White Bordal)	8 ounces | 230 g	10 to 12 hours	6 cups (1.41 l) to simmer; 4 cups (960 ml) to pressure-cook	1 to 2 hours simmered; 25 minutes in the pressure cooker plus 10 to 15 minutes natural pressure release	3½ cups (1 pound, 3½ ounces | 555 g)
Kidney Beans	8½ ounces | 240 g	10 to 12 hours	6 cups (1.41 l) to simmer; 4 cups (960 ml) to pressure-cook	60 to 90 minutes simmered; 15 minutes in the pressure cooker plus 10 to 15 minutes natural pressure release	4 cups (1 pound, 5 ounces | 595 g)
Pinto Beans	9½ ounces | 270 g	10 to 12 hours	6 cups (1.41 l) to simmer; 4 cups (960 ml) to pressure-cook	60 to 90 minutes simmered; 15 minutes in the pressure cooker plus 10 to 15 minutes natural pressure release	4 cups (1 pound, 9¾ ounces | 730 g)
Red Lentils	9¾ ounces | 275 g	Do not soak	3 cups (720 ml)	20 minutes simmered; do not pressure-cook	3 cups (2 pounds | 910 g)

USING CANNED BEANS

Drain and thoroughly rinse two 15½-ounce (440 g) cans of beans. Transfer to a medium pot and cover with filtered water. Bring to a boil over high heat, reduce the heat to low, and simmer for 1 to 2 minutes, until the beans are heated through. Drain well and use in any of the recipes in this chapter. Be sure to measure or weigh your beans after they are drained, as the liquid is included in the weight of the beans in a can.

- One 15½-ounce | 440 g can = 1½ cups drained beans
- 3 cups cooked and drained beans = 15½ ounces | 440 g

Marinated Beans

MAKES 3 CUPS | ABOUT 1 POUND, 1½ OUNCES | ABOUT 500 G | SERVES 4

3 cups cooked beans (see Bean Cooking Times on the preceding pages), preferably just cooked and still warm, drained well

3 tablespoons (45 ml) extra-virgin olive oil

2 tablespoons (30 ml) raw apple cider vinegar, plus more to taste

½ teaspoon fine sea salt, plus more to taste

Put the beans in a medium bowl, add the olive oil, vinegar, and salt, and stir to combine. Adjust the seasoning to taste. Set aside for 30 minutes to marry the flavors if you have time, or serve immediately. Store the beans in a jar in the fridge for up to 4 days.

NOTE: Weights and serving size depend on the type of bean used.

Chickpeas with Chili and Parsley

MAKES 3 CUPS | 1 POUND, 2 OUNCES | ABOUT 510 G | SERVES 4

1 recipe Marinated Beans, using chickpeas

½ cup (½ ounce | 15 g) coarsely chopped fresh flat-leaf parsley

1 teaspoon red chili pepper flakes, or more to taste

Make the beans following the instructions for the base recipe. Add the parsley and red chili pepper flakes, stir to combine, and adjust the seasoning to taste. **Pictured on page 151**

Herbed Corona Beans

MAKES 3 CUPS | ABOUT 1 POUND, 6 OUNCES | 625 G
SERVES 4 TO 6

1 recipe Marinated Beans, using Corona or gigante beans, or other heirloom beans

¼ cup (½ ounce | 15 g) chopped fresh dill

¼ cup (¼ ounce | 8 g) chopped fresh flat-leaf parsley

1 teaspoon umeboshi vinegar (optional)

Make the beans following the instructions for the base recipe. Let the beans cool if they are not already at room temperature, then add the herbs and umeboshi vinegar, if using, stir to combine, and adjust the seasoning to taste. **Pictured on the following page**

Adzuki Beans with Tamari, Scallions, and Toasted Sesame Seeds

MAKES 3 CUPS | 1 POUND, 2¾ OUNCES | 530 G | SERVES 4

1 recipe Marinated Beans, using adzuki beans, replacing the apple cider vinegar with brown rice vinegar, and reducing the salt to ¼ teaspoon

2 tablespoons (½ ounce | 15 g) raw unhulled sesame seeds, toasted (see page 390), plus more for garnish

2 teaspoons tamari

1 scallion, thinly sliced

Chopped fresh flat-leaf parsley for garnish

Make the beans following the instructions for the base recipe, adding the sesame seeds, tamari, and scallion along with the other ingredients, then season to taste with salt; you'll need less salt than in the base recipe because of the tamari. Serve with additional sesame seeds, and chopped parsley. **Pictured on page 151**

Heirloom Beans with Tomatoes and Basil

MAKES 5 CUPS | ABOUT 1 POUND. 12½ OUNCES | 810 G
SERVES 4

1 recipe Marinated Beans, using Scarlet Runner, white Corona, or other extra-large creamy beans and replacing the apple cider vinegar with red wine vinegar

2 cups (10 ounces | 290 g) cherry tomatoes in assorted colors, halved

½ cup (⅓ ounce | 10 g) fresh basil leaves, torn

2 tablespoons (30 ml) extra-virgin olive oil

2 tablespoons (30 ml) red wine vinegar

Flaky sea salt and freshly ground black pepper

Make the beans following the instructions for the base recipe, adding the cherry tomatoes, basil, olive oil, and red wine vinegar along with the other ingredients, then season with flaky salt and pepper to taste. **Pictured on the following page**

NOTE: Because of the fresh tomatoes, this recipe won't keep as long as the other variations and should be eaten within a few hours of making it. If you want to make it ahead, don't add the tomatoes until just before serving.

BEAN TOPPINGS AND FLAVORINGS

Beans love vinegar and olive oil. Their creamy, starchy texture absorbs flavor easily. You can dress up beans in so many ways with added herbs, seeds, and chiles. Try these recipes (pictured from left to right):

- Heirloom Beans with Tomatoes and Basil (page 149)

- Herbed Corona Beans (page 149)

- Adzuki Beans with Tamari, Scallions, and Toasted Sesame Seeds (page 149)

- Chickpeas with Chili and Parsley (page 148)

Red Lentil Pâté

MAKES 2 CUPS | 1 POUND, 2 OUNCES | 510 G | SERVES 4

1 cup (6½ ounces | 185 g)
red lentils

1½ cups (360 ml) filtered water

One 2-inch (5 cm) piece kombu

3 large garlic cloves

3 tablespoons (45 ml) extra-virgin
olive oil, plus more for serving

½ teaspoon fine sea salt, or to taste

Put the lentils in a medium pot, cover them with tap water, swish them around with your fingers, and drain. Repeat and return the drained lentils to the pot. Add the filtered water, kombu, and garlic and bring to a boil over high heat. Cover the pot, reduce the heat to low, and simmer for 20 minutes, or until the lentils are soft and all the water has been absorbed. Remove from the heat and remove the kombu (compost it).

Add the olive oil and salt and stir vigorously until the lentils and garlic are smooth and creamy. Drizzle with olive oil and serve warm or at room temperature. Store the cooled pâté in a jar or an airtight container in the fridge for up to 4 days.

NOTE: The pâté will firm up when chilled. To serve, heat it in a covered saucepan with a splash of water over low heat, stirring frequently, until warmed through and creamy. Season with salt if needed.

Red Lentil Pâté with Dukkah

MAKES 2 CUPS | 1 POUND, 3 OUNCES | 540 G |
SERVES 4

1 recipe Red Lentil Pâté

⅓ cup (1 ounce | 32 g) Hazelnut Dukkah
(recipe follows), plus more for serving

Make the pâté following the instructions for the
base recipe. When the lentils are cooked, stir in
the dukkah and continue as directed, keeping in
mind when seasoning the mixture that the dukkah
contains salt. Serve sprinkled with more dukkah.

Hazelnut Dukkah

MAKES 1¾ CUPS | 5½ OUNCES | 155 G

½ cup (2½ ounces | 70 g) raw unhulled sesame
seeds

2 tablespoons (⅓ ounce | 10 g) coriander seeds

2 tablespoons (⅓ ounce | 10 g) cumin seeds

1 tablespoon fennel seeds

½ cup (2¼ ounces | 65 g) raw hazelnuts, toasted
(see page 390) and skinned

1 teaspoon flaky sea salt

1 teaspoon freshly ground black pepper

Warm a large skillet over low-medium heat. Add the
sesame, coriander, cumin, and fennel seeds and toast,
stirring frequently, for 4 to 5 minutes, until deeply
fragrant. Transfer to a food processor and grind until
the spices are cracked. Add the hazelnuts and pulse
until crushed. Add the salt and pepper and pulse to
combine, then transfer to a jar. Secure with the lid
once the dukkah has cooled and store in a cool, dark
place for up to 3 months. **Pictured on page 339**

Red Lentil Pâté with Lemon and Herbs

MAKES 2 CUPS | 1 POUND, 3¼ OUNCES | 545 G |
SERVES 4

1 recipe Red Lentil Pâté

3 tablespoons (45 ml) freshly squeezed lemon juice

2 teaspoons minced fresh oregano

1 teaspoon minced fresh thyme

Make the pâté following the instructions for the
base recipe. When the lentils are cooked, stir in the
lemon juice, oregano, and thyme and continue as
directed. **Pictured on page 163**

Butter Bean Pâté

MAKES 2 CUPS | ABOUT 1 POUND, 1¼ OUNCES | 490 G | SERVES 4

3 cups (15½ ounces | 440 g) cooked butter beans or two 15½-ounce (440 g) cans beans, drained and well rinsed

¼ cup (60 ml) extra-virgin olive oil

½ teaspoon finely grated or pressed garlic (see the sidebar)

½ teaspoon fine sea salt, or more to taste

Freshly ground black pepper

Put the beans, olive oil, garlic, salt, and pepper in a food processor and process until completely smooth, with a fluffy whipped texture; this will take a couple of minutes to achieve. Season to taste with more salt and pepper if necessary. Serve, or store in an airtight container in the fridge for up to 4 days.

GRATED GARLIC

The quickest, easiest, and, in my opinion, best way to add a little garlic to dressings, sauces, or other dishes is to grate the clove on a Microplane. This technique results in the same texture you get from using a garlic press, but cleanup is much easier.

In these pâtés, I add grated garlic because it's easier to measure than a whole garlic clove.

Beet and Cashew Butter Bean Pâté

MAKES 2¾ CUPS | 1 POUND, 5¾ OUNCES | 620 G | SERVES 4 TO 6

1 recipe Butter Bean Pâté, using 2 tablespoons (30 ml) olive oil

1 small (3½ ounces | 100 g) red beet, cooked (see page 223)

¼ cup (2 ounces | 60 g) raw cashew butter

1 teaspoon raw apple cider vinegar

2 teaspoons balsamic vinegar

Make the pâté following the instructions for the base recipe, adding the beet, cashew butter, cider vinegar, and balsamic vinegar to the processor along with the other ingredients and blending until completely smooth, then continue as directed. **Pictured on page 61**

Herbed Butter Bean Pâté with Leeks and Spinach

MAKES ABOUT 2¾ CUPS | 1 POUND, 7 OUNCES | 650 G | SERVES 4 TO 6

1 recipe Butter Bean Pâté, using 2 tablespoons (30 ml) olive oil

1 tablespoon extra-virgin coconut oil

1 medium (8 ounces | 230 g) leek (see Note, page 129), sliced (2 heaping cups)

¼ teaspoon fine sea salt, plus more to taste

4 cups (3 ounces | 85 g) baby spinach leaves

2 tablespoons (30 ml) freshly squeezed lemon juice

2 tablespoons (⅕ ounce | 6 g) chopped fresh dill

Freshly ground black pepper

Make the pâté following the instructions for the base recipe and leave the mixture in the food processor.

Warm the coconut oil in a large skillet over medium heat. Add the leeks and salt and cook, stirring frequently, for 5 minutes. Cover the pan, reduce the heat to low, and cook for another 5 minutes, or until the leeks are soft. Add the spinach, cover the pan, and let the spinach wilt for 3 minutes. Remove the lid and stir until the spinach is cooked. Transfer the leeks and spinach to the food processor, add the lemon juice and dill, and blend until smooth. Adjust the seasoning with more salt and pepper to taste. **Pictured on page 163**

Chickpea Pâté

MAKES ABOUT 2 CUPS | 1 POUND, 1¼ OUNCES | 460 G | SERVES 4

1 cup whole raw nuts (weight depends on the nuts used; see the variations for measures), toasted (see page 390)

2 tablespoons (30 ml) extra-virgin olive oil, plus more for drizzling

1½ cups (7½ ounces | 215 g) cooked chickpeas, drained, reserving ⅓ cup (80 ml) liquid, or one 15½-ounce (440 g) can chickpeas, drained and rinsed well

½ cup (120 ml) filtered water if using canned chickpeas

1 teaspoon fine sea salt, plus more to taste

½ teaspoon grated or pressed garlic (see the sidebar on page 154)

½ teaspoon raw apple cider vinegar

Put the nuts and oil in a food processor and blend until completely smooth, scraping down the sides as necessary. It will take a few minutes to reach a runny consistency. Add the chickpeas, cooking liquid (or water), salt, garlic, and vinegar and blend until completely smooth. Add more cooking liquid or water if necessary to get the desired consistency; this will take a couple of minutes. Add more salt to taste and serve, drizzled with olive oil. Or store in an airtight container in the fridge for up to 4 days.

Chickpea Pâté with Almond, Chili, and Sumac

MAKES ABOUT 2¼ CUPS | 1 POUND, 3 OUNCES | 540 G | SERVES 4

1 recipe Chickpea Pâté, using 1 cup (5 ounces | 140 g) whole raw almonds, toasted (see page 390), ¼ cup (60 ml) olive oil, and ¾ cup (180 ml) chickpea cooking liquid or water

2 tablespoons (½ ounce | 15 g) ground sumac, plus more for garnish

1 tablespoon red chili pepper flakes

1 Medjool date, pitted and roughly chopped

Chopped toasted almonds for garnish

Make the pâté following the instructions for the base recipe, adding the sumac, red chili pepper flakes, and date along with the chickpeas and other ingredients. Continue as directed and serve garnished with chopped almonds, a sprinkling of sumac, and a drizzle of olive oil. **Pictured on page 163**

NOTE: If you've made the Salted Almond Butter with Sumac and Chili (page 114), you can use ½ cup (4¾ ounces | 135 g) here in place of the almonds, sumac, red chili pepper flakes, and salt. Season to taste with extra sumac and red chili pepper flakes once mixture is combined.

Pine Nut Chickpea Pâté with Rosemary

MAKES ABOUT 2 CUPS | 1 POUND, 1 OUNCE | 480 G | SERVES 4

1 recipe Chickpea Pâté, using 1 cup (5 ounces | 120 g) raw pine nuts, toasted (see page 242), and 1 teaspoon freshly squeezed lemon juice in place of the apple cider vinegar, plus more to taste

1 tablespoon minced fresh rosemary

Cracked black pepper

Make the pâté following the instructions for the base recipe, adding the rosemary when blending the nuts and oil, then continue as directed. Add the lemon juice and salt to taste. Serve topped with cracked black pepper. **Pictured on page 15**

Cashew Chickpea Pâté with Turmeric, Chili, and Lime

MAKES 2 CUPS | 1 POUND, 3¾ OUNCES | 560 G | SERVES 4

1 recipe Chickpea Pâté, using 1 cup (4½ ounces | 130 g) raw cashews, toasted (see page 390)

1 tablespoon finely grated peeled fresh turmeric

2 tablespoons (30 ml) freshly squeezed lime juice, plus more to taste

½ teaspoon cayenne pepper

½ teaspoon tamari

Make the pâté following the instructions for the base recipe, adding the turmeric when the cashews and oil are smooth and blending well to combine. Add the lime, cayenne, and tamari along with the chickpeas and continue as directed. Add more lime juice and salt to taste. **Pictured on page 61**

Quick Bean Sauce

MAKES 3 CUPS | 720 ML | SERVES 4

2 tablespoons (30 ml) extra-virgin coconut or olive oil

1 medium (8 ounces | 230 g) onion, diced

½ teaspoon fine sea salt, plus more to taste

3 large garlic cloves, finely chopped

2 teaspoons chopped fresh thyme

3 cups (15½ ounces | 440 g) cooked beans (see the chart on pages 146–147), such as pinto, cannellini, navy, or black beans, drained, 1 cup (240 ml) liquid reserved, or two 15½-ounce (440 g) cans beans, drained and rinsed well

1 cup (240 ml) filtered water if using canned beans

2 teaspoons raw apple cider vinegar

Warm the oil in a large skillet over medium-high heat. Add the onion and salt and cook for 5 minutes, or until the onion is light golden. Cover the pan, reduce the heat to low, and cook the onion for another 5 minutes, or until soft and beginning to brown. Stir in the garlic and cook, uncovered, for 3 to 4 minutes, until fragrant. Add the thyme and cook for 2 minutes. Stir in the beans and the reserved cooking liquid (or water), raise the heat, and bring the mixture to a boil, then cover the pan, reduce the heat to low, and simmer for 5 minutes. Remove the lid and cook for another 5 minutes, or until the mixture is creamy and the beans are very soft. (If you would like a thicker sauce, continue cooking, uncovered, until the sauce reaches the desired consistency.) You can crush some of the beans with the back of a spoon to create a creamier, smoother sauce if you like; this works best with smaller varieties like black, navy, pinto, or kidney beans. Stir in the vinegar and season with more salt to taste. Serve immediately, or let cool and store in an airtight container in the fridge for up to 4 days.

Pinto Bean Sauce with Tomatoes and Oregano

MAKES ABOUT 3½ CUPS | 840 ML | SERVES 4 TO 6

1 cup (7 ounces | 220 g) canned tomatoes, with their juice

1 recipe Quick Bean Sauce, using pinto beans and ½ cup (120 ml) bean cooking liquid or water and replacing the apple cider vinegar with balsamic vinegar

1 tablespoon chopped fresh oregano

Freshly cracked black pepper

Extra-virgin olive oil for drizzling (optional)

Put the tomatoes in a bowl and crush them with your hands; set aside. Make the bean sauce following the instructions for the base recipe, adding the oregano along with the thyme and adding the tomatoes (with their juices) along with the beans. Continue as directed, and season to taste with pepper as well as more salt. Serve drizzled with olive oil, if desired.

Creamy White Bean Sauce with Greens

MAKES ABOUT 4 CUPS | 960 ML | SERVES 4

1 recipe Quick Bean Sauce, using cannellini or navy beans and ½ cup (120 ml) bean cooking liquid or water

4 cups (5 ounces | 140 g) thinly sliced mixed greens, such as Swiss chard, tatsoi, and spinach

Freshly ground black pepper

Extra virgin olive oil, for drizzling (optional)

Make the bean sauce following the instructions for the base recipe, adding the greens once the beans have simmered, covered, for 5 minutes. Continue cooking as directed, or until the greens are tender and the mixture is creamy. Season to taste with pepper as well as more salt. Serve drizzled with olive oil, if desired. **Pictured on page 161**

OPPOSITE: Ingredients for Pinto Bean Sauce with Tomatoes and Oregano; **ABOVE:** Creamy White Bean Sauce with Greens

BEANS—HOW TO USE

Method	Pairings
Marinated	Chickpeas with Chili and Parsley (page 148) + Toasted sourdough, rubbed with a raw garlic clove and drizzled with extra-virgin olive oil Adzuki Beans with Tamari, Scallions, and Toasted Sesame Seeds (page 149) + Short-grain brown rice (see page 391) + Sliced avocado
Red Lentil Pâté	Red Lentil Pâté with Dukkah (page 153) + Warmed bread + Cucumbers Red Lentil Pâté with Lemon and Herbs (page 153) + Pickled Carrots with Coriander and Chile (page 194) + Lacto-Fermented Radishes (page 195)
Butter Bean Pâté	Beet and Cashew Butter Bean Pâté (page 155) + Black Rice–Black Sesame Crackers (page 287) Herbed Butter Bean Pâté with Leeks and Spinach (page 155) + Seasonal crudités + Toasted sourdough + Olives

Method	Pairings
Chickpea Pâté	Chickpea Pâté with Almond, Chili, and Sumac (page 157) + Lettuce cup + Grated carrot + Sliced avocado + Sliced scallions + Olive-oil-and-lemon drizzle Pine Nut Chickpea Pâté with Rosemary (page 157) + Roasted seasonal vegetables (see pages 178–179)
Bean	Pinto Bean Sauce with Tomatoes and Oregano (page 159) + Short-grain brown rice or quinoa (see page 391) + Crumbled feta or avocado Creamy White Bean Sauce with Greens (page 159) + Steamed kabocha (see page 171)
Any Bean, Cooked	Chickpeas + Fennel and Green Cabbage Kraut (page 194) + Sliced avocado + Steamed broccoli (see page 170) + Sliced scallions Heirloom beans + Extra-virgin olive oil + Apple cider vinegar + Chopped parsley + Sliced scallions + Crumbled feta or nut cheese

OPPOSITE, CLOCKWISE FROM TOP LEFT: Herbed Butter Bean Pâté with Leeks and Spinach; Chickpea Pâté with Almond, Chili, and Sumac; Red Lentil Pâté with Lemon and Herbs; Lacto-Fermented Radishes

Vegetables: Land and Sea

—

The vegetable recipes in this chapter are super simple and quick to prepare, and I urge you to get in the habit of making these and other dishes with produce chosen intuitively—that is, just get the vegetables that look the best at the farmers' market or wherever you are shopping. If an ingredient you have on your list does not look fresh and appealing, reach for another one instead. Unlike the porridges, breads, and bean and grain dishes in this book, vegetables don't require much advance planning (except for the recipes that require fermentation). The preparation technique can depend on what you're craving or think your dining partners will enjoy that day, and, of course, it should always be a reflection of the season.

Since there's no question that increasing our vegetable intake is absolutely beneficial to our health and well-being, it makes sense to put vegetables at the center of many of your meals, and the recipes you'll find in this chapter will allow you to do just that. Plus, the simple methods of steaming, roasting, sautéing, and quick-pickling fresh, seasonal vegetables, outlined in the following sections, can provide delicious results. If you have not introduced sea vegetables—especially the sustainable, wild-harvested kind from nearby oceans—into your diet, do try the recipes for them included here.

According to Chinese medicine and Ayurvedic tradition, an excess of raw foods can diminish one's digestive fire, so most of the food I eat is cooked, especially in the winter. Along with sprouts and microgreens from the farmers' market, the raw foods I enjoy year-round are naturally fermented vegetables and sauerkrauts, and you will find recipes for those here as well.

STEAMED VEGETABLES

Steaming is one of the fastest ways to get a healthy, flavorful, and satisfying meal on the table. One night you might enjoy a bowl of steamed sliced squash and greens topped with a poached egg, scallions, and a drizzle of dressing; another night it might be steamed broccoli tossed with fermented vegetables, chickpeas, toasted seeds, and sliced avocado. And even when you are making a dish that doesn't contain greens, you can quickly steam kale, collard greens, or chard to have on the side. The steamer is also handy for warming up leftover beans or grains; add sliced dark, leafy greens, and you have a one-pot meal.

In fact, while most vegetables are best when freshly steamed, with some, it's worth making extra to ensure that you have leftovers. For example, steamed squash still tastes good for a few days, and it can be a welcome sweet note in a bean or grain bowl or on sandwiches or toast. You'll find recipes here for a Leftover Steamed Vegetable Miso Bowl, as well as two steamed vegetable salads, which are delicious with any of the dressings on pages 214–229. Steamed vegetable salads are a lovely way to eat an array of vegetables and are more substantial and nourishing than just raw leaves; they can be served year-round, warm or at room temperature.

BASIC METHOD

Fill the bottom of a steamer pot or another large pot with about 2 inches (5 cm) of filtered water (make sure the water level is below your steamer basket or rack). Bring to a boil over high heat and set the steamer basket in place. Add your prepped vegetables, cover, and steam until the vegetables are cooked; check the chart below for timing. With tender green vegetables, it's best to remove them just before they're completely cooked through, as they will continue cooking as they sit. On the other hand, it's not a problem if you overcook large wedges of winter squash by a minute or two, since their flavor won't be diminished, unlike that of most vegetables.

STEAMED VEGETABLE COOKING TIMES

These times are for a steamer that is 9 inches (23 cm) in diameter. If you are using a smaller steamer and the vegetables are layered, they may take longer to cook. If there is a vegetable that you don't see here, please check the Spring/Summer Steamed Vegetable Salad (page 173) or the Fall/Winter Steamed Vegetable Salad (page 173) for steaming instructions.

Vegetable	Amount	Cut	Cooking Time	Yield
Asparagus, Medium	1 pound | 455 g	Whole, ends trimmed	2 minutes	Serves 2
Bok Choy	1 medium | 14 ounces | 400 g	Stems chopped into ½-inch (1.25) cm pieces	2 minutes	Serves 2 to 4
Broccoli	1 medium head | 10 ounces | 285 g	Medium florets; stems peeled and cut into ¼-inch (6 mm) slices	3 minutes	Serves 2 to 4
Butternut Squash	4 cups | 1½ pounds | 680 g	Peeled, seeded, and cut into 1-inch (2.5 cm) triangles	8 minutes	Serves 4
Cabbage	2 cups sliced | 6 ounces | 170 g	¼-inch (6 mm) slices	3 to 4 minutes	Serves 2

Vegetable	Amount	Cut	Cooking Time	Yield
Carrots	3 cups, sliced | 5 medium | 1 pound | 455 g	¼-inch (6 mm) slices	3 minutes	Serves 4
Cauliflower	½ medium head | 8 ounces | 230 g	Medium florets	5 to 6 minutes	Serves 2 to 4
Chard/Spinach/ Japanese Turnip Greens	5 ounces | 140 g	Leaves cut into 1-inch (2.5 cm) slices (spinach left whole)	1 to 2 minutes	Serves 2
Daikon	1 medium | 1 pound | 455 g	Peeled and cut into ¼-inch (6 mm) slices	4 minutes	Serves 4
English Peas, Fresh	2 pounds | 910 g	Shelled	4 minutes	Serves 4
English Peas, Frozen	2 cups | 10 ounces | 385 g	Frozen	1 minute	Serves 4
Green Beans	8 ounces | 230 g	Whole, stem end trimmed	2 to 3 minutes	Serves 4
Japanese Turnips	2 cups | 12 ounces | 340 g	Halved	3 minutes	Serves 2 to 4
Kabocha Squash	½ medium | 1½ pounds | 680 g	1 x 3-inch (2.5 x 7.5 cm) wedges	12 to 15 minutes	Serves 4
Kale/Collards	1 large bunch | 12 ounces | 340 g	Tough stems removed; cut into 1-inch (2.5 cm) slices	2 to 3 minutes	Serves 4
Kohlrabi	1 medium | 8 ounces | 230 g	Peeled and cut into ¼-inch (6 mm) slices	3 to 4 minutes	Serves 2
Radishes, Small	1 large bunch | 10 ounces | 285 g	Halved	3 to 4 minutes	Serves 2 to 4
Snow Peas	2 cups | 5 ounces | 140 g	Whole, strings removed	1½ minutes	Serves 2
Sugar Snap Peas	2 cups | 6 ounces | 170 g	Whole, strings removed	2 minutes	Serves 2
Sweet Corn	2 ears	Shucked	3 minutes	Serves 2
Sweet Potato	1 medium | 14 ounces | 400 g	Halved lengthwise and cut into ¼-inch (6 mm) slices	5 minutes	Serves 2 to 4
Watermelon Radish	1 large | 12 ounces | 340 g	Peeled, halved and cut into ¼-inch (6 mm) slices	3 minutes	Serves 2
Zucchini/Summer Squash	1 medium | 8 ounces | 230 g	Cut into ¼-inch (6 mm) slices	2 minutes	Serves 2

Spring/Summer Steamed Vegetable Salad

Spring/Summer Steamed Vegetable Salad

SERVES 4

8 ounces (230 g) asparagus, cut diagonally into 1-inch (2.5 cm) lengths (about 2 cups)

6 medium (4 ounces | 115 g) radishes, cut into 6 wedges each (about 2 cups)

2 cups (6 ounces | 170 g) sugar snap peas, strings removed and halved lengthwise on a diagonal

2 medium (1 pound | 455 g) golden zucchini, cut into ¼-inch (6 mm) slices (about 2½ cups)

2 medium (6 ounces | 115 g) carrots, cut into ¼-inch (6 mm) slices (about 2 cups)

½ cup (2½ ounces | 70 g) fresh or frozen peas

1 medium (5 ounces | 140 g) watermelon radish, peeled, halved, and sliced into ¼-inch (6 mm) slices

1 cup (240 ml) dressing of your choice (see pages 214–229)

Set up a steamer and fill the pot with about 2 inches (5 cm) of filtered water. Bring to a boil over high heat and set the steamer basket in place. Steam each vegetable separately, spreading the vegetables out in the basket to ensure even steaming: Steam the asparagus, radishes, sugar snaps, and zucchini for 2 minutes each, or until just tender. Remove swiftly when they are done, transfer to a flat plate, and spread out to cool. Steam the carrots and fresh peas, if using, for 3 minutes each and transfer to separate plates to cool; if using frozen peas, steam them for about a minute, or until just heated through. Finally, steam the watermelon radish for 3 minutes, or until tender, and transfer to a plate to cool. Once the vegetables are cool, drain the liquid from each plate, transfer the vegetables to a bowl, and toss to combine. The vegetables can be stored, undressed, in the fridge in an airtight container for up to 3 days, though they will lose their bright color after a day or so. Serve at room temperature, with the dressing of your choice.

Fall/Winter Steamed Vegetable Salad

SERVES 4 TO 6

1 medium (8 ounces | 230 g) kohlrabi, peeled, halved, and cut into ¼-inch (6 mm) slices

4 medium (5 ounces | 140 g) Japanese turnips, cut into ¾-inch (2 cm) wedges (1½ cups)

1 medium (5 ounces | 140 g) watermelon radish, peeled, halved, and cut into ¼-inch (6 mm) slices (1 cup)

1 medium (5 ounces | 140 g) purple daikon radish, peeled and cut into ¼-inch (6 mm) slices (1 cup)

3 medium (8 ounces | 230 g) carrots, cut diagonally into ¼-inch (6 mm) slices (2 cups)

2 cups (4½ ounces | 130 g) small broccoli florets

½ cup (2 ounces | 60 g) ¼-inch | 6 mm slices leek (see Note, page 129)

1 cup (240 ml) dressing of your choice (see pages 214–229)

Set up a steamer and fill the pot with about 2 inches (5 cm) of filtered water. Bring to a boil over high heat and set the steamer basket in place. Steam each vegetable separately, spreading them out in the basket to ensure even steaming: Steam the kohlrabi for 3 to 4 minutes, until tender, then swiftly remove from the steamer and spread out on a large plate to cool. Steam the turnips, watermelon radish, purple radish, and carrots for 3 minutes each, or until tender, and transfer to separate plates to cool. Wipe out the steamer basket if any of the darker-colored vegetables have bled. Steam the broccoli and leeks for 2 minutes each and spread out on another plate. Once the vegetables are cool, drain the liquid from each plate, transfer the vegetables to a large bowl, and toss to combine. The vegetables can be stored, undressed, in the fridge in an airtight container for up to 3 days, though they will lose their bright color after a day or so. Serve at room temperature, with the dressing of your choice.

Steamed Kabocha Squash with Nori and Scallions

SERVES 4 AS A SIDE DISH

½ medium (1½ pounds | 680 g) kabocha squash, seeded (skin left on) and cut into 1 x 3-inch (2.5 x 7.5 cm) wedges

1 sheet nori, toasted and crushed (see the sidebar on page 202)

2 scallions, thinly sliced, plus more for garnish

2 tablespoons (30 ml) tamari

1 tablespoon mirin

2 tablespoons (½ ounce | 15 g) raw unhulled sesame seeds, toasted (see page 390)

Set up a steamer and fill the pot with about 2 inches (5 cm) of filtered water. Bring to a boil over high heat and set the steamer basket in place. Arrange the kabocha wedges skin side down in the basket in a single layer and steam for 12 to 15 minutes, until the flesh is soft when pierced with a paring knife.

Meanwhile, combine the nori, scallions, tamari, and mirin in a small bowl; set aside.

When the squash is cooked, transfer to a serving platter and drizzle the nori mixture over the top. Sprinkle with the sesame seeds and scallions and serve. (Any leftovers can be stored in the fridge for 2 to 3 days.)

Leftover Steamed Vegetable Miso Bowl

SERVES 2

3 cups (about 12 ounces | 340 g) steamed vegetables (such as winter squash, radishes, broccoli, cabbage, and/or peas; see the chart on pages 170–171)

2 cups (480 ml) filtered water

2 teaspoons finely grated peeled fresh ginger

2 teaspoons finely grated peeled fresh turmeric (optional)

3 tablespoons (1½ ounces | 45 g) unpasteurized chickpea miso, mellow white miso, or brown rice miso, or a combination

Thinly sliced scallions or fresh chives

Put the vegetables and water in a medium pot and bring to a boil over high heat, stirring to ensure that the vegetables reheat evenly. Reduce the heat to a simmer and stir in the ginger and turmeric, if using. Transfer about ⅓ cup (80 ml) of the liquid to a small bowl and stir in the miso until dissolved, then stir into the vegetables and remove from the heat (be careful not to let the miso boil, as that would destroy the enzymes). Divide between two bowls, top with scallions or chives, and serve.

NOTE: If you have greens like kale, chard, spinach, or tatsoi on hand, you can stir some sliced greens into the vegetables and cook lightly before adding the miso. You can also add Ginger-Marinated Wakame (page 204) or Quick Marinated Arame (page 204) and heat through before adding the miso.

OPPOSITE: Leftover Steamed Vegetable Miso Bowl

ROASTED VEGETABLES

Just about any vegetable tastes good roasted. You can use the technique when you want a more concentrated and richer taste, and you can also use it to make food ahead of time. Roasted vegetables taste great at room temperature, and they keep very well in the fridge for a few days.

In the fall, there's nothing like plain roasted winter squash, with its velvety texture and deep, sweet flavor. In winter, roasted cabbage wedges, with their crispy outer leaves, are addictive. And then in warmer weather, there are succulent roasted eggplant and juicy collapsed tomatoes as summer comes to a close. There are limitless combinations of vegetables you can roast together in one pan, and even more options when you add herbs or spices to the mix. Sometimes just a simple scattering of fennel seeds and ground turmeric before roasting will be enough; other times, a heavy shower of chopped fresh herbs and a squeeze of lemon after they've been removed from the oven are all that's needed to make a meal out of roasted vegetables. And because they store well, you can keep some on hand to be easily added to lunch boxes, salads, and bowls.

BASIC METHOD

Preheat the oven to 400°F (200°C).

Line a baking sheet with parchment paper and spread the vegetables over it in a single layer. They can touch a little, but the pan shouldn't be crowded, or the vegetables will steam, not roast—they need room to get crispy and browned around the edges, and juicier vegetables will release liquid. Drizzle with 1 to 2 tablespoons (15 to 30 ml) melted extra-virgin coconut oil or ghee (these oils can withstand this high temperature, although I do sometimes make an exception for tomatoes and use extra-virgin olive oil), sprinkle with a large pinch of salt, and use your hands to toss the vegetables, making sure each piece is lightly coated in oil. Spread them out in a single layer again, largest flat surface down if the vegetables are cut, and place in the oven. See the chart on the following pages for roasting times. Most vegetables need to be turned over or the tray rotated after 20 minutes. Then return to the oven and roast for another 10 to 15 minutes. Harder vegetables are ready when they are soft inside (test by cutting into one with a knife) and well browned on all sides; softer vegetables should be browned and reduced in size. Most vegetables will shrink quite a bit as they roast. Remove the pan from the oven, lift the parchment paper, and slide the vegetables onto a serving dish or platter. Or leave them to cool on the baking sheet and then store in airtight containers in the fridge for up to 4 days.

If your oven has a convection setting, it's great to use for roasting vegetables with a higher water content like tomatoes, zucchini, and radishes. It can also work well for speeding up the bake time of whole roasted sweet potatoes and denser-fleshed vegetables that are not cut into large pieces—otherwise the center won't cook through before the edges brown. When using the convection setting, reduce the oven temperature to 375°F (190°C) and check the vegetables halfway through the bake times listed in the chart on the following pages. They cook quite a bit faster using convection, so keep an eye on them.

ROASTED VEGETABLE COOKING TIMES

The roasting times in this chart are approximate, as actual time will depend on the size of your pan and your oven—these vegetables are all roasted on one half sheet pan, which is a rimmed baking sheet that is 17 x 12 inches (43 x 30 cm). The best oils to use are coconut oil and ghee—they need to be melted before measuring. If you roast two baking sheets at a time, switch the positions of the pans and rotate them halfway through; you will most likely have to increase the time, as there will be more moisture in the oven.

Vegetable	Amount	Cut	Amount of Oil + Sea Salt	Cooking Temperature	Cooking Time	Yield
Asparagus	1½ pounds | 680 g	Whole, ends trimmed	4 teaspoons | 20 ml + ½ teaspoon	400°F | 200°C	20 to 30 minutes (depending on thickness)	Serves 2 to 4
Beets	8 small-medium beets | 1½ pounds | 680 g	Scrubbed, sliced into ¼-inch (6 mm) rounds	2 tablespoons | 30 ml + 1 teaspoon	400°F | 200°C	20 minutes, then stir and roast another 10 minutes	Serves 4 to 6
Bell Peppers	4 medium | 1½ pounds | 680 g	Halved and seeded and cut into ¾-inch (2 cm) strips	2 tablespoons | 30 ml + 1 teaspoon	400°F | 200°C	20 minutes, then stir and roast another 15 minutes	Serves 6
Broccoli	1¼ pounds | 565 g	Cut into florets, stems peeled and cut into ½-inch (1.25 cm) slices	2 tablespoons | 30 ml + ¾ teaspoon	400°F | 200°C	20 minutes, then stir and roast another 10 minutes	Serves 4
Brussels Sprouts	1½ pounds | 680 g	Trimmed and halved	2 tablespoons | 30 ml + 1 teaspoon	400°F | 200°C	20 minutes, then stir and roast another 10 minutes	Serves 4
Butternut Squash	1 medium | 3 pounds | 1.36 kg	Peeled, seeded, and cut into 1-inch (2.5 cm) triangles	2 tablespoons | 30 ml + 1 teaspoon	400°F | 200°C	20 minutes, then stir and roast another 10 minutes	Serves 4 to 6
Cabbage	1 large | 2 pounds | 910 g	Cut into 1½-inch (4 cm) wedges (about 10)	2 tablespoons | 30 ml + 1 teaspoon	400°F | 200°C	50 minutes	Serves 4
Cauliflower	1 medium | 2 pounds | 910 g	Cut into ¾-inch (2 cm) florets	2 tablespoons | 30 ml + 1 teaspoon	400°F | 200°C	30 minutes, then stir and roast another 10 minutes	Serves 4 to 6

Vegetable	Amount	Cut	Amount of Oil + Sea Salt	Cooking Temperature	Cooking Time	Yield
Delicata Squash	2 medium | 1½ pounds | 680 g	Seeded and sliced into ½-inch (1.25 cm) rounds	2 tablespoons | 30 ml + 1 teaspoon	400°F | 200°C	25 minutes, then turn the squash over and roast another 10 minutes	Serves 4 to 6
Eggplant	1 medium to large | 1½ pounds | 680 g	½ inch x 3-inch (1.25 cm x 7.5 cm) wedges	3 tablespoons | 45 ml + 1 teaspoon	400°F | 200°C	25 minutes, then turn over and roast another 15 minutes	Serves 4
Garlic Scapes	8 ounces | 230 g	Whole	1 tablespoon + ½ teaspoon	400°F | 200°C	20 minutes	Serves 2
Green Beans	1 pound | 455 g	Whole stem, end trimmed	1 tablespoon + ½ teaspoon	400°F | 200°C	20 to 25 minutes	Serves 2 to 4
Jerusalem Artichokes	1½ pounds | 680 g	Halved lengthwise	2 tablespoons | 30 ml + 1 teaspoon	400°F | 200°C	Cut side down for 30 to 40 minutes	Serves 6
Kale, Curly	1 bunch | 8 ounces | 230 g	Stems removed, torn into 2-inch (5 cm) pieces, washed and dried well	1 tablespoon + ½ teaspoon	300°F | 150°C	15 minutes, then rotate trays and roast another 10 to 15 minutes	Serves 2 to 4
Potatoes	2½ pounds | 1.13 kg	Scrubbed, cut into 1-inch (2.5 cm) cubes	2 tablespoons | 30 ml + 1 teaspoon	400°F | 200°C	30 minutes, then stir and roast another 25 to 30 minutes	Serves 6
Sweet Potatoes, Cut	1½ pounds | 680 g	Halved lengthwise, then cut into 1 x 3-inch (2.5 x 7.5 cm) wedges	2 tablespoons | 30 ml + 1 teaspoon	400°F | 200°C	Cut side down, roast 20 minutes, turn over and roast another 10 minutes	Serves 4
Sweet Potatoes, Whole	1 medium | 14 ounces | 400 g	Whole, skin on, pricked with a fork	None	400°F | 200°C	60 minutes	Serves 1 to 2
Tomatoes, plum	10 medium | 2 pounds | 900 g	Quartered	2 tablespoons | 30 ml + 1 teaspoon	400°F | 200°C	30 minutes, then rotate the tray and roast for another 30 minutes	Serves 6

Spicy Miso-Roasted Tomatoes and Eggplant

SERVES 4 TO 6 AS A SIDE DISH

- 1 medium (1 pound | 455 g) eggplant, cut into 1 x 3-inch (2.5 x 7.5 cm) wedges
- 4 medium (1½ pounds | 680 g) tomatoes, cut into 6 wedges each
- 1 medium (8 ounces | 230 g) yellow onion, cut into ¼-inch (6 mm) slices
- 3 tablespoons (45 ml) melted extra-virgin coconut oil or olive oil
- 2 tablespoons (1 ounce | 30 g) unpasteurized sweet white miso
- 2 tablespoons (30 ml) mirin (or substitute 1 teaspoon honey or maple syrup)
- 1 tablespoon freshly squeezed lemon juice
- 1 large garlic clove, grated or pressed (see the sidebar on page 154)
- 1 teaspoon ground coriander
- 1 teaspoon red chili pepper flakes
- ½ teaspoon ground turmeric
- ½ teaspoon fine sea salt, plus more to taste
- ¾ cup (4 ounces | 115 g) cooked chickpeas (see page 146), well drained
- Chopped fresh flat-leaf parsley or cilantro leaves for garnish
- Thick coconut or whole-milk yogurt for serving

Preheat the oven to 400°F (200°C).

Line a large baking sheet with parchment paper and put the eggplant, tomatoes, and onion on it. Combine the oil, miso, mirin, lemon juice, garlic, coriander, red chili pepper flakes, turmeric, and salt in a small bowl and stir until smooth. Pour over the vegetables and toss until evenly coated. Spread the vegetables out on the pan; they should almost be in a single layer, with just a few overlapping.

Roast for 20 to 25 minutes, until the vegetables are browned on the bottom. Remove the vegetables from the oven and turn them over as best you can; you may end up just stirring them, as they will be juicy. Roast for another 15 to 20 minutes, until the vegetables are completely soft and browned in spots. Scatter the chickpeas over the vegetables, sprinkle with a little more salt, and return to the oven for 5 more minutes to warm the chickpeas through. Transfer the vegetables to a serving platter and top with the herbs. Serve warm or at room temperature, with yogurt on the side. Any leftovers can be stored in an airtight container in the fridge for up to 3 days.

Mustard-Roasted Beets and Shallots with Thyme

SERVES 6 AS A SIDE DISH

- 8 medium (2 pounds | 910 g) mixed-color beets
- 8 large (1 pound | 455 g) shallots
- 3 large garlic cloves, finely chopped
- 2 tablespoons (⅛ ounce | 4 g) coarsely chopped fresh thyme
- 3 tablespoons (45 ml) melted extra-virgin coconut oil
- 3 tablespoons (¼ ounce | 7 g) Dijon mustard
- 1 tablespoon black mustard seeds
- 1 tablespoon balsamic vinegar
- 1½ teaspoons fine sea salt

Preheat the oven to 400°F (200°C). Line a rimmed baking sheet with parchment paper and set aside.

Peel the beets, halve lengthwise, and cut each half into ½-inch (1.25 cm) wedges; transfer to the lined

OPPOSITE: Spicy Miso-Roasted Tomatoes and Eggplant

pan. Cut the shallots into 6 wedges each (cut any smaller ones into quarters) and add to the pan, along with the garlic and thyme. Stir together the oil, mustard, mustard seeds, balsamic vinegar, and salt in a small bowl and drizzle over the vegetables. Use your hands to toss until thoroughly coated and then spread the vegetables out in a single layer on the pan.

Roast the vegetables for 20 to 25 minutes, then stir and roast for another 20 minutes, or until tender and browning in spots. Serve warm or at room temperature. Any leftovers can be stored in an airtight container in the fridge for up to 4 days.

Lemony Roasted Cauliflower with Coriander

SERVES 4 TO 6 AS A SIDE DISH

1 medium (2 pounds | 910 g) cauliflower, cut into 1-inch (2.5 cm) florets

¼ cup (2 ounces | 60 g) raw cashew butter

2 tablespoons (30 ml) filtered water

Grated zest of 1 lemon

2 tablespoons (30 ml) freshly squeezed lemon juice

2 tablespoons (30 ml) melted extra-virgin coconut oil

2 teaspoons ground coriander

1 teaspoon fine sea salt

1 large garlic clove, grated or pressed (see the sidebar on page 154)

¼ teaspoon ground turmeric

Preheat the oven to 400°F (200°C). Line a rimmed baking sheet with parchment paper and set aside.

Set up a steamer and fill the pot with about 1 inch (2.5 cm) of filtered water. Bring to a boil over high heat and set the steamer basket in place. Arrange the cauliflower evenly in the basket and steam for 5 minutes, or until a knife slides easily into a floret. Transfer to a bowl and set aside.

Combine the cashew butter, water, lemon zest, and lemon juice in a small bowl and stir until smooth. Add the coconut oil, coriander, salt, garlic, and turmeric and stir to combine. Pour over the cauliflower and use your hands to gently and thoroughly mix, making sure every floret is thoroughly coated.

Spread the cauliflower out on the parchment-lined baking sheet and roast for 20 to 25 minutes, until browned on the bottom. Remove from the oven and turn each piece over, then roast for another 10 to 15 minutes, until golden brown. Serve warm. This is best served right away, but any leftovers can be stored in an airtight container in the fridge for 2 to 3 days.

SAUTÉED VEGETABLES

Sautéing fits the bill when you're in a hurry and you want something tasty and loaded with vegetables, or it's hot outside and you don't want to heat up the oven. Sautéing is one of the best ways to take advantage of the new arrivals at the farmers' market in spring and early summer—from the first tender greens like ramps (wild leeks), dandelion, and nettles to peas, asparagus, and baby zucchini, and their blossoms. Once the vegetables are sautéed, you can turn them into a one-pot meal by adding leftover beans or grains. Then finish them with a squeeze of lemon or a scattering of chopped fresh herbs to brighten everything up.

BASIC METHOD

Place a large skillet or wok over medium-high heat and heat 1 to 2 tablespoons (15 to 30 ml) extra-virgin coconut oil or ghee. Add 1 to 2 chopped garlic cloves, if you like, and sauté, stirring frequently, until fragrant and light golden. Add 6 to 8 cups (about 5 ounces | 140 g) chopped greens or 2 to 3 cups (about 12 ounces | 340 g) other thinly sliced vegetables and a pinch of fine sea salt. If using greens, stir until they begin to wilt, and then continue cooking until tender and just cooked through. Vegetables like zucchini, sugar snap peas, carrots, and asparagus will take only a few minutes to cook and are nice served a little crisp.

Broccolini on Fire

SERVES 2 AS A SIDE DISH

1 bunch (10½ ounces | 300 g) broccolini

2 tablespoons (30 ml) extra-virgin coconut oil

4 large garlic cloves, cut into ¼-inch (6 mm) slices

¼ teaspoon fine sea salt

½ teaspoon red chili pepper flakes

Trim the bottom ends of the broccolini stems. Cut the florets off the stems and cut each floret into 2 or 3 pieces. Slice the stems in half lengthwise.

(continued)

ABOVE: Broccolini on Fire; OPPOSITE: Ingredients for Sautéed Root Vegetables with Parsley, Poppy Seeds, and Lemon

Warm the oil in a large heavy skillet, preferably cast iron, over medium heat. Add the garlic and sauté for 4 to 5 minutes, until golden. Using a slotted spoon, remove the garlic from the pan, leaving the oil behind, and set aside. Add the broccolini and stems to the pan and sauté for 12 to 15 minutes, stirring every couple of minutes, until it is tender and starting to brown in parts. Remove from the heat and stir in the salt and red chili pepper flakes and reserved garlic. Serve warm. Any leftovers can be stored in an airtight container in the fridge for up to 3 days. **Pictured on page 184**

Sautéed Root Vegetables with Parsley, Poppy Seeds, and Lemon

SERVES 4 AS A SIDE DISH

2 tablespoons (30 ml) extra-virgin coconut oil

2 large garlic cloves, finely chopped

1 pound (455 g) root vegetables, such as carrots, turnips, parsnips, and/or rutabagas, grated on the large holes of a box grater (about 5 cups)

1 teaspoon fine sea salt, plus more to taste

1 tablespoon poppy seeds

Grated zest of 1 small lemon

1 tablespoon freshly squeezed lemon juice

1½ cups (¾ ounce | 22 g) fresh flat-leaf parsley leaves, coarsely chopped

Warm the oil in a large skillet over medium heat. Add the garlic and sauté for 1 minute, or until golden. Stir in the grated vegetables and salt and cook for 8 minutes, or until the vegetables are softened. Remove from the heat and stir in the poppy seeds, lemon zest, lemon juice, and parsley. Season to taste with more salt and serve warm or at room temperature. Any leftovers can be stored in an airtight container in the fridge for up to 3 days.

Summer Squash and Blossom Sauté with Mint and Peas

SERVES 2 TO 4 AS A SIDE DISH

½ cup (2½ ounces | 70 g) fresh or frozen peas

1 pound (455 g) mixed zucchini and pattypan squash, preferably small ones

1 tablespoon extra-virgin coconut oil

About 15 large (4 ounces | 115 g) zucchini blossoms, stems removed and chopped into ½-inch (1.25 cm) pieces

A handful of fresh mint leaves, torn

1½ ounces (45 g) drained goat's-milk feta or nut cheese, crumbled (optional)

If you're using fresh peas, bring a small saucepan of water to a boil, add the peas, and simmer for 3 minutes, or until tender. Drain and set aside.

Slice baby zucchini lengthwise in half and then crosswise into 2-inch (5 cm) pieces. Cut larger zucchini into ½-inch (1.25 cm) slices. Cut pattypan squash into ½-inch (1.25 cm) wedges. Warm the oil in a wide skillet over medium-high heat. Add the squash and sauté, stirring frequently, until tender and beginning to brown in parts, 2 to 3 minutes. Add the peas and zucchini blossoms and cook for another minute or so, until the blossoms have softened and the peas are heated through. Remove from the heat. Top with the mint and feta or nut cheese, if using, and serve. This is best served fresh, but any leftovers can be stored for a day or two in the fridge.

OPPOSITE: Summer Squash and Blossom Sauté with Mint and Peas

QUICK-PICKLED VEGETABLES

The easy pickling method described at right is a great way to transform raw ingredients almost instantly into crisp, bright, and refreshing garnishes or accompaniments. Unlike brine-pickled vegetables, these are ready in a flash and can be served immediately, though the flavor will develop further as they sit. All the pickles keep for up to 2 weeks in the fridge, and they can be used to jazz up everything from sandwiches to salads and bowls of all kinds. Leftover pickling juice is also a tasty addition to salad dressings and marinades.

It's fun to watch the colors develop when you are pickling different-colored radishes or when adding grated fresh turmeric. Most of these recipes call for raw apple cider vinegar, but you can use different types of vinegars or lemon or lime juice, or even a combination. Citrus zest of any kind is a lovely way to change up the flavors.

Unlike the krauts and fermented vegetables in this chapter, these quick pickles don't contain live active enzymes, so it's best not to substitute them for your daily dose of the fermented variety.

BASIC METHOD

Put 4 cups shaved or thinly sliced vegetables (the weight will vary according to the type) in a medium bowl. Add 1 teaspoon fine sea salt and 6 tablespoons (90 ml) raw apple cider vinegar and mix well; using your hands to massage the vegetables will accelerate the release of juices and get the salt and vinegar into the vegetables. Taste and add more salt and/or vinegar if necessary. Serve right away, or let sit for up to 2 hours to allow the flavors and colors to develop before serving. Store the pickles in their liquid in a tightly sealed jar in the fridge for up to 2 weeks.

NOTE: A mandoline (see Resources, page 393) is a great and efficient way to thinly slice vegetables, and you can shave them directly into the bowl.

Radish Turmeric Pickle

MAKES 2½ CUPS | 1 POUND, 1 OUNCE | 480 G | SERVES 6

1 pound (455 g) medium radishes (about 24)

6 tablespoons (90 ml) raw apple cider vinegar

1 teaspoon fine sea salt, or more to taste

One 2-inch (5 cm) piece (½ ounce | 15 g) fresh turmeric

Trim the tail ends of the radishes and thinly slice the radishes on a mandoline, holding them by their greens, or slice paper-thin with a sharp knife.

Transfer to a medium bowl, add the vinegar and salt, and mix until well combined.

Peel and finely grate the turmeric, then stir it into the radishes and season with more salt if necessary. Serve immediately, or transfer to a jar, cover, and store in the fridge for up to 2 weeks. Invert the jar after an hour or two to make sure all the radishes are combined with liquid and evenly colored by the turmeric.

OPPOSITE, FROM TOP TO BOTTOM: Daikon Beet Pickle with Lime; Radish Turmeric Pickle; Jicama-Citrus Pickle (left); Shaved Fennel and Lemon Pickle (right)

Shaved Fennel and Lemon Pickle

MAKES 2½ CUPS | 8½ OUNCES | 245 G | SERVES 4 TO 6

1 large (12 ounces | 340 g) fennel

3 tablespoons (45 ml) freshly squeezed lemon juice, or more to taste

¾ teaspoon fine sea salt, or more to taste

Trim off the fennel stalks (reserve the fronds to use as a garnish, or add the stalks and fronds to the Restorative Mineral-Mushroom Broth, page 207). Remove any tough outer layers from the fennel bulbs, quarter each one, and remove the cores. Shave on a mandoline or slice paper-thin with a sharp knife. Put the fennel in a medium bowl, add the lemon juice and salt, and mix well to combine. Season to taste with more salt and/or lemon juice if necessary. Serve immediately, or store in a jar in the fridge for up to 1 week. **Pictured on the preceding page**

Jicama-Citrus Pickle

MAKES 3 CUPS | 1 POUND, 1 OUNCE | 480 G | SERVES 6

1 small-medium (1 pound | 455 g) jicama, peeled

2 tablespoons (30 ml) raw apple cider vinegar, or more to taste

1 teaspoon grated orange zest

1 teaspoon grated lime zest

1 teaspoon grated lemon zest

¼ cup (60 ml) freshly squeezed orange juice

2 teaspoons freshly squeezed lime juice

2 teaspoons freshly squeezed lemon juice

1¼ teaspoons fine sea salt, or more to taste

Cut the jicama crosswise into 1-inch (2.5 cm) slices. Shave lengthwise on a mandoline or slice paper-thin with a sharp knife. Transfer to a medium bowl, add the vinegar, citrus zest and juice, and salt, and mix well to combine. Add more vinegar and/or salt to taste if necessary. Serve immediately, or store in a jar in the fridge for up to 1 week. **Pictured on the preceding page**

Daikon Beet Pickle with Lime

MAKES 1½ CUPS | 14 OUNCES | 400 G | SERVES 6

1 medium-large (12 ounces | 340 g) daikon radish, peeled

2 small (3½ ounces | 100 g) beets, preferably 1 red and 1 yellow, peeled

¼ cup (60 ml) freshly squeezed lime juice, or more to taste

1 teaspoon fine sea salt, or more to taste

Thinly shave the daikon and beets on a mandoline, or slice paper-thin with a sharp knife. Transfer to a medium bowl, add the lime juice and salt, and mix well to combine. Add more lime juice and/or salt to taste if necessary. Serve immediately, or store in a jar in the fridge for up to 2 weeks. The color will intensify as the pickle sits. **Pictured on the preceding page**

FERMENTED VEGETABLES

Salt, time, and air are all you need for the magical alchemy of fermentation; this centuries-old practice of preservation and transformation never ceases to amaze me. Fermented vegetables are an essential part of a balanced diet, not only as a means of incorporating probiotics and live enzymes into your everyday meals but also as a way of adding a deliciously bright flavor and texture to everything from crackers and toast to soups, salads, and grain or bean bowls. There is no better or easier way to get a deeply nutritious serving of vegetables in your bowl than with natural ferments—and they don't even need a dressing or sauce. While there are now many different flavors available in just about every health food store and farmers' market, it is, of course, more cost effective to make your own—and you can tailor them to your own tastes, adding different flavors each time.

In this section, you will find instructions for two different fermentation methods. One uses lacto fermentation, with an added brine, and the other is based on the method used for making sauerkraut. Neither of them requires a fermentation crock; a large widemouthed jar with a tight-fitting lid works fine. You will also need something to weight down the vegetables as they ferment. Small glass jars or flat glass lids work fine; there are also glass weights made especially for fermenting (see Resources, page 393), which I highly recommend as they do the best job of keeping vegetables submerged at all times.

BASIC METHODS

These two basic methods for fermentation both use a brine of sorts. The fermented carrots and the kraut create their own brine with the addition of salt to the grated or sliced vegetables—this draws out the juices from the vegetables, which become the brine needed for fermentation to take place. The carrot pickles and lacto-fermented radishes are submerged in a brine you make with salt and water. This method is best for vegetables that won't create a lot of juice on their own, like the large carrots or radishes in the recipes here, or whole pickling cucumbers, cauliflower, green beans, and so on.

For krauts, I recommend including some green cabbage in the mix, as it consistently ferments well and helps create a good amount of brine. Combine the sliced or grated vegetables, salt, and any spices you want to include in a large bowl and mix well, squeezing the vegetables to help them release their juices. Taste the mixture; it should be slightly saltier than you want your kraut to end up. If you're adding spices, keep in mind that their flavors will intensify as the vegetables ferment, and because the volume of the mixture will reduce as it pickles, you really don't need much to get a good kick of flavor. Pack the kraut into a large jar or fermentation crock, pressing each handful down with your fist and using your body weight to release any air bubbles; then add any liquid from the bowl, making sure the vegetables are well submerged. If for some reason the vegetables are not completely submerged, you can make a brine, using the recipe on page 195, and add it as necessary. Be sure to leave about 3 inches (7.5 cm) headspace above the surface of the vegetables. Place a weight on top of the vegetables. Secure the lid, label and date the jar or crock, and store in a cool, dark place (about 65°F | 18°C) to ferment. I start checking mine after about 10 days. It's good to release air every week if you're using a jar as gases build up; you can do this by slowly opening the lid. These ferments are usually ready after 2 to 3 weeks of fermenting and can be stored in the fridge for months.

The term *lacto fermentation* refers to the lactic acid that is created when lactobacillus and other beneficial bacteria found on the skins of vegetables convert the sugars and starches in vegetables to lactic acid. When fermenting vegetables this way, I like to use several smaller jars, which give you the option of fermenting a few different kinds or flavoring the same vegetable in different ways. Prepare a sea salt brine using the recipe on page 195. Cut up the vegetables or leave them whole, depending on the size and type, place them in a jar, along with any herbs or spices you like, then pour the cooled brine over them. Be sure you leave about 1 inch (2.5 cm) of headspace above the vegetables. Press the vegetables down to release any air bubbles, then use a glass weight or small glass lid to keep the vegetables submerged. Secure the lid, put the jar on a plate, and set aside in a cool, dark place (about 65°F | 18°C) for 1 week. Slowly unscrew the lid—some gases may have built up—and sample the pickle. If the texture and flavor are to your liking, then transfer it to the fridge; if not, set it aside for another few days before sampling again. Larger vegetables will take longer. Once you're happy with the flavor and texture, store the pickles in brine in the fridge for up to 6 months.

NOTES: When using a widemouthed jar as your fermenting vessel, it can be a challenge to find a glass lid or jar the right size to use as a weight and still be able to seal the lid. I recommend purchasing glass fermentation weights (see Resources, page 393). They're very affordable and a great and easy way to hold the vegetables beneath the brine.

If for any reason your kraut does not produce enough brine to cover the surface after being packed into jars (or a crock), you can make Sea Salt Brine (page 195) and pour over enough to cover the vegetables.

Fermented Carrots with Turmeric and Ginger

MAKES ABOUT 8 CUPS | 2¼ POUNDS | 1 KG

10 medium-large (2 pounds | 910 g) carrots, grated (about 10 cups)

½ medium (12 ounces | 340 g) cabbage, cored and thinly sliced (4 cups); reserve a whole cabbage leaf for covering the kraut

One 3-inch (7.5 cm) piece (¾ ounce | 22 g) fresh turmeric, peeled and finely grated (2 tablespoons)

One 2-inch (5 cm) piece (1 ounce | 30 g) fresh ginger, peeled and finely grated (1½ tablespoons)

1 small (1 ounce | 30 g) shallot, finely chopped

5 teaspoons (⅔ ounce | 20 g) fine sea salt

Sea Salt Brine (page 195), only if necessary

Combine the carrots, cabbage, turmeric, ginger, shallot, and salt in a large bowl and use clean hands to mix the vegetables together, squeezing and softening them until they are juicy and wilted. (The turmeric will temporarily dye your hands; use food service gloves if you want to avoid that.) Transfer a handful of the mixture to a large widemouthed jar or a fermentation crock and press it down well with your fist. Repeat with the remaining carrot mixture, a handful at a time, and then add any liquid left in the bowl. The liquid should completely cover the mixture; if it does not, keep pressing the mixture down until it does. If they don't create enough liquid, add cooled brine to cover. You should have at least 3 inches (7.5 cm) of headspace above the vegetables. Clean the edges of the jar or crock of any stray pieces of vegetable. Place the reserved cabbage leaf on top of the vegetables. Add a weight, such as a small glass jar filled with water, a flat glass plate or lid, or a fermentation weight, to keep the vegetables

OPPOSITE, CLOCKWISE FROM TOP RIGHT: Pickled Carrots with Coriander and Chile; Fennel and Green Cabbage Kraut; Pickled Carrots with Coriander and Chile in brine; Fennel and Green Cabbage Kraut; Fermented Carrots with Turmeric and Ginger; Lacto-Fermented Radishes

submerged, then seal the jar or crock. Label and date it and put it in a cool, dark place (about 65°F | 18°C) for 10 days.

After 10 days, carefully remove the lid, as it might pop off because of the gases that have built up, then remove the weight and cabbage leaf and use a clean fork to remove a little of the carrots to taste. If the level of tanginess and complexity of flavor are to your liking, transfer the jar or crock to the fridge, or transfer the mixture to smaller jars and refrigerate. If not, replace the leaf and the weight, tighten the lid, set aside for a few more days, and taste again. Usually 2 to 3 weeks of fermentation results in a good flavor. The fermented carrots will keep in the fridge for months. The flavor will continue to develop, but at a much slower rate. **Pictured on the preceding page**

Fennel and Green Cabbage Kraut

MAKES ABOUT 8 CUPS | 2½ POUNDS | 1.13 KG

1 medium (1¾ pounds | 800 g) green cabbage, cored and thinly sliced; reserve a whole cabbage leaf for covering the kraut

1 large (1 pound | 455 g) fennel bulb, trimmed, cored, and shaved on a mandoline or thinly sliced

5 teaspoons (⅔ ounce | 20 g) fine sea salt

2 teaspoons fennel seeds

Combine the cabbage, shaved or sliced fennel, salt, and fennel seeds in a large bowl and use clean hands to mix the vegetables together, squeezing and softening them until they are juicy and wilted. Transfer a handful of the mixture to a large widemouthed jar or a fermentation crock and press it down with your fist. Repeat with the remaining mixture, a handful at a time, and then add any liquid left in the bowl. The liquid should completely cover the mixture; if it does not, keep pressing the mixture

down until it does. You should have at least 3 inches (7.5 cm) of headspace above the vegetables. Clean the edges of the jar or crock of any stray pieces of vegetable. Place the reserved cabbage leaf on top of the vegetables. Add a weight, such as a small glass jar filled with water, a flat glass plate or lid, or a fermentation weight, to keep the vegetables submerged, then seal the jar or crock. Label and date it and put it in a cool, dark place (about 65°F | 18°C) for 10 days.

After 10 days, carefully remove the lid, as it might pop off because of the gases that have built up, then remove the weight and cabbage leaf and use a clean fork to remove a little of the kraut to taste. If the level of tanginess and complexity of flavor are to your liking, transfer the jar or crock to the fridge, or transfer the kraut to smaller jars and refrigerate. If not, replace the leaf and the weight, tighten the lid, set aside for a few more days, and taste again. Usually 2 to 3 weeks of fermentation results in a good flavor. The kraut will keep in the fridge for months. The flavor will continue to develop, but at a much slower rate. **Pictured on the preceding page**

Pickled Carrots with Coriander and Chile

MAKES ABOUT 3 CUPS | 12 OUNCES | 340 G

2 large garlic cloves, cut into ¼-inch (6 mm) slices

1 tablespoon coriander seeds

4 medium-large (14 ounces | 400 g) carrots, cut into 3-inch (7.5 cm) strips

6 dried red chiles

1 recipe Sea Salt Brine (recipe follows), cooled

Put the garlic and coriander seeds in a clean 1-quart (940 ml) widemouthed glass jar. Add the carrot strips, standing them up in the jar and squeezing them in snugly. Poke the chiles in between the carrots and lay any remaining carrots on top. Pour the brine over the vegetables and press them down to remove any air bubbles. Make sure there is at least 1 inch (2.5 cm) of headspace above the vegetables. Place a small glass lid or glass weight on top of the carrots to hold them down. Secure the lid, label and date the jar, put it on a plate, and set aside in a cool, dark place (about 65°F | 18°C) to ferment for 10 days.

After 10 days, remove the lid and weight and remove a carrot piece to taste. The carrots will be tangy and crisp when ready, with a good kick from the chile. If the texture and flavor are to your liking, transfer the jar to the fridge. If not, replace the weight and lid and set aside for a few more days before checking again. Once they are ready, the carrots can be stored in the fridge for up to 3 months. **Pictured on page 193**

Sea Salt Brine

MAKES 2 CUPS | 480 ML

4 teaspoons (½ ounce | 16 g) fine sea salt

2 cups (240 ml) filtered water

Put the salt in a heatproof jar or bowl. Bring the water to a boil, pour into the jar, and stir to dissolve the salt. Let cool before using.

Lacto-Fermented Radishes

MAKES ABOUT 3 CUPS | 13½ OUNCES | 380 G

14 ounces (400 g) radishes, washed and cut into ½-inch (1.25 cm) wedges (about 3 cups)

1 recipe Sea Salt Brine (opposite), cooled

Put the radishes in a clean 1-quart (940 ml) widemouthed glass jar and pour the brine over them. Press the radishes down to release any air bubbles. Make sure there is at least 1 inch (2.5 cm) of headspace above the radishes. Place a glass weight or heavy glass lid on top of the radishes to hold them down. Secure the lid, label and date the jar, put it on a plate, and set aside in a cool, dark place (about 65°F | 18°C) for 1 week.

After 1 week, remove the lid and weight and remove a piece of radish to taste. When ready, the radishes should have a pleasant crisp texture and lovely tangy flavor. If the texture and flavor are to your liking, transfer the jar to the fridge. If not, replace the weight and lid and set aside for a few more days before checking again. Once they are ready, the radishes can be stored in the fridge for up to 3 months. **Pictured on page 193**

CLOCKWISE FROM TOP LEFT: Wild Atlantic kombu; dulse; instant wakame; alaria; wakame; arame; kombu; nori sheets

SEA VEGETABLES

The advantages of including sea vegetables, or seaweeds, in your diet are immense—they're some of the most nutritious foods you can eat. Sea vegetables boast elevated levels of minerals like iron, calcium, and iodine and are high in protein. And because they do not need land or fresh water to grow, they're one of the most environmentally sustainable food choices available. Seaweeds contain naturally occurring glutamate, an amino acid that also acts as a natural flavor enhancer and is responsible for seaweed's umami appeal. However, it can be difficult to make sea vegetables part of your regular diet. Adding kombu to beans or stocks or eating a sheet of toasted nori with your meal is easy; it's more challenging to include other varieties, such as wakame, dulse, and arame. So, the best way to include seaweeds consistently in your diet is to have them already prepared and ready to add to meals. Even a small amount as a garnish or side dish is enough to reap their benefits.

This chapter describes two basic methods that can be used to prepare any type of seaweed: toasting and soaking and simmering. All of the recipes included here can be made ahead, and some will keep for weeks or even months. Among them you'll find interesting condiments and sprinkles that are an easy way to add minerals to your meals along with the flavor-enhancing qualities of seaweed. Try the Dulse Rose Za'atar sprinkled over eggs, hummus, yogurt, or simple vegetable dishes. The Toasted Seed and Nori Salad Topper and the Magic Mineral Dust, an umami-rich powder made from sesame seeds and toasted and ground kombu, are easy ways to add a nutritional boost to any dish.

Since our oceans are becoming increasingly polluted, it's important that you seek out companies that are harvesting seaweeds from clean waters and frequently checking radiation levels (see Resources, page 393). It's exciting to see small hand-harvested-seaweed companies springing up around the world. Many of them offer unusual varieties, but these same preparation methods can be applied to any of them.

OPPOSITE: Miso Nori Chips

Toasted Sea Vegetables

Nori, which is probably the most popular seaweed, has a mild flavor and goes well with many different types of foods. It needs to be lightly toasted to transform its slightly chewy texture to light and crisp. Toasting also brings out its flavor and makes it easy to crush or to enjoy as a chip. Nori can be purchased toasted or untoasted, but it's easy to toast it yourself; see below. Dulse has a soft, pliable texture and is quite chewy if eaten right out of the package. Once toasted, though, it crushes easily and, with its natural smoky flavor, makes a delicious seasoning. Kombu can be either toasted or simmered; also see Soaked and Simmered Sea Vegetables (page 203).

BASIC METHODS

There are three basic methods that I use for toasting seaweed such as nori, dulse, kelp, or wakame (which are described in more detail in the individual recipes).

FLAME: Using a gas flame is best for toasting nori, as it toasts incredibly fast. Using this method also enables you to toast it evenly and gives you complete control over how long you toast it. If you don't have a gas stove, hold a piece of nori over an electric element until it turns light green. You can also buy pre-toasted nori.

CAST-IRON SKILLET: A cast-iron skillet works well for toasting dulse when you don't want to turn on the oven (it can't be used for nori or kombu). Warm the skillet over medium-high heat, add the dulse, and stir constantly until the color darkens and the texture is crispy. It will crisp up further as it cools.

OVEN: The even heat of a moderate oven (350°F | 180°C) is best for thicker seaweeds such as kombu. You can also toast wakame in the oven, but since it's more delicate than kombu, be sure to check it frequently. Dulse can also be toasted in the oven.

Dulse Rose Za'atar

MAKES 6 TABLESPOONS | 1½ OUNCES | 45 G

¼ cup (1¼ ounces | 35 g) raw unhulled sesame seeds, toasted (see page 390)

2 tablespoons (1 g) dried organic rose petals (see the sidebar on page 301)

1 tablespoon Toasted Dulse Flakes (see the sidebar)

1 teaspoon ground sumac

1 teaspoon dried thyme

½ teaspoon flaky sea salt

Combine the sesame seeds, rose petals, dulse, sumac, thyme, and salt in a small jar or bowl and stir to combine. Store in a tightly sealed jar for up to 3 months.

TOASTED DULSE FLAKES

To toast dried dulse, spread ½ cup (¼ ounce | 8 g) over a baking sheet and toast in a 350°F (180°C) oven for 10 minutes, or until crisp to the touch and lightly browned in spots. Allow to cool slightly, and use your fingertips to crush the dulse into flakes. Store in a tightly sealed jar for up to 6 months. This makes a scant 3 tablespoons (½ ounce | 15 g).

OPPOSITE, CLOCKWISE FROM TOP: Steamed broccoli (see page 170) with Fennel and Green Cabbage Kraut, chickpeas, and avocado; Dulse Rose Za'atar; boiled eggs with Dulse Rose Za'atar

Miso Nori Chips

MAKES 48 CHIPS | SERVES 8

6 tablespoons (3 ounces | 85 g) almond or cashew butter, store-bought or homemade (see page 112)

¼ cup (2 ounces | 60 g) unpasteurized chickpea miso or sweet white miso

4 teaspoons (20 ml) mirin

1 tablespoon melted extra-virgin coconut oil

1 tablespoon filtered water

8 sheets (½ ounce | 16 g) nori (both toasted and untoasted work)

½ cup (2½ ounces | 70 g) raw unhulled sesame seeds, toasted (see page 390)

Preheat the oven to 300°F (150°C). Line a rimmed baking sheet with parchment paper and set aside.

Combine the nut butter, miso, mirin, oil, and water in a small bowl and stir until smooth. Place one sheet of nori on a cutting board, top with 3 tablespoons (45 ml) of the miso mixture, and spread it evenly over the nori, all the way to the edges. Sprinkle with 2 tablespoons (½ ounce | 15 g) of the sesame seeds, top with another sheet of nori, and press to seal. Cut the stacked nori lengthwise in half and cut each half crosswise into 6 strips, to get 12 pieces. Arrange on the baking sheet and repeat with the remaining nori and miso mixture.

Bake for 10 to 15 minutes, until the nori is crinkled; the chips will crisp up as they cool. Remove from the oven and allow to cool. Store the chips in an airtight container for up to 2 weeks. **Pictured on page 198**

Toasted Seed and Nori Salad Topper

MAKES 2 CUPS | 8 OUNCES | 230 G

½ cup (2½ ounces | 70 g) raw pumpkin seeds

½ cup (2½ ounces | 70 g) raw unhulled sesame seeds

½ cup (2¼ ounces | 65 g) raw sunflower seeds

1 teaspoon raw apple cider vinegar

1 teaspoon tamari

½ teaspoon fine sea salt

¼ teaspoon cayenne pepper

⅛ teaspoon garlic powder (optional)

½ cup (⅙ ounce | 5 g) Crushed Nori (see the sidebar)

Preheat the oven to 300°F (150°C). Line a rimmed baking sheet with parchment paper and set aside.

Put the pumpkin, sesame, and sunflower seeds in a medium strainer and rinse under cold running water. Set aside to drain well.

Transfer the drained seeds to a medium bowl and add the vinegar, tamari, salt, cayenne, and garlic powder, if using. Mix well, then spread the seeds out on the lined baking sheet in a single layer. Toast for 10 minutes, stir, and toast for another 6 to 8 minutes, until the seeds are fragrant and golden. Remove from the oven and set aside to cool.

Transfer the seeds to a dry bowl, add the nori flakes, and mix well. Store in an airtight jar for up to 6 weeks.

Magic Mineral Dust

MAKES ⅓ CUP | 1 OUNCE | 28 G

3 tablespoons (¾ ounce | 22 g) raw black sesame seeds, toasted (see page 390)

1 tablespoon Kombu Powder (see the sidebar)

Put the sesame seeds in an electric spice grinder, or use a suribachi or mortar and pestle, and pulse briefly or crush until the seeds are coarsely ground. Transfer to a small bowl or jar and stir in the kombu powder. Store in a tightly sealed jar for up to 3 months.

CRUSHED NORI

Hold a sheet of untoasted nori about 5 inches (13 cm) above a medium gas flame, moving it constantly to prevent burning. The nori is toasted when it is a light green color (you only need to toast one side). Crush the nori sheet with your hands into about ½-inch (1.25 cm) pieces. Store in a tightly sealed jar for up to 1 month. Sprinkle over salads, soups, and grain or bean dishes. You can also lightly toast nori sheets that were purchased toasted but have become stale from being exposed to air. One sheet makes ¼ cup (2.5 g).

KOMBU POWDER

Add four 4-inch (10 cm) pieces of kombu to a baking sheet and toast in a 350°F (180°C) oven for 8 to 10 minutes, until fragrant and the color has slightly changed from green to brown-green. The kombu won't be crisp until it cools. Break it up and add it to an electric spice grinder, a suribachi, or a mortar and grind to a powder. This makes about 5 teaspoons (⅓ ounce | 10 g.)

Soaked and Simmered Sea Vegetables

Many dried seaweeds need to be soaked and/or simmered before eating. Some are ready to use after a 20-minute soak; others, such as wakame (except the instant kind), need to be trimmed of their tough stems and simmered until tender. The water you use to soak seaweed can be used for watering your garden or houseplants, or you can add it to broths and soups—but be sure to strain it in that case, since it can contain a little bit of sand.

Plain soaked seaweeds like arame or wakame are pretty bland on their own, so they are best marinated before being added to salads, noodle dishes, or grain or bean bowls. When purchasing local and wild varieties of seaweeds, soak them and then taste a piece; if it's tender enough to eat, there is no need to simmer the seaweed. Just like any plants, seaweeds vary in thickness and some will need more simmering than others; test every 5 minutes or so until the desired tenderness is achieved. Kombu can be added to a broth or pot of beans or grains without soaking. And if you are planning on adding your seaweed to, say, a stir-fry, soup, or stew, just soak, drain, chop it if necessary, and add to the dish.

If you're new to seaweeds, start with the Restorative Mineral-Mushroom Broth (page 207). You'll get all the amazing benefits of seaweed without its distinct briny flavor or unfamiliar texture. This broth is a fantastic vegan alternative to bone broth, with a deliciously deep, savory flavor. You can use it during a cleanse (see Soup and Broth Cleanse, page 381), or any time you want a satisfying, nourishing, and savory alternative to herbal tea.

BASIC METHOD

To soak the seaweed, put it in a medium bowl and cover with plenty of filtered water. I use boiling water for arame, since I do not simmer it, but room-temperature water is fine for softening any seaweed you will simmer. Drain the seaweed in a strainer once it's completely hydrated, which can take anywhere from 5 to 20 minutes.

To simmer the drained seaweed, put it in a small to medium pot and cover with filtered water. Bring to a boil, cover the pot, reduce the heat to low, and simmer for 5 to 20 minutes, depending on the thickness of the seaweed. Drain as soon as it is cooked, or, depending on the variety, it can become slimy.

Ginger-Marinated Wakame

MAKES 1 CUP | 6½ OUNCES | 185 G

Six 4-inch (10 cm) strips (½ ounce | 15 g) wakame
(see Note)

2 cups (480 ml) warm filtered water

1 tablespoon brown rice vinegar

2 teaspoons tamari

1 teaspoon toasted sesame oil

1 teaspoon finely grated fresh ginger

Put the wakame in a medium bowl, cover with the
warm water, and set aside to soak for 20 minutes.

Thoroughly drain the wakame in a sieve set over
a bowl (reserve the soaking liquid to water your
garden or houseplants, or use it to replace some of
the water in the Restorative Mineral-Mushroom
Broth, page 207). Lay the wakame flat on a cutting
board and cut away the tough stems. Cut the
wakame into 1-inch (2.5 cm) squares and transfer to
a small pot. Cover with 2 cups (480 ml) filtered
water and bring to a boil over high heat. Cover the
pot, reduce the heat to low, and simmer for 5 to
15 minutes, until the wakame is tender; some types
will cook a lot faster than others, so test as you go.
Once the wakame is tender, drain well and set aside
to cool. Transfer to a bowl, add the vinegar, tamari,
oil, and ginger, and mix well. Store in a tightly sealed
container in the fridge for up to 1 week.

NOTE: You can make this with instant or
"ready to use" wakame. Use ½ cup
(½ ounce | 15 g) and soak, drain, chop,
and marinate as above; there is no need to
cook it. The wakame can also be replaced
with alaria, which is a seaweed harvested
off the coast of Maine.

Quick Marinated Arame

MAKES 2 CUPS | 6¾ OUNCES | 190 G

1½ cups (1 ounce | 30 g) dried arame

4 cups (960 ml) boiling filtered water

1 tablespoon extra-virgin olive oil or
toasted sesame oil

1 tablespoon tamari

1 tablespoon brown rice vinegar

1 tablespoon mirin

Fine sea salt if needed

2 tablespoons (½ ounce | 15 g) raw unhulled sesame
seeds, toasted (see page 390)

Thinly sliced scallions to serve

Put the arame in a medium bowl, cover with the
boiling water, and set aside for 20 minutes to hydrate
and soften.

Thoroughly drain the arame in a sieve set over
a bowl (reserve the soaking liquid to water your
garden or houseplants). Transfer to a bowl and
add the oil, tamari, vinegar, and mirin. Taste and
season with a pinch of salt if needed. Stir in the
sesame seeds. The arame can be stored in a jar
in the fridge for up to 1 week. Serve sprinkled
with scallions.

OPPOSITE: Ginger-Marinated Wakame (top) and
Quick Marinated Arame (bottom)

Restorative Mineral-Mushroom Broth

MAKES 5 TO 6 QUARTS | 4.7 TO 5.6 L

½ large (2 pounds | 900 g) unpeeled winter squash, such as kabocha or Red Kuri, coarsely chopped and seeds reserved (5 cups)

3 large (12 ounces | 340 g) burdock roots, scrubbed and coarsely chopped (about 3 cups), or 1 cup (4 ounces | 115 g) dried burdock

1 large (12 ounces | 340 g) leek (see Note, page 129), chopped

½ medium-large (1 pound | 455 g) cabbage, coarsely chopped (5 cups)

1 large (1 pound | 455 g) fennel bulb with fronds, coarsely chopped

Four 4-inch (10 cm) strips (⅓ ounce | 10 g) dried kombu

1 cup (½ ounce | 15 g) dried dulse

1½ cups (1 ounce | 30 g) dried maitake mushrooms

12 ounces (340 g) fresh shiitake mushrooms, finely chopped (6 cups)

1 cup (1 ounce | 30 g) dried shiitake mushrooms

10 inches (25 cm) of fresh turmeric (2½ ounces | 70 g), peeled and chopped, or 2 tablespoons (⅓ ounce | 10 g) ground turmeric

6 inches (15 cm) of fresh ginger (3 ounces | 85 g), peeled and chopped

3 large garlic cloves

20 sprigs (½ large bunch) fresh parsley

7 quarts (6.6 l) filtered water

2 large bunches fresh cilantro, coarsely chopped (including stems)

Combine the squash and seeds, burdock, leek, cabbage, fennel, kombu, dulse, maitake, fresh and dried shiitakes, turmeric, ginger, garlic, parsley, and water in a large stockpot and bring to a boil over high heat. Cover the pot, reduce the heat to low, and simmer gently for 2½ hours, stirring every 30 minutes or so to help distribute the flavors. Taste the broth. It should have a good rich flavor; if not, continue simmering for another 30 minutes. Remove from the heat, stir in the cilantro, and set aside for 30 minutes to 3 hours, uncovered, to steep.

Strain the broth through a colander into a large pot or bowl, pressing out as much liquid as possible from the vegetables (you can use a large plate to press the cooked vegetables down to extract more liquid). Then strain the broth through a fine-mesh strainer into jars or containers for storage; if you plan to freeze some of the broth, be sure to leave at least 1½ inches (4 cm) of headspace. Allow to cool completely, then secure the lids and refrigerate for up to 1 week or freeze for up to 6 months. **Pictured on page 382**

NOTE: Serve the hot broth on its own, or garnish with thinly sliced scallions, fresh cilantro leaves, chopped fresh parsley, grated lemon (or Meyer lemon) or yuzu zest, and/ or finely grated peeled ginger, turmeric, or horseradish.

Dressings

When it comes to easy, vibrant, and healthy whole food meals, dressings are one of the keys to success. The dressings in this chapter are not like your ordinary vinaigrette. Made by blending vegetables with herbs and citrus juice until creamy, they are light, super flavorful, and addictive. The six base recipes and the more than a dozen variations are really all you need to transform any meal. And once you've made a few of the variations, you will be able to create dozens of your own flavorful dressings.

All of these dressings will keep for up to 3 days, so you can blend one up at the beginning of the week to have on hand for several meals. If you're cooking for more than yourself, make a few different dressings so you can change up the flavor and visual appeal of almost any dish with very little effort. Try the Carrot-Turmeric Dressing with Macadamia on a grain bowl or drizzle the Fennel, Cilantro, and Mint Dressing over roasted sweet potatoes topped with avocado and black beans (pictured on page 231). In summer, spoon one of the Sweet Corn Dressings or Shiso-Lime Zucchini Dressing over wedges of ripe tomatoes for a refreshing side dish. The Dill, Mint, and Lime Zucchini Dressing is the answer to brightening up simple tacos or steamed vegetables. Toss the Fennel and Pine Nut Dressing with sturdy greens for a salad, or serve the Artichoke Dressing as a dip for roasted potatoes or other roasted or raw vegetables. (See more ways to use these dressings on page 230.)

The idea for blending vegetables into dressings came from a lovely woman I used to cook for named Nisha. She asked me to use zucchini and fennel in dressings as a way to keep the oil to a minimum. Thanks to Nisha's adventurous palate and creativity, we ended up with an array of completely-new-to-me recipes that inspired a number of the variations in this chapter.

Notes

TEXTURE

All of these dressings are blended in an upright blender until smooth and creamy. Using a high-powered blender will result in the best consistency, especially with more fibrous vegetables like fennel and carrots. If you are using a regular blender, stick to the zucchini, artichoke, and beet dressings, and grate the carrots first for the carrot dressings. When blending the zucchini dressings for the first time, most people are sure they will need more liquid, but trust me—you don't. Be patient and wait for the mixture to start coming together, or press the ingredients down in the blender jar to help them blend. The dressings will thicken up overnight; to thin them, just stir in a little water.

FLAVOR

Most of these dressing bases are flavored with fresh lime juice. You can use lemon juice or raw apple cider vinegar instead, but in that case, start with less, as the flavor will be more pronounced. Fresh herbs like cilantro, mint, basil, dill, shiso, and rosemary feature prominently in many of these recipes, but there are also options for strictly pantry-based dressings, like the Wasabi–Black Sesame Zucchini Dressing and the Spicy Carrot-Miso Dressing. And when you don't have any of these fresh vegetables on hand, turn to the recipes made with a jar of artichokes, which go beautifully with beans, roasted vegetables, and simple potato salads.

It's important to use good-quality olive oil in these dressings. Many extra-virgin olive oils taste bitter because they have been sitting around for too long, exposed to heat and light. A good extra-virgin olive oil should be on the expensive side; if it is not, despite what the label says, it is most likely a blend that also contains a refined oil. Cold-pressed flax oil also tastes great in most of these base recipes and variations. Coconut oil is not suitable, as it's solid at room temperature.

ADD-INS

Because these dressings are made in a blender, it's easy to add fresh turmeric or ginger, chiles, herbs, or any spices you love. You can blend in a slice of fresh turmeric (finely chop it first if you don't have a high-speed blender) to any dressing if you want a slightly golden hue, like a lemon dressing; or use just a pinch of dried turmeric—no more, or the flavor will be dusty and flat.

Since chiles can vary significantly in heat, you might want to add a pinch of cayenne at the end if your dressing doesn't have the heat you want. Most of these dressings use fresh herbs rather than dried spices, but you can certainly experiment by adding a pinch of toasted and ground cumin or coriander to either of the cilantro dressings.

Many of these dressings are nut- and seed-free, and some are quite low in oil; however, you can add a tablespoon or more of nuts or seeds when blending them for a richer version. Stick to hemp seeds, cashews, and macadamias, or the added fiber from other nuts will be noticeable. You can use nut or seed butter in their place, but you'll need only half as much.

GARNISHES

These colorful dressings are a lovely garnish for almost any dish; for a pretty touch, add a sprinkling of the herbs or seeds used in the dressing—a scattering of small cilantro sprigs with the Fennel, Cilantro, and Mint Dressing, for example, or toasted black sesame seeds with the Wasabi–Black Sesame Zucchini Dressing or Golden Citrus Zucchini Dressing.

STORING

Stored in airtight glass jars in the fridge, all of these dressings will keep for up to 3 days. The dressings cannot be frozen.

DRESSING FLAVORS

Blended vegetables combined with herbs, citrus, chile, turmeric, or wasabi along with oil and salt are all you need to make a versatile and flavorful dressing. Here are some of the possibilities (pictured clockwise from left):

- Sweet Corn and Basil Dressing (page 229)

- Tangy Beet-Cashew Dressing with Chile (page 223)

- Golden Citrus Zucchini Dressing (page 215)

- Shiso-Lime Zucchini Dressing (page 215)

- Carrot-Turmeric Dressing with Macadamia (page 219)

- Wasabi–Black Sesame Zucchini Dressing (page 215)

- Fennel, Cilantro, and Mint Dressing (page 227)

- Artichoke–Meyer Lemon Dressing with Chives (page 221)

- Dill, Mint, and Lime Zucchini Dressing (page 215)

Zucchini Dressing

MAKES ABOUT 1 CUP | 240 ML

1 medium (8 ounces | 230 g) zucchini, cut into 1-inch (2.5 cm) chunks (about 1¾ cups)

One 3-inch (7.5 cm) piece scallion, white and light green parts only, coarsely chopped

3 tablespoons (45 ml) freshly squeezed lime juice

3 tablespoons (45 ml) extra-virgin olive oil or cold-pressed flax seed oil

½ teaspoon fine sea salt, plus more to taste

Combine the zucchini, scallion, lime juice, oil, and salt in an upright blender (see Note) and blend until smooth, starting on a lower speed and gradually increasing it as the dressing comes together. Use a rubber spatula (with the blender off) to help move the ingredients around as necessary, or use the tamper stick if using a high-powered blender. Adjust the seasoning to taste—some variations with lots of extra herbs will need more salt. Scrape down the sides and blend again. Use immediately, or store in a glass jar in the fridge for up to 3 days. Shake well before using. The dressing will thicken once chilled; thin it out with a little water if needed.

NOTE: Some blender pitchers are wide at the base, which makes blending small amounts difficult. If yours is wide, I suggest doubling the recipes in this chapter that make 1 cup.

Golden Citrus Zucchini Dressing

MAKES ABOUT 1½ CUPS | 360 ML

1 recipe Zucchini Dressing, using golden zucchini or a peeled green zucchini and 2 tablespoons (30 ml) lime juice

One 2-inch (5 cm) piece (½ ounce | 15 g) fresh turmeric, peeled and chopped (finely chopped if using a regular blender)

2 tablespoons (30 ml) freshly squeezed orange juice

2 tablespoons (1 ounce | 30 g) raw cashew butter

2 teaspoons nutritional yeast

One ¼-inch (6 mm) slice of a large garlic clove

Make the dressing following the instructions for the base recipe, adding the turmeric, orange juice, cashew butter, nutritional yeast, and garlic to the blender along with the other ingredients. **Pictured on page 213**

Dill, Mint, and Lime Zucchini Dressing

MAKES ABOUT 1¼ CUPS | 300 ML

1 recipe Zucchini Dressing

1 cup (1 ounce | 30 g) chopped fresh dill, including tender stems

½ cup (⅕ ounce | 6 g) fresh mint leaves

Make the dressing following the instructions for the base recipe, adding the dill and mint to the blender along with the other ingredients. **Pictured on page 212**

Shiso-Lime Zucchini Dressing

MAKES ABOUT 1 CUP | 240 ML

1 recipe Zucchini Dressing

10 large (¼ ounce | 8 g) fresh green shiso leaves, chopped (see Note)

Make the dressing following the instructions for the base recipe, adding the shiso to the blender along with the other ingredients. **Pictured on page 213**

NOTE: Be sure to use green (not purple) shiso leaves; otherwise the dressing will be brown.

Wasabi–Black Sesame Zucchini Dressing

MAKES ABOUT 1 CUP | 240 ML

1 recipe Zucchini Dressing

2 teaspoons wasabi powder

1 tablespoon raw black sesame seeds, toasted (see page 390)

Make the dressing following the instructions for the base recipe, adding the wasabi to the blender along with the other ingredients. After adjusting the seasoning, add the black sesame seeds and pulse a few times to combine and break up some of the seeds; be careful not to overblend, or the dressing will turn gray. **Pictured on page 213**

ABOVE: Steamed vegetables (see pages 170–171) and poached egg (see page 383) with Dill, Mint, and Lime Zucchini Dressing; **OPPOSITE:** Creamy Carrot Dressing

Creamy Carrot Dressing

MAKES 1½ CUPS | 360 ML

2 medium (6 ounces | 115 g) carrots, chopped if using a high-powered blender (about 1¼ cups), grated if using a regular blender

½ cup (120 ml) filtered water

¼ cup (1¼ ounces | 35 g) raw cashews

¼ cup (60 ml) extra-virgin olive oil

3 tablespoons (45 ml) freshly squeezed lime juice

One 3-inch (7.5 cm) piece scallion, white and light green parts only, coarsely chopped

One ½-inch (1.25 cm) slice of a large garlic clove

½ teaspoon fine sea salt, plus more to taste

1 teaspoon tamari, plus more to taste

Combine the carrots, water, cashews, olive oil, lime juice, scallion, garlic, salt, and tamari in an upright blender and blend until completely smooth; this will take at least 1 minute. Scrape down the sides with a rubber spatula and blend again. Adjust the seasoning to taste and blend again. Use immediately, or store in a glass jar in the fridge for up to 3 days. Shake well before using. The dressing will thicken once chilled; thin it out with a little water if needed. **Pictured on the preceding page**

Spicy Carrot-Miso Dressing

MAKES 1½ CUPS | 360 ML

1 recipe Creamy Carrot Dressing, omitting the salt and using brown rice vinegar in place of the lime juice

1 tablespoon unpasteurized chickpea miso or sweet white miso

One 1-inch (2.5 cm) piece (½ ounce | 15 g) fresh ginger, peeled and chopped (finely chopped if using a regular blender)

⅛ teaspoon cayenne pepper, plus more to taste

Make the dressing following the instructions for the base recipe, adding the miso, ginger, and cayenne to the blender along with the other ingredients. Adjust the seasoning with cayenne as well as more salt to taste.

Carrot-Turmeric Dressing with Macadamia

MAKES 1½ CUPS | 360 ML

1 recipe Creamy Carrot Dressing, using raw macadamia nuts in place of the cashews

One 3-inch (7.5 cm) piece (¾ ounce | 22 g) fresh turmeric, peeled and chopped (finely chopped if using a regular blender)

Make the dressing following the instructions for the base recipe, adding the turmeric to the blender along with the other ingredients. **Pictured on page 213**

VERSATILE CARROT DRESSINGS

The beauty of these carrot-based dressings is that they work just as well drizzled over leafy green and sprout salads as they do stirred into noodle salads. You can adjust the water to create a thicker or thinner dressing—they will thicken further in the fridge overnight. These dressings look particularly striking with a forbidden black rice bowl and make a great dip for summer rolls or nori rolls.

Artichoke Dressing

MAKES ABOUT 1 CUP | 240 ML

1 cup (5¾ ounces | 165 g) drained jarred or canned artichoke hearts (9 medium hearts)

One 3-inch (7.5 cm) piece scallion, white and light green parts only, coarsely chopped

¼ cup (60 ml) extra-virgin olive oil

1 tablespoon freshly squeezed lemon juice, plus more to taste

6 tablespoons (75 ml) filtered water

½ teaspoon fine sea salt, plus more to taste

Combine the artichokes, scallion, olive oil, lemon juice, water, and salt in an upright blender (see Note, page 214) and blend until completely smooth. Scrape down the sides with a rubber spatula and blend again. Adjust the seasoning and lemon juice to taste and blend again. Use immediately, or store in a glass jar in the fridge for up to 3 days. Shake well before using.

Pictured on page 208

MORE THAN A DRESSING

Although delicious on its own, the Artichoke Dressing base recipe is the ideal foundation for adding herbs. You can simply chop them and stir them in or blend them with the other ingredients. The lovely silky texture and creamy color of these dressings makes them incredibly versatile. Try them drizzled over bitter green salads or steamed vegetable salads and (if you reduce the water) as a dip for roasted vegetables and crudités or as a mayonnaise replacement on sandwiches.

Artichoke–Meyer Lemon Dressing with Chives

MAKES ABOUT 1 CUP | 240 ML

2 teaspoons grated Meyer lemon zest

2 tablespoons (⅕ ounce | 6 g) finely chopped fresh chives

1 recipe Artichoke Dressing, omitting the lemon juice and using 3 tablespoons (45 ml) water

¼ cup (60 ml) freshly squeezed Meyer lemon juice

Combine the lemon zest and chives in a small jar and set aside. Make the dressing following the instructions for the base recipe, adding the Meyer lemon juice to the blender along with the other ingredients. After adjusting the seasoning, pour the dressing into the jar with the lemon zest and chives and stir or shake to combine. **Pictured on page 213**

Artichoke-Tarragon Dressing

MAKES ABOUT 1 CUP | 240 ML

1 recipe Artichoke Dressing

2 tablespoons (⅕ ounce | 6 g) fresh tarragon leaves, plus more to taste

Make the dressing following the instructions for the base recipe, adding the tarragon to the blender along with the other ingredients.

Beet Dressing

MAKES ABOUT 1 CUP | 240 ML

1 small-medium (6 ounces | 170 g) cooked and cooled red beet (see the sidebar opposite)

¼ cup (60 ml) filtered water

3 tablespoons (1½ ounces | 45 g) raw cashew butter, coconut butter, or tahini

2 tablespoons plus 1 teaspoon (35 ml) raw apple cider vinegar

2 tablespoons (30 ml) extra-virgin olive oil

One ¼-inch (6 mm) slice of a large garlic clove

½ teaspoon fine sea salt, plus more to taste

Put the beet, water, nut or coconut butter or tahini, vinegar, olive oil, garlic, and salt in an upright blender (see Note, page 214) and blend until completely smooth. Scrape down the sides with a rubber spatula and blend again. Adjust the seasoning to taste and blend again. Use immediately, or store in a glass jar in the fridge for up to 3 days. Shake well before using. The dressing will thicken once chilled; thin it out with a little water if needed.

Tangy Beet-Cashew Dressing with Chile

MAKES ABOUT 1 CUP | 240 ML

1 recipe Beet Dressing, using raw cashew butter

1 small (1 ounce | 30 g) red chile, seeded and chopped

Make the dressing following the instructions for the base recipe, adding the chile to the blender along with the other ingredients. **Pictured on page 212**

Beet, Coconut, and Lime Dressing

MAKES ABOUT 1 CUP | 240 ML

1 recipe Beet Dressing, using ¼ cup (2 ounces | 60 g) coconut butter and freshly squeezed lime juice in place of the apple cider vinegar

Pinch of cayenne pepper, or more to taste

Make the dressing following the instructions for the base recipe, adding the cayenne to the blender along with the other ingredients.

COOKED BEETS

MAKES 3 MEDIUM BEETS | 14 OUNCES | 400 G

1 pound (455 g) beets, preferably the same size (about 3 medium)

Trim any greens off the beets, leaving about a ½-inch (1.25 cm) stem attached (there's no need to wash them). Put the beets in a medium-large pot, cover completely with filtered water, and bring to a boil over high heat. Cover the pot, reduce the heat to low, and simmer until tender. Test by inserting the tip of a sharp knife into the center of a beet. It will slide in easily when the beets are cooked. If the beets vary in size, remove the smaller ones once they're cooked. Drain the beets, slip off and discard their skins, and rinse briefly. Cool and use, or store the cooked beets in a sealed jar in the fridge for up to 4 days.

OPPOSITE AND ABOVE: Preparing Tangy Beet-Cashew Dressing with Chile

Fennel-Citrus Dressing

MAKES ABOUT 1½ CUPS | 360 ML

1 medium (12 ounces | 340 g) fennel bulb

5 tablespoons (75 ml) extra-virgin olive oil

3 tablespoons (45 ml) freshly squeezed lemon or lime juice

¼ cup (1¼ ounces | 35 g) raw cashews or 2 tablespoons (1 ounce | 30 g) raw cashew butter

One 3-inch (7.5 cm) piece scallion, white and light green parts only, coarsely chopped

One ½-inch (1.25 cm) slice of a large garlic clove

¾ teaspoon fine sea salt, plus more to taste

1 teaspoon nutritional yeast (optional)

½ teaspoon tamari (optional)

Remove any tough outer layers from the fennel, then halve, core, and dice. You should have 1½ cups (6 ounces | 170 g). Transfer the fennel to a high-powered blender (this dressing won't become smooth enough in a regular blender), add the olive oil, lemon juice, cashews, scallion, garlic, salt, nutritional yeast, and tamari, if using, and blend until completely smooth. This dressing is quite thick and creamy, but you can thin it out with a little water, if desired. Use immediately, or store in a glass jar in the fridge for up to 3 days. Shake well before using.

Fennel, Cilantro, and Mint Dressing

MAKES ABOUT 1½ CUPS | 360 ML

1 recipe Fennel-Citrus Dressing, using lime juice

1½ cups (¾ ounce | 22 g) fresh cilantro leaves

½ cup (⅕ ounce | 6 g) fresh mint leaves

Make the dressing following the instructions for the base recipe, adding the cilantro and mint to the blender along with the other ingredients. **Pictured on page 213**

Fennel and Pine Nut Dressing

MAKES ABOUT 1½ CUPS | 360 ML

1 recipe Fennel-Citrus Dressing, using lemon juice and replacing the cashews with raw pine nuts

Freshly cracked black pepper

Make the dressing following the instructions for the base recipe. After adjusting the seasoning, season to taste with cracked black pepper.

Sweet Corn Dressing

MAKES ABOUT 2 CUPS | 480 ML

2 large ears sweet corn,
husked and kernels cut off
(2 cups | 10 ounces | 285 g)

6 tablespoons (90 ml) extra-virgin
olive oil

¼ cup (60 ml) freshly squeezed
lime juice, plus more to taste

Two 3-inch (7.5 cm) pieces
scallion, white and light green
parts only, coarsely chopped

One ½-inch (1.25 cm) slice of a
large garlic clove

¾ teaspoon fine sea salt, plus more
to taste

Combine the corn kernels, olive oil, lime juice, scallion, garlic, and salt in an upright blender and blend until completely smooth and velvety. Scrape down the sides with a rubber spatula. Adjust the seasoning and lime juice to taste and blend again. Use immediately, or store in a glass jar in the fridge for up to 3 days. Shake well before using.

Sweet Corn and Basil Dressing

MAKES ABOUT 2 CUPS | 480 ML

1 recipe Sweet Corn Dressing

1 cup (½ ounce | 16 g) fresh basil leaves

Make the dressing following the instructions for the base recipe. After adjusting the seasoning, add the basil leaves and pulse until the basil is finely chopped.

OPPOSITE: Tomatoes with Sweet Corn and Basil Dressing

Sweet Corn Dressing with Cilantro and Jalapeño

MAKES ABOUT 2 CUPS | 480 ML

1 recipe Sweet Corn Dressing

2 tablespoons (½ ounce | 16 g) chopped seeded jalapeño

1 cup (½ ounce | 15 g) fresh cilantro leaves

Make the dressing following the instructions for the base recipe, adding the jalapeño and cilantro to the blender along with the other ingredients.

DRESSINGS—HOW TO USE

Vegetable Base	Pairings
Zucchini	Dill, Mint, and Lime Zucchini Dressing (page 215) + Spring/Summer Steamed Vegetable Salad (page 173) Shiso-Lime Zucchini Dressing (page 215) + Tomato wedges + Cooked heirloom beans (see page 147) + Thinly sliced red onions
Creamy Carrot	Spicy Carrot-Miso Dressing (page 219) + Cabbage salad + Sunflower sprouts + Toasted sunflower seeds (see page 390) + Sliced scallions Carrot-Turmeric Dressing with Macadamia (page 219) + Forbidden black rice (see page 391) + Boiled egg (see page 383) + Daikon Beet Pickle with Lime (page 190)
Artichoke	Artichoke Dressing (page 220) + Quinoa (see page 391) + Daikon Beet Pickle with Lime (page 190) + Cooked chickpeas (see page 146) + Salad greens Artichoke-Tarragon Dressing (page 221; reducing the water) + Roasted potatoes (see page 179)

Vegetable Base	Pairings
Beet	Beet, Coconut, and Lime Dressing (page 223) + Quick Panfried Tempeh (see page 240) + Steamed broccoli (see page 170) + Sprouts Tangy Beet-Cashew Dressing with Chile (page 223) + Brown rice or quinoa (see page 391) + Steamed vegetables (see pages 170–171) + Fermented Carrots with Turmeric and Ginger (page 192) + Cooked chickpeas (see page 146)
Fennel-Citrus	Fennel, Cilantro, and Mint Dressing (page 227) + Whole roasted sweet potato (see page 179) + Cooked heirloom beans (see page 147) + Crumbled feta or nut cheese + Sliced avocado Fennel and Pine Nut Dressing (page 227) + Bitter greens + Roasted squash (see page 179)

OPPOSITE: A whole roasted sweet potato with cooked heirloom beans, crumbled feta, sliced avocado, and Fennel, Cilantro, and Mint Dressing

Sauces

Sauces have the same magical ability as dressings (see pages 214–229) to transform the simplest of dishes into deeply satisfying and delicious meals. These nut- and seed-based sauces offer up not only bright flavors but also a good amount of protein. There are three types here: Creamy Nut Sauces, Easy Pine Nut Pasta Sauces, and Quick Tahini Sauces. All are versatile and can be made in a multitude of variations, and all can be made days ahead. Whether you're folding the Golden Cashew Sauce with Chile and Lime into rice noodles, drizzling Zesty Turmeric Tahini Sauce over a bowl of steamed veggies, or dipping roasted sweet potato wedges into Whipped Chipotle-Lime Tahini Sauce, these sauces offer up lush flavors and great texture.

The Creamy Nut Sauce variations have distinctly different flavors, and you can create your own by following the base recipe using your favorite nuts. If you don't have nuts on hand, you can use nut butter instead. Use these sauces to dress up plain grains, steamed veggies, panfried tempeh, or tofu, or toss them with whole-grain noodles.

Until I made the first version of the Easy Pine Nut Pasta Sauce a few years ago, I had never had a really good bowl of vegan pasta. You know, the kind of ultrasimple pasta that feels like a hug, the sauce gently coating each strand and bringing all the ingredients into union. The lack of umami-rich Parmigiano-Reggiano is noticeable in many vegan pasta dishes, but combining crushed lightly toasted pine nuts with a little lemon, olive oil, and salt results in the "more-ish" flavor and texture of a successful pasta, sans dairy. Once your pasta is coated in this sauce, you can add anything from lightly cooked spring vegetables to a hearty red sauce.

The Quick Tahini Sauce base recipe can become the foundation for a wide range of variations, including some as simple as just adding citrus juice or zest, sweet white miso, chile sauce, or store-bought harissa paste; a pinch of ground sumac will add another dimension to this base. And these sauces can be thinned with water to drizzle over salads or vegetables. Left as they are, they can also be served as a dip.

Notes

TEXTURE

The texture you want for any of these sauces will depend on how you plan to use them. To adjust the consistency of the nut or tahini sauces, simply use more or less water. These will also thicken as they sit and may need to be adjusted when you take them from the fridge. A splash of boiling water will take the edge off a refrigerator-cold sauce while making it easier to pour or drizzle. The Easy Pine Nut Pasta Sauce can be thinned with a little of the pasta cooking water if necessary, as noted in the recipes.

FLAVOR

With nuts and seeds being the main ingredient, these sauces are rich in good fats. Since fat carries flavor, they will enhance the taste of anything you pair them with. With the addition of sautéed onions and garlic, the Creamy Nut Sauces have an extra layer of flavor that is beautifully enhanced by a dash of citrus or vinegar. The Easy Pine Nut Pasta Sauce has a neutral flavor and is a clever replacement for Parmesan. It tastes great with just about every ingredient you might add to pasta, such as tomato sauce, roasted eggplant, or lemon and broccoli. The Quick Tahini Sauces have a few distinct flavor variations that you can choose to suit your mood.

ADD-INS

You can add chopped fresh chiles or ginger to any of the Creamy Nut Sauces when cooking the garlic, or adjust the flavors of the finished sauces in the same ways as suggested opposite for the Quick Tahini Sauces. For the Easy Pine Nut Pasta Sauce, you could add chopped fresh herbs, black pepper or red chili pepper flakes, capers, olives, or a handful of baby spinach leaves. Possible additions for the Quick Tahini Sauces can be as simple as a squeeze of ginger juice (see page 239), a pinch of cayenne or a few drops of hot sauce, or a spoonful of miso; see the variations for more inspiration.

GARNISHES

Any of the base recipes and variations will benefit from a garnish of fresh herbs. The pasta dishes are great finished with a generous amount of black pepper and a drizzle of olive oil, and you might want to dust the nut or tahini sauces with a pinch of red chili pepper flakes, cayenne, or sumac.

STORING AND FREEZING

All of the nut and tahini sauces will keep for at least 4 days in airtight jars in the fridge, and the Easy Pine Nut Pasta Sauce base recipe can be stored for over a month. The Creamy Nut Sauces can be frozen for up to 3 months, but they may separate and so should be reblended before serving. Freezing the tahini sauce is not recommended.

USING SAUCES

Creamy nut sauces are delicious folded into noodles; served with grains, steamed vegetables, panfried tempeh (see page 240), or tofu; or used as a dip for roasted vegetables. Try the Tangy Red Pepper–Almond Sauce with crusty bread, or the Walnut Miso Sauce with Lemon with soba noodles and sautéed greens.

Quick to make and mostly lighter in texture, the tahini sauces in this chapter are great for drizzling over raw, steamed, or roasted vegetables, or as a topping for plain cooked grains. The Whipped Chipotle–Lime Tahini Sauce can be smeared over a burger or served as a dip and the Spiced Tahini-Yogurt Sauce with Sumac is a favorite for spooning into pita pockets or over roasted eggplant.

Pictured here from left to right:

TOP ROW

○ Tangy Red Pepper–Almond Sauce (page 239)

○ Tamarind, Date, and Ginger Tahini Sauce (page 247)

○ Zesty Turmeric Tahini Sauce (page 246)

MIDDLE ROW

○ Walnut Miso Sauce with Lemon (page 239)

○ Whipped Chipotle–Lime Tahini Sauce (page 247)

○ Green Herb Tahini Sauce (page 247)

BOTTOM ROW

○ Golden Cashew Sauce with Chile and Lime (page 240)

○ Spiced Tahini Yogurt Sauce with Sumac (page 247)

Creamy Nut Sauce

MAKES ABOUT 2 CUPS | 480 ML

1 tablespoon extra-virgin coconut oil

1 medium (8 ounces | 230 g) onion, diced

3 large garlic cloves, finely chopped

½ teaspoon fine sea salt, plus more to taste

1 tablespoon mirin

¼ cup (60 ml) filtered water

1 cup raw or toasted cashews, walnuts, or almonds (weight depends on the nuts used; see the variations for measures)

¾ cup (180 ml) boiling filtered water (see Note)

1 teaspoon tamari

Warm the oil in a medium skillet over medium-high heat. Add the onion and cook for 6 to 8 minutes, until golden. Stir in the garlic and salt and cook for 3 to 4 minutes, until the garlic is golden and fragrant. Add the mirin and the ¼ cup (60 ml) water, then raise the heat and bring to a simmer, stirring for a couple of minutes to deglaze the pan.

Remove from the heat and transfer the mixture to an upright blender, scraping the skillet with a rubber spatula. Add the nuts, boiling water, and tamari and blend until smooth, scraping the sides as necessary. Season to taste with more salt and serve immediately, or let cool and store in an airtight jar in the fridge for up to 4 days.

NOTE: The nut sauce recipes call for boiling water so that the sauce can be served immediately without having to be reheated after blending. If you want a room-temperature sauce or are making the sauce ahead, use cool water.

Walnut Miso Sauce with Lemon

MAKES 2 CUPS | 480 ML

1 recipe Creamy Nut Sauce, using 1½ cups (5¼ ounces | 150 g) raw walnuts, toasted (see page 390), and omitting the salt and tamari

1 tablespoon unpasteurized red miso or other dark miso

2 tablespoons (1 ounce | 30 g) unpasteurized sweet white miso or chickpea miso

1 tablespoon fresh lemon juice, plus more to taste

Fine sea salt (optional)

Make the sauce following the instructions for the base recipe, adding the miso and lemon juice when blending the sauce. Season to taste with salt and lemon juice, if needed. **Pictured on page 236**

Tangy Red Pepper–Almond Sauce

MAKES 2½ CUPS | 600 ML

1 recipe Creamy Nut Sauce, using ⅔ cup (3 ounces | 85 g) whole raw almonds, toasted (see page 390), and omitting the ¼ cup (60 ml) filtered water

2 small-medium (12 ounces | 340 g) red bell peppers, cored, seeded, and diced (2 cups)

2 teaspoons red chili pepper flakes

1 tablespoon brown rice vinegar

2 teaspoons fresh ginger juice (see the sidebar), or more to taste

Start the sauce following the instructions for the base recipe, adding the bell pepper along with the garlic and salt. Cook for a couple of minutes, until the peppers have begun to soften. Then cover the pan, reduce the heat to low, and cook for 10 minutes, or until the peppers have cooked through. Remove the lid, add the red chili pepper flakes, and cook, uncovered, for a few more minutes, until any pan juices have cooked away. There is no need to deglaze the pan as in the base recipe; just add the red pepper mixture to the blender along with the mirin, nuts, boiling water, tamari, vinegar, and ginger juice. Continue as directed and season to taste with more salt and ginger juice if needed. **Pictured on page 236**

GINGER JUICE

To make ginger juice, finely grate unpeeled gingerroot on the small holes of a box grater or Microplane zester—you can also use a grater especially designed for grating ginger. Place the pulp in the palm of your hand and squeeze it over a small bowl or cup to extract the juice. You will need about a 1-inch (2.5 cm) piece of fresh ginger (½ ounce | 15 g) to get 2 teaspoons ginger juice.

Golden Cashew Sauce with Chile and Lime

MAKES ABOUT 2 CUPS | 480 ML

1 recipe Creamy Nut Sauce, using 1 cup (4½ ounces | 130 g) raw cashews

One 3-inch (7.5 cm) piece (¾ ounce | 22 g) fresh turmeric, peeled and finely chopped

One 1½-inch (3.75 cm) piece fresh ginger (¾ ounce | 22 g), peeled and finely chopped

1 medium (1½ ounces | 45 g) red jalapeño or Thai chile, seeded and finely chopped

1 tablespoon freshly squeezed lime juice

Make the sauce following the instructions for the base recipe, adding the turmeric, ginger, and chile to the pan along with the garlic and cooking for 5 minutes. Continue as directed, adding the lime juice when blending the sauce.

QUICK PANFRIED TEMPEH

SERVES 2

2 tablespoons (30 ml) extra-virgin coconut oil, plus more as needed (see Note)

½ pound (230 g) tempeh, cut into ¼-inch (6 mm) slices

Flaky or fine sea salt

Warm a large skillet over medium heat. Add the coconut oil and tilt the pan to coat. Add the sliced tempeh in a single layer and cook until golden, 3 to 4 minutes. Turn the tempeh over and cook the other side until golden and crisp, adding more oil if needed. Repeat with any remaining tempeh, adding more oil to the pan before adding the sliced tempeh. Transfer the tempeh to a serving plate and sprinkle with salt; serve warm.

NOTE: Be generous with the coconut oil when cooking tempeh this way; it will help the tempeh get the golden crisp edges and delicious flavor you're looking for.

OPPOSITE: Golden Cashew Sauce with Chile and Lime served with forbidden black rice (see page 391) and Quick Panfried Tempeh with sunflower and radish sprouts.

Easy Pine Nut Pasta Sauce

MAKES ½ CUP | 120 ML | ENOUGH FOR 12 OUNCES (340 G) PASTA

½ cup (2½ ounces | 60 g) raw pine nuts

3 tablespoons (45 ml) extra-virgin olive oil

1 tablespoon freshly squeezed lemon juice

½ teaspoon fine sea salt, or more to taste

Warm a medium skillet over medium heat for 2 minutes. Toss in the pine nuts, reduce the heat to low, and toast, stirring frequently, for 5 minutes, or until fragrant and golden. Transfer to a mortar or mini food processor (see Note) and add the olive oil, lemon juice, and salt. Use a pestle to crush the nuts and grind until a paste forms. Or, if you're using a mini food processor, blend until smooth, scrape the sides, and blend again. Use immediately, or store the sauce in a glass jar in the fridge for up to 1 month.

NOTE: If you only have a regular-size food processor, you may need to double this recipe to get it to blend up smooth; if you don't want to make extra sauce, just blend until it is as smooth as possible, stopping to move the mixture around to help it blend.

Preparing Easy Pine Nut Pasta Sauce

Lemon, Red Chili Pepper, and Parsley Pasta

SERVES 4

2 tablespoons (30 ml) extra-virgin olive oil

3 large garlic cloves, finely chopped

5 cups (3 ounces | 85 g) fresh flat-leaf parsley leaves, chopped

½ teaspoon flaky sea salt, plus more to taste

2 teaspoons red chili pepper flakes, plus more to taste

One 12-ounce (340 g) package gluten-free or whole-grain penne or spaghetti

1 recipe Easy Pine Nut Pasta Sauce

4 teaspoons (20 ml) freshly squeezed lemon juice

Lemon wedges for serving

Warm the olive oil in a large skillet over medium-low heat. Add the garlic and cook for 3 minutes, or until golden. Add the parsley and cook for 2 minutes, or until wilted. Remove from the heat, add the flaky salt and red chili pepper flakes, and stir to combine. Set aside.

Cook the pasta according to the package directions. Drain, reserving ½ cup (120 ml) of the cooking water, and return the pasta to the pot. Add the pine nut sauce and stir to evenly coat the pasta, then add the parsley and garlic mixture and lemon juice and stir to combine. Add a splash of the reserved pasta water to loosen the sauce if needed (you probably won't need additional liquid if you are using gluten-free pasta). Season to taste with salt and serve immediately, with lemon wedges on the side. Leftover pasta can be stored in the fridge for up to 2 days; steam in a steamer basket to reheat, or serve at room temperature.

Green Pea Pasta

SERVES 4 TO 6

1 recipe Easy Pine Nut Pasta Sauce

2 tablespoons (30 ml) extra-virgin olive oil

2 large garlic cloves, finely chopped

2 cups (10 ounces | 285 g) frozen peas

¼ teaspoon fine sea salt

One 16-ounce (455 g) package gluten-free or whole-grain penne or fusilli

3 cups (2 ounces | 60 g) micro pea greens

2 teaspoons freshly squeezed lemon juice, plus more to taste

Flaky sea salt and freshly cracked black pepper

Lemon wedges for serving

Make the pine nut sauce using a food processor (any size processor will work here); leave the sauce in the processor.

Warm the olive oil in a large skillet over medium-low heat. Add the garlic and cook for 3 minutes, or until golden. Add the peas and salt and cook for 6 to 8 minutes, until the peas are tender but still bright green. Remove from the heat and transfer ½ cup (about 2½ ounces | 70 g) of the peas to the food processor; set the rest of the peas aside. Blend the peas with the pine nut sauce until creamy.

Cook the pasta according to the package directions. Drain, reserving ½ cup (120 ml) of the cooking water, and return the pasta to the pot. Add the pea–pine nut sauce and stir to evenly coat the pasta, adding a splash of the reserved pasta water to loosen the sauce if needed (you probably won't need any additional liquid if you are using gluten-free pasta). Stir in the reserved peas, half the pea greens, the lemon juice, and flaky salt and pepper to taste. Serve topped with the remaining pea greens, with lemon wedges on the side. Leftover pasta can be stored in the fridge for up to 2 days; steam in a steamer basket to reheat, or serve at room temperature.

Summer Tomato and Basil Pasta

SERVES 4

1½ pounds (680 g) ripe tomatoes

1 cup (½ ounce | 16 g) fresh basil leaves, torn

2 tablespoons (30 ml) extra-virgin olive oil

2 teaspoons balsamic vinegar

1 large garlic clove, pressed or grated (see the sidebar on page 154)

¾ teaspoon fine sea salt, plus more to taste

Freshly ground black pepper

One 12-ounce (340 g) package gluten-free or whole-grain penne, spaghetti, or fettuccine

1 recipe Easy Pine Nut Pasta Sauce

Core the tomatoes, cut into ½-inch (1.25 cm) chunks, and transfer to a large serving bowl, along with their juice. Add the basil, olive oil, vinegar, garlic, salt, and pepper to taste and toss to thoroughly combine. Set aside to marinate while you cook the pasta (you can prepare the tomatoes up to 3 hours in advance).

Cook the pasta according to the package directions. Drain the pasta well and return to the pot. Add the pine nut sauce and stir to evenly coat the pasta. Add to the tomatoes and gently toss to combine. Season to taste with more salt and pepper and serve.

NOTE: This dish is best eaten immediately, as the tomatoes don't stand up well in the fridge.

OPPOSITE: Green Pea Pasta (top) and Summer Tomato and Basil Pasta (bottom)

Quick Tahini Sauce

MAKES 1¼ CUPS | 300 ML

½ cup (4½ ounces | 120 ml) tahini

½ cup (120 ml) filtered water (see Note)

2 tablespoons (30 ml) extra-virgin olive oil

2 tablespoons (30 ml) freshly squeezed lemon juice

1 small garlic clove, finely grated or pressed

½ teaspoon fine sea salt, plus more to taste

Combine the tahini, water, olive oil, lemon juice, garlic, and salt in a food processor and blend until smooth. (If you are not making a variation recipe, you can make this sauce in a bowl; stir the tahini and water together and then add the remaining ingredients.) Season to taste. Use immediately, or store the sauce in a glass jar in the fridge for up to 5 days. Bring to room temperature before using and add water to thin if needed.

NOTE: If you have particularly runny tahini, reduce the water by half and add more as needed to achieve the desired consistency.

Zesty Turmeric Tahini Sauce

MAKES 1½ CUPS | 360 ML

1 recipe Quick Tahini Sauce

One 4-inch (10 cm) piece (1 ounce | 30 g) fresh turmeric, peeled and finely grated (2½ tablespoons)

¼ cup (60 ml) freshly squeezed orange juice

2 Medjool dates, pitted and chopped

1 teaspoon tamari

¼ teaspoon cayenne pepper, plus more to taste

Make the sauce following the instructions for the base recipe, adding the turmeric, orange juice, dates, tamari, and cayenne to the food processor along with the other ingredients. Adjust the salt and cayenne to taste. **Pictured on page 237**

Tamarind, Date, and Ginger Tahini Sauce

MAKES ABOUT 2 CUPS | 480 ML

⅓ cup (3 ounces | 85 g) seedless tamarind paste

½ cup (120 ml) boiling water

1 recipe Quick Tahini Sauce

2 Medjool dates, pitted and chopped

1 tablespoon fresh ginger juice (see the sidebar on page 239)

Combine the tamarind and boiling water in a bowl. Stir until smooth, then press through a strainer into a bowl, scraping the bottom of the strainer with a rubber spatula to collect all the tamarind. You should have 5 tablespoons (75 ml) strained tamarind.

Make the sauce following the instructions for the base recipe, adding the strained tamarind, dates, and ginger juice to the food processor along with the other ingredients. Adjust the seasoning to taste as directed. **Pictured on page 237**

Whipped Chipotle-Lime Tahini Sauce

MAKES 1¾ CUPS | 420 ML

1 recipe Quick Tahini Sauce, using ¼ cup (60 ml) lime juice in place of the lemon juice

½ cup (4½ ounces | 100 g) roasted sweet potato flesh (see page 179)

½ teaspoon chipotle powder

Make the sauce following the instructions for the base recipe, using a food processor, adding the sweet potato and chipotle powder along with the other ingredients and adding extra water to get the desired consistency. Add salt to taste. **Pictured on page 237**

Spiced Tahini-Yogurt Sauce with Sumac

MAKES 1¾ CUPS | 420 ML

1 recipe Quick Tahini Sauce, using 2 tablespoons (30 ml) water

4 ounces (120 ml) thick full-fat dairy or coconut yogurt

2 teaspoons ground sumac

1 teaspoon ground coriander

1 teaspoon ground cumin

Pinch of cayenne pepper, plus more to taste

Make the sauce following the instructions for the base recipe, adding the yogurt, sumac, coriander, cumin, and cayenne to the food processor along with the other ingredients. Add cayenne and salt to taste. **Pictured on page 237**

Green Herb Tahini Sauce

MAKES 1⅓ CUPS | 320 ML

1 recipe Quick Tahini Sauce

2 cups (1 ounce | 30 g) fresh cilantro leaves

2 cups (1 ounce | 30 g) fresh parsley leaves

½ cup (⅕ ounce | 6 g) fresh mint leaves

1 Medjool date, pitted and chopped (optional)

Make the sauce following the instructions for the base recipe and leave it in the food processor. Add the cilantro, parsley, mint, and date, if using, and process again until the herbs are finely chopped, then adjust the salt to taste. **Pictured on page 249**

ABOVE: Preparing Green Herb Tahini Sauce; **OPPOSITE:** Roasted sweet potatoes (see page 179) with Green Herb Tahini Sauce

Baked Marinated Tempeh

Tempeh is a tasty, sliceable fermented bean product traditionally made from soybeans. A source of highly absorbable protein and fiber, it originated in Java and has been around for thousands of years. Tempeh has a much firmer consistency than tofu and is nutritionally more beneficial thanks to the fermentation process, which increases the digestibility of its nutrients. Unfortunately, the commercially made tempeh available in most health food and grocery stores has been pasteurized to keep it shelf stable, which gives it a flat taste and a denser texture than the traditionally made product.

If you seek out artisan-made tempeh, you will be rewarded with a far more appetizing taste and texture. You will also discover a whole world of tempeh made with ingredients such as white beans or adzuki beans and brown rice, like those from Barry's Tempeh in New York City. And the fava bean and chickpea versions from Byron Bay Tempeh in Australia are so good plain, you won't even want to marinate them.

Due to its dense texture, it's difficult to infuse the readily available pasteurized tempeh with flavor, but a super-flavorful, relatively thin marinade can work wonders. Steaming commercial tempeh before marinating it also helps it open up and absorb the marinade better. For the recipes in this chapter, the marinating time is minimal, so there is no need to plan ahead. You simply blend the marinade while the oven heats up, then steam the tempeh, transfer it to a baking dish, cover generously with the marinade, and bake. Slicing the tempeh quite thin also helps it absorb the marinade. If you do find unpasteurized tempeh, you can skip the steaming step.

The baked tempeh can be eaten warm from the oven or at room temperature, and the leftovers enjoyed over the next few days. The generous amount of marinade acts as a sauce and keeps the tempeh moist. Serve the tempeh as a hearty high-protein side dish with a salad or steamed vegetables, or add it to a grain bowl. It also makes a great sandwich filling or topping for toast.

Notes

TEXTURE

The base recipe here is baked for 30 minutes covered and then 20 to 25 minutes uncovered; with the thicker marinades in the variations, baking the tempeh covered for a longer time helps it stay moist and become well infused with flavor. The thicker marinades also result in a delicious glaze of sorts when the tempeh is cooked. The baked tempeh is moist and succulent when freshly made; it firms up slightly when stored in the fridge.

FLAVOR

Because tempeh has a slightly bitter flavor, it benefits from a marinade that is on the sweeter side. These marinades use orange and apple juice rather than maple syrup or honey, so those on sugar-free diets can also enjoy the tempeh. Although the base marinade has a slightly Asian flavor, it is very versatile and can be used as a starting point for whatever direction you choose to head in. Replace the tamari with a teaspoon of salt, for example, or use a different oil or vinegar.

ADD-INS

You can add herbs, spices, miso, or mustard directly to the blender when making the marinade. Or sprinkle chopped herbs or other ingredients such as citrus zest, capers, or sliced fresh chile over the tempeh right before you pour on the marinade and bake it.

GARNISHES

The tempeh in many of these recipes comes out golden, bubbling, and pretty enticing just as it is. I usually serve it in the baking dish because it looks best left undisturbed. But you can certainly scatter fresh herbs over the tempeh before serving to add flavor and color, or sprinkle it with toasted seeds, grated citrus zest, or chopped olives—depending on the flavor of the marinade.

STORING AND FREEZING

The marinated tempeh can be refrigerated for up to a day before baking. Once cooled, the baked tempeh can be stored in an airtight container in the fridge for up to 4 days. To reheat, it can be briefly steamed or warmed, covered, in the oven, but it's actually best at room temperature. I don't recommend freezing baked tempeh because the texture will change (if you don't want too many leftovers, these recipes can easily be halved).

Marinated Tempeh

SERVES 8

16 ounces (455 g) plain tempeh

1 cup (240 ml) pure apple juice

1 cup (240 ml) freshly squeezed orange juice

¼ cup (60 ml) extra-virgin coconut oil

3 tablespoons (45 ml) tamari

1 tablespoon raw apple cider vinegar

2 large garlic cloves

If you intend to bake the tempeh right away, preheat the oven to 350°F (180°C).

Cut the tempeh into ¼-inch (6 mm) slices. Layer the tempeh in a steamer basket and steam over boiling water for 5 minutes, or until heated through. Skip this step if you are using unpasteurized tempeh. Meanwhile, make the marinade: Put the apple juice, orange juice, oil, tamari, vinegar, and garlic in an upright blender and blend until completely smooth.

Arrange the tempeh in a single snug layer in two 12 x 8-inch (30 x 20 cm) or equivalent-size baking dishes. Pour the marinade over the warm tempeh; it should be submerged. You can bake the tempeh right away, set it aside for up to 1 hour, or refrigerate, covered, for up to 1 day before baking.

To bake the tempeh, cover each baking dish first with parchment paper and then with foil and seal tightly. Bake for 30 minutes. Remove the foil and parchment paper (save the foil for another use) and bake for another 25 to 30 minutes, until the marinade is absorbed and the tempeh is lightly browned. Remove from the oven and serve. Store leftover tempeh in an airtight container in the fridge for up to 4 days.

Miso-Turmeric Baked Tempeh

SERVES 8

1 recipe Marinated Tempeh, using 1 tablespoon tamari

5 tablespoons (2½ ounces | 75 g) unpasteurized chickpea miso, mellow white miso, or sweet white miso

One 3-inch (7.5 cm) piece (¾ ounce | 22 g) fresh turmeric, peeled and chopped (finely chopped if using a regular blender)

Make the marinade following the instructions for the base recipe, adding the miso and turmeric to the blender along with the other ingredients and blending until completely smooth. Continue as directed and bake the tempeh covered for 50 minutes. Remove the cover and bake for 5 to 10 minutes longer, until the edges of the tempeh are browning and the marinade has reduced and thickened to a glaze.

Golden Ginger-Sesame Baked Tempeh

SERVES 8

1 recipe Marinated Tempeh, using 3 tablespoons (45 ml) coconut oil

One 3-inch (7.5 cm) piece fresh turmeric (¾ ounce | 22 g), peeled and chopped (finely chopped if using a regular blender)

OPPOSITE, CLOCKWISE FROM TOP RIGHT: Marinade for Spicy Olive and Tomato Baked Tempeh; marinade for Carrot-Coriander Baked Tempeh; marinade for Chile-Coconut-Lime Baked Tempeh; marinade for Rosemary-Mustard Baked Tempeh; marinade for Miso-Turmeric Baked Tempeh; marinade for Golden Ginger-Sesame Baked Tempeh

One 1½-inch (3.75 cm) piece (¾ ounce | 22 g) fresh ginger, peeled and chopped (finely chopped if using a regular blender)

3 tablespoons (45 ml) mirin

2 scallions, coarsely chopped, plus sliced scallions for garnish

1 tablespoon toasted sesame oil

½ cup (2½ ounces | 70 g) raw unhulled sesame seeds, toasted (see page 390)

Make the marinade following the instructions for the base recipe, adding the turmeric, ginger, mirin, chopped scallions, and sesame oil to the blender along with the other ingredients. Continue as directed, sprinkling the sesame seeds over the tempeh before adding the marinade. Cover and bake for 50 minutes, then remove the cover and bake for 5 to 10 minutes longer, until the tempeh is golden brown.

Rosemary-Mustard Baked Tempeh

SERVES 8

1 recipe Marinated Tempeh, using 2 tablespoons (30 ml) tamari

¼ cup (½ ounce | 14 g) chopped fresh rosemary

6 tablespoons (2½ ounces | 70 g) Dijon mustard

½ teaspoon fine sea salt

4 teaspoons (½ ounce | 14 g) black mustard seeds

Make the marinade following the instructions for the base recipe, adding the rosemary, Dijon mustard, and salt to the blender along with the other ingredients. Continue as directed, sprinkling the mustard seeds over the tempeh before adding the marinade. Cover and bake for 50 minutes, then remove the cover and bake for 5 to 10 minutes longer, until the edges of the tempeh are browning and the marinade is absorbed.

OPPOSITE AND ABOVE: Marinade for Miso-Turmeric Baked Tempeh

Spicy Olive and Tomato Baked Tempeh

SERVES 8

1 recipe Marinated Tempeh, using ½ cup (120 ml) each apple juice and orange juice, replacing the coconut oil with extra-virgin olive oil, omitting the tamari, and replacing the apple cider vinegar with balsamic vinegar

One 14½-ounce (410 g) can tomatoes

1 teaspoon sea salt

½ cup (3 ounces | 85 g) Kalamata or other olives, pitted and torn or coarsely chopped

¼ cup (¾ ounce | 22 g) thinly sliced shallots

2 teaspoons red chili pepper flakes

Chopped fresh flat-leaf parsley for garnish

Make the marinade following the instructions for the base recipe, adding the tomatoes and salt to the blender along with the other ingredients. Continue as directed. After you pour the marinade over the tempeh, top with the olives, shallots, and red chili pepper flakes. Cover and bake for 40 minutes, then remove the cover and bake for 10 to 15 minutes longer, until the edges of the tempeh are beginning to brown. Serve garnished with parsley.

Carrot-Coriander Baked Tempeh

SERVES 8

2 large (8 ounces | 230 g) carrots, peeled and grated (3 cups)

1 recipe Marinated Tempeh

4 teaspoons (⅛ ounce | 4 g) ground coriander

½ teaspoon ground cumin

½ teaspoon fine sea salt

Fresh cilantro leaves for garnish

Set aside 1 cup (2½ ounces | 70 g) of the grated carrot and put the rest in an upright blender, along with the marinade ingredients for the base recipe. Add the coriander, cumin, and salt and blend until smooth. Continue as directed, then stir the reserved grated carrots into the marinade and pour over the tempeh. Cover and bake for 50 minutes, then remove the cover and bake for 5 to 10 minutes more, until the tempeh is beginning to brown. Serve garnished with cilantro leaves.

Chile-Coconut-Lime Baked Tempeh

SERVES 8

1 recipe Marinated Tempeh, using ½ cup (120 ml) each apple juice and orange juice and omitting the coconut oil and apple cider vinegar

One 13½-ounce (400 ml) can full-fat coconut milk

¼ cup (60 ml) freshly squeezed lime juice

One 1-inch (2.5 cm) piece (½ ounce | 15 g) fresh ginger, peeled and coarsely chopped

2 medium (3 ounces | 85 g) red Thai chiles or jalapeños, thinly sliced

1 cup (½ ounce | 15 g) fresh cilantro leaves, plus more for garnish

Make the marinade following the instructions for the base recipe, adding the coconut milk, lime juice, and ginger to the blender along with the other base recipe ingredients—you can blend in a few slices of the chile if you like it spicy. Continue as directed. After you pour the marinade over the tempeh, arrange the chile slices and cilantro on top. Bake as directed and garnish with more cilantro leaves before serving. **Pictured on page 250**

Cauliflower Bakes

—

The base recipe in this chapter is for an extremely versatile cauliflower topping that is superb spread and baked over a variety of vegetable fillings. It can turn just about any vegetable dish into a delectable meal. There's a mysterious flavor magic that happens when steamed cauliflower is whipped with pine nuts, seasoned with nutritional yeast, and baked until golden; it's pure comfort food delivered in the healthiest way.

These bakes, or casseroles, can be assembled as individual portions and stored in the fridge or freezer until you are ready to serve them. Since both the filling and topping are already cooked, all you have to do is heat them thoroughly in the oven until browned on top.

You'll find four of my favorite bakes here, including a Leek and Greens Bake that is made for anyone avoiding grains or starches—and also happens to be one of the most enjoyable ways there is to eat a meal of greens. Once you get a feel for the kind of fillings that work best, you will be able to create many variations of your own. The filling should be like a thick vegetable stew, not at all brothy. Depending on the ingredients, you may need to add a little arrowroot to bring the filling together. The Leek and Greens Bake and the Shiitake Mushroom, Caramelized Onion, and Chickpea Bake with Swiss Chard both contain arrowroot, so the filling stays together when it's scooped out.

These bakes involve more steps than most of the other recipes in this book, but they are intended to be complete meals, with a leafy green salad on the side if you like. They all contain greens and lots of veggies and, except for the Leek and Greens Bake, plenty of protein. To add protein to that bake, serve it with Marinated Beans (page 148) or a poached egg on top or stir cooked chickpeas or other beans into the greens before adding the topping.

Notes

TEXTURE

The velvety texture of the cauliflower topping is achieved by blending it in a high-powered blender with nuts and olive oil; you'll need to use the tamper stick to get it all moving. Resist the urge to add more liquid, as it will whip into soft, shiny folds after a minute or two. I have also included instructions for using a food processor for those who don't have a high-powered blender.

FLAVOR

You can vary the flavor of the topping by using different nuts. My favorites are pine nuts, but macadamias, cashews, and walnuts also work well here.

ADD-INS

There is one possible addition to this topping that is especially worth mentioning: rutabaga. Blending a small steamed rutabaga into the topping results in a deeper, layered taste—it seems to enhance the other flavors, and it also makes the topping thicker and creamier. I chose not to include it in the base recipe, however, because it's not always available, and any rutabagas that have sat around after their fall season often have a stringy texture that doesn't blend well. To use rutabaga, peel, dice, and steam a small one (separately) until soft. Add it to the blender along with the cauliflower and blend until smooth, adding a little water as needed.

GARNISH

The only "garnish" these bakes need is the golden brown tinge the topping acquires with a couple of minutes under the broiler right after it's baked.

STORING AND FREEZING

Once assembled, the bakes can be frozen for up to 3 months and then baked when you are ready to serve them. They can be made in one large baking dish, as directed in the recipes, or divided among 4 to 6 smaller (4-inch | 10 cm) ovenproof containers. Be sure you leave about ¾ inch (2 cm) of room above the filling, then cover tightly and freeze. Defrost in the fridge overnight or on the counter for a few hours and bake as directed. The bakes made in smaller containers will cook in less time, 15 to 20 minutes, until heated through and browning on top. Once cooked and cooled, the bakes can be stored in the fridge for 2 to 3 days and then reheated in the oven.

ABOVE: Cauliflower Bake Topping; OPPOSITE: Leek and Greens Bake filling

Cauliflower Bake Topping

MAKES ABOUT 4 CUPS | 960 ML | SERVES 4 TO 6

---

1 large head (2½ pounds | 1.13 kg) cauliflower, cut into 1½-inch (4 cm) florets (about 8 cups)

½ cup (about 2½ ounces | 75 g) raw pine nuts, cashews, or macadamia nuts

½ cup (120 ml) filtered water if using a food processor

2 tablespoons (30 ml) extra-virgin olive oil

3 tablespoons (½ ounce | 15 g) nutritional yeast, plus more to taste (see Note)

½ teaspoon fine sea salt, plus more to taste

Set up a steamer pot with about 2 inches (5 cm) of filtered water in the bottom (the water shouldn't touch the bottom of the basket) and bring to a boil over high heat. Arrange the cauliflower florets in the steamer basket, cover, and steam for 10 to 12 minutes, until the cauliflower is cooked through but not falling apart. Remove from the heat and set aside.

High-Powered-Blender Method: Put the nuts, olive oil, yeast, and salt in a high-powered blender and add the steamed cauliflower. Starting on low speed and using the tamper stick to help press the cauliflower down, blend, gradually increasing the speed to high, until completely smooth and thick; use the tamper stick to keep the mixture moving and to scrape down the sides as you go. This will take a couple of minutes. Season with more nutritional yeast and salt to taste and blend to combine.

Food-Processor Method: Put the steamed cauliflower in a food processor. Combine the nuts, water, olive oil, yeast, and salt in a regular upright blender and blend until completely smooth. Pour into the food processor with the cauliflower and process until completely smooth, scraping down the sides as necessary. Season with more yeast and salt to taste.

The topping is ready to be baked on a filling of your choice, or it can be stored in an airtight container in the fridge for up to 3 days or frozen for up to 3 months.

NOTE: You can skip the nutritional yeast and the topping will still be delicious, but be sure to season it with extra salt.

Leek and Greens Bake

SERVES 4 TO 6

1 tablespoon extra-virgin coconut oil

1 large (12 ounces | 340 g) leek (see Note, page 129), cut into ½-inch (1.25 cm) slices

1 small or ½ medium (12 ounces | 340 g) green cabbage, cored and sliced into ½-inch (1.25 cm) strips (about 6 cups)

¼ teaspoon fine sea salt, plus more to taste

1 large (1 pound | 455 g) bunch lacinato kale, tough stems removed, sliced (about 12 cups; see Note)

2 tablespoons plus 2 teaspoons (40 ml) filtered water

2 tablespoons (30 ml) mirin

2 teaspoons tamari, plus more to taste

2 teaspoons arrowroot powder

1 recipe Cauliflower Bake Topping

Preheat the oven to 375°F (190°C).

Warm a deep skillet or large pot over medium-high heat. Pour in the oil, then add the leek and cook for 2 minutes, or until wilted. Stir in the cabbage and

salt and cook for 2 minutes, or until the cabbage is beginning to soften. Cover the pot and cook, stirring every minute or so, for 6 to 8 minutes, until the leek and cabbage are tender. Stir in the kale one handful at a time, then cover and cook for 2 to 3 minutes, until the kale is tender. Add the 2 tablespoons (30 ml) water, the mirin, and tamari and stir. Dissolve the arrowroot in the remaining 2 teaspoons water and drizzle into the greens, then cook for 1 minute, stirring constantly, or until any liquid has thickened and the greens are glossy. Remove from the heat and season to taste with more salt and tamari.

Transfer the mixture to an 8-inch (20 cm) square or equivalent baking dish and smooth the surface. Spread the cauliflower topping evenly over the greens. Bake for 30 minutes, or until the filling is bubbling and the topping has begun to set. Turn on the broiler and broil the bake for 3 to 6 minutes, until the topping is golden and browning in parts. Remove from the oven and allow to sit for a few minutes before serving.

Once cooled, leftovers can be stored in the fridge in an airtight container for up to 3 days. To reheat, cover and warm in a 400°F (200°C) oven until heated through.

NOTE: To change up the flavor, you can also sauté finely chopped garlic, ginger, and fresh turmeric in the oil before adding the leek.

French Lentil Tomato Bake with Kale and Capers

SERVES 6

¾ cup (5 ounces | 140 g) French lentils, soaked overnight in 3 cups (720 ml) filtered water

One 2-inch (5 cm) piece kombu

2 cups (480 ml) filtered water

2 tablespoons (30 ml) extra-virgin olive oil

1 medium (8 ounces | 230 g) onion, diced

3 large garlic cloves, finely chopped

¼ teaspoon fine sea salt, plus more to taste

1 medium (8 ounces | 230 g) leek (see Note, page 129), cut into ½-inch (1.25 cm) slices

One 14½-ounce (410 g) can diced tomatoes

½ cup (⅓ ounce | 10 g) fresh basil leaves, coarsely chopped

6 cups (8 ounces | 230 g) thinly sliced kale (tough stems removed)

3 tablespoons (1 ounce | 30 g) drained capers in brine

2 teaspoons balsamic vinegar

Freshly ground black pepper

1 recipe Cauliflower Bake Topping

Drain and rinse the lentils and transfer them to a medium pot. Add the kombu and the 2 cups (480 ml) water and bring to a boil over high heat, then cover the pot, reduce the heat to low, and simmer for 20 minutes, or until the lentils are soft. Remove from the heat and remove the kombu (compost it). Drain the lentils and set aside.

Preheat the oven to 375°F (190°C).

Warm the olive oil in a large skillet over medium heat. Add the onion and cook for 6 to 8 minutes, until golden. Stir in the garlic and salt and cook for 3 minutes, or until the garlic is golden. Add the leek and cook for 5 minutes, or until softened. Stir in the tomatoes, cooked lentils, and basil, raise the heat to high, and bring to a simmer. Add the kale and cook just until wilted. Stir in the capers and balsamic vinegar and season to taste with salt and pepper.

Transfer the mixture to an 8-inch (20 cm) square or equivalent baking dish and smooth the surface. Spread the cauliflower topping evenly over the filling. Bake for 30 minutes, or until the filling is bubbling and the topping has begun to set. Turn on the broiler and broil the bake for 3 to 6 minutes, until the topping is golden and browning in parts. Remove from the oven and allow to sit for a few minutes before serving.

Once cooled, leftovers can be stored in the fridge in an airtight container for up to 3 days. To reheat, cover and warm in a 400°F (200°C) oven until heated through.

Beet, Cannellini Bean, and Fennel Bake with Dill

SERVES 4 TO 6

2 tablespoons (30 ml) extra-virgin coconut oil

1 medium (8 ounces | 230 g) onion, quartered and thinly sliced lengthwise

1 medium (10 ounces | 285 g) leek (see Note, page 129), cut into ½-inch (1.25 cm) slices

3 large garlic cloves, finely chopped

1 large (1¼ pounds | 570 g) fennel bulb, quartered, cored, and thinly sliced crosswise

1 teaspoon fine sea salt, plus more to taste

1 medium (6 ounces | 170 g) red beet, grated (2 cups)

1 large (5 ounces | 140 g) carrot, grated (1 cup)

1½ cups (7½ ounces | 215 g) cooked cannellini beans (see page 146), drained, or one 15-ounce (425 g) can cannellini beans, drained and rinsed thoroughly

2 teaspoons balsamic vinegar

1 cup (1 ounce | 30 g) chopped fresh dill (about 1 small bunch)

6 cups (4 ounces | 115 g) spinach, coarsely chopped, or baby spinach leaves

Freshly ground black pepper

1 recipe Cauliflower Bake Topping

Preheat the oven to 375°F (190°C).

Warm the oil in a deep skillet or large pot over medium heat. Add the onion and cook for 10 minutes, or until golden brown. Stir in the leek, garlic, fennel, and salt and cook for 6 to 8 minutes, until the fennel has softened. Add the beet and carrot and cook for 6 to 8 minutes more, until the beets are tender. Stir in the beans, vinegar, and dill. Add the spinach and stir until wilted, then season to taste with pepper and more salt. Remove from the heat.

Transfer the mixture to an 8-inch (20 cm) square or equivalent baking dish and smooth the surface. Spread the cauliflower topping evenly over the filling. Bake for 30 minutes, or until the filling is bubbling and the topping has begun to set. Turn on the broiler and broil the bake for 3 to 6 minutes, until the topping is golden and browning in parts. Remove from the oven and allow to sit for a few minutes before serving.

Once cooled, leftovers can be stored in the fridge in an airtight container for up to 3 days. To reheat, cover and warm in a 400°F (200°C) oven until heated through.

Shiitake Mushroom, Caramelized Onion, and Chickpea Bake with Swiss Chard

SERVES 4 TO 6

3 tablespoons (45 ml) extra-virgin coconut oil

1½ pounds (680 g) shiitake mushrooms, stems removed and caps thinly sliced (about 10 cups)

2 tablespoons (⅛ ounce | 4 g) chopped fresh thyme

3 medium (1½ pounds | 680 g) onions, quartered and thinly sliced lengthwise

½ teaspoon fine sea salt, plus more to taste

6 cups (6 ounces | 170 g) sliced Swiss chard (tough stems removed)

1½ cups (7½ ounces | 215 g) cooked chickpeas (see page 146), drained, ¼ cup (60 ml) cooking liquid reserved, or one 15-ounce (425 g) can chickpeas, drained and rinsed thoroughly

1 tablespoon tamari

2 teaspoons balsamic vinegar

¼ cup (60 ml) filtered water if using canned chickpeas

2 teaspoons arrowroot powder

1 tablespoon filtered water

Freshly ground black pepper

1 recipe Cauliflower Bake Topping

Preheat the oven to 375°F (190°C).

Warm a large skillet over medium-high heat and pour in 1 tablespoon of the oil. Add half the shiitakes and the thyme, stir to coat with oil, and cook for 10 to 12 minutes, stirring only every minute or two (to allow the mushrooms to brown), until the shiitakes are golden brown. Transfer to a bowl and set aside. Repeat with another tablespoon of oil and the remaining mushrooms. Wash and dry the skillet if there are blackened bits on the bottom.

Add the remaining tablespoon oil to the pan, then add the onions and cook over medium heat for 8 minutes, or until beginning to brown. Cover the pan, reduce the heat to low, and cook for 10 minutes, or until the onions are soft and lightly browned. Remove the lid, add the salt, and cook uncovered for another 5 minutes, or until the onions are caramelized. Add the chard, cover, and allow to steam for 3 minutes, or until tender. Add the chickpeas, cooked mushrooms, tamari, balsamic vinegar, and chickpea cooking liquid or ¼ cup (60 ml) water, raise the heat, and bring to a simmer. Dissolve the arrowroot in the 1 tablespoon water, stir, and drizzle into the simmering mixture, stirring constantly. When the mixture has returned to a simmer, remove from the heat and season to taste with pepper and more salt.

Transfer the mixture to an 8-inch (20 cm) square or equivalent baking dish and smooth the surface. Spread the cauliflower topping evenly over the filling. Bake for 30 minutes, or until the filling is bubbling and the topping has begun to set. Turn on the broiler and broil the bake for 3 to 6 minutes, until the topping is golden and browning in parts. Remove from the oven and allow to sit for a few minutes before serving.

Once cooled, leftovers can be stored in the fridge in an airtight container for up to 3 days. To reheat, put the bake in a baking dish, cover, and warm in a 400°F (200°C) oven until heated through.

Seeded Crackers

—

The satisfying crunch and the delicious toasty flavor of these crackers is thanks to the generous amount of seeds mixed with blended whole grains or almond pulp (reserved from making almond milk). When you try one of these crackers, you'll realize that even the most expensive artisanal brands often taste stale, and many store-bought crackers are really just a vehicle for cheese or dips. These crackers are different: they taste just as good plain as they do topped with anything from sliced avocado or pickles and krauts to bean pâtés (see pages 152–157), as well as cheese of all kinds. They also keep extremely well. And, as a bonus, any crumbs left on the pan after you break up the sheets of baked crackers make tasty toppers for salads or soups.

In this chapter, you'll find two extremely versatile and reliable cracker bases that can be flavored in any way you choose—use the variations as guidelines for your own creations. The grain-free crackers were the result of my quest to find a good use for all the pulp left over from making almond milk. To make them, almond pulp is blended with oil, psyllium husks, and a little water and then combined with lots of seeds; the result is a great canvas for any number of flavor directions. Keep a container of almond pulp in the freezer, adding more each time you make a batch of almond milk, and soon you'll have enough for a batch of crackers. If you're cutting back on grains in your diet, these crackers can step in when you're missing something to serve with your soup or salad, and they make a delicious high-protein snack.

The second base recipe is made with cooked whole grains. The next time you're making grains, make extra so you will have enough to bake a batch of crackers. And if you don't have either cooked grains or nut pulp on hand, make the Oat Pecan Crackers with Rosemary and Raisins. They need no advance planning and are delicious served with a soft, tangy goat cheese, smooth nut cheese, or cultured butter.

When experimenting with your own flavors, keep in mind that some additions will make the dough more moist, which translates into a longer baking time. But if you have to break off the crisp parts after baking a sheet of crackers (as noted in the recipes that follow) and then return the rest to the oven, it's not a big deal; just watch carefully so they don't burn.

Notes

TEXTURE

The addictive texture of these crackers is the result of the high proportion of seeds, bound by a combination of blended whole grains or nut pulp with psyllium husks. Psyllium husks bind ingredients and are ideal for gluten-free recipes or in vegan recipes made without eggs. Although the crackers are crisp and light, most are sturdy enough to support a generous amount of topping—even a smear of dip and a small dressed salad, as you might serve on a flatbread. Because the grain-free dough is more fragile than the whole-grain one, the seeds you incorporate need to be small, which is why larger seeds like pumpkin seeds should be roughly chopped in the food processor before proceeding with the recipe.

FLAVOR

Since both of the base recipes are packed with a mixture of sunflower, pumpkin, and sesame seeds, the crackers are already full of flavor. The whole-grain crackers have a subtle, nutty taste that varies depending on the grain you choose. But you can add chopped fresh herbs, such as thyme, sage, or rosemary, and whole or ground spices, such as cumin, fennel, or coriander seeds, to change the flavor as you like. Cayenne or sumac will take the crackers in another direction, and adding crumbled or crushed dried seaweed is another easy option for either base recipe.

A NOTE ON ROLLING

When rolling out any of the doughs, you may find that the edges start to get crumbly. If that happens, remove the top sheet of parchment, fold one edge of the bottom sheet up and over the edge of the dough, press the paper down, and smooth the dough with your fingers to create a straight edge; repeat as necessary on the other edges, then replace the top sheet of parchment and continue rolling out.

ADD-INS

You can add chopped nuts or dried fruit (see the Oat Pecan Crackers with Rosemary and Raisins) to either of the base recipes, but be sure the pieces are not too large, or the dough will be difficult to roll. Because of their water content, which can make the crackers dense, vegetables are perhaps the most challenging addition to these doughs, and they will usually make the baking time longer; see the Carrot-Sumac Crackers and the Beet-Millet Crackers with Dill Seeds for guidance.

STORING

These crackers store like a dream for 3 weeks, and even with longer storage, they are fresher tasting than many you can buy. Store them in airtight containers, and if you make a few different batches, put them in separate containers so they don't all get exposed to air each time you reach for one. Since the crackers keep so well at room temperature, there is no need to freeze them.

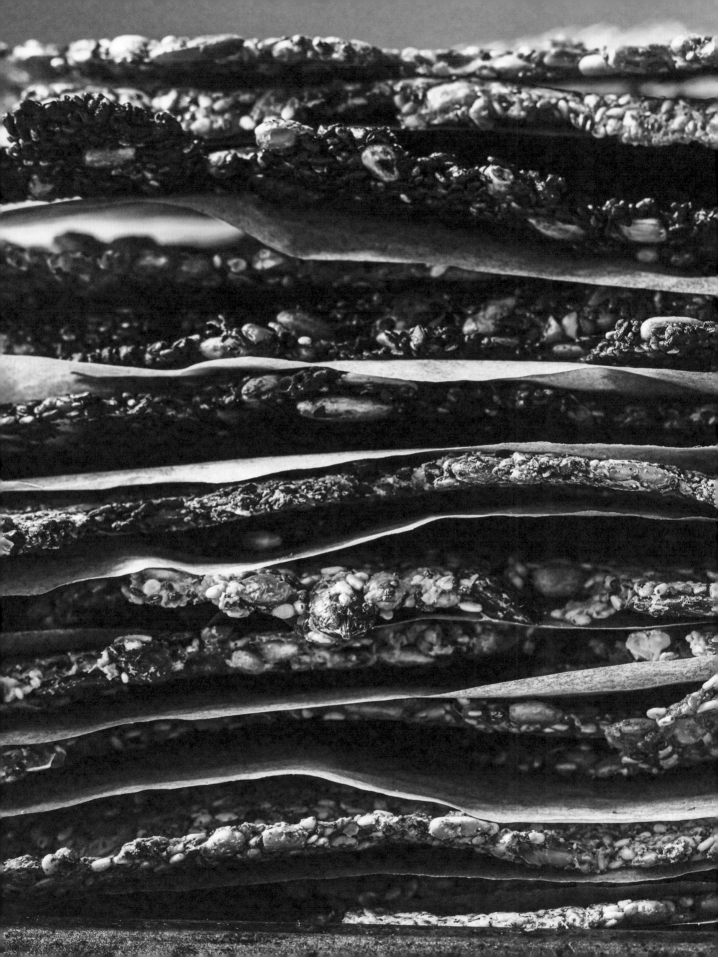

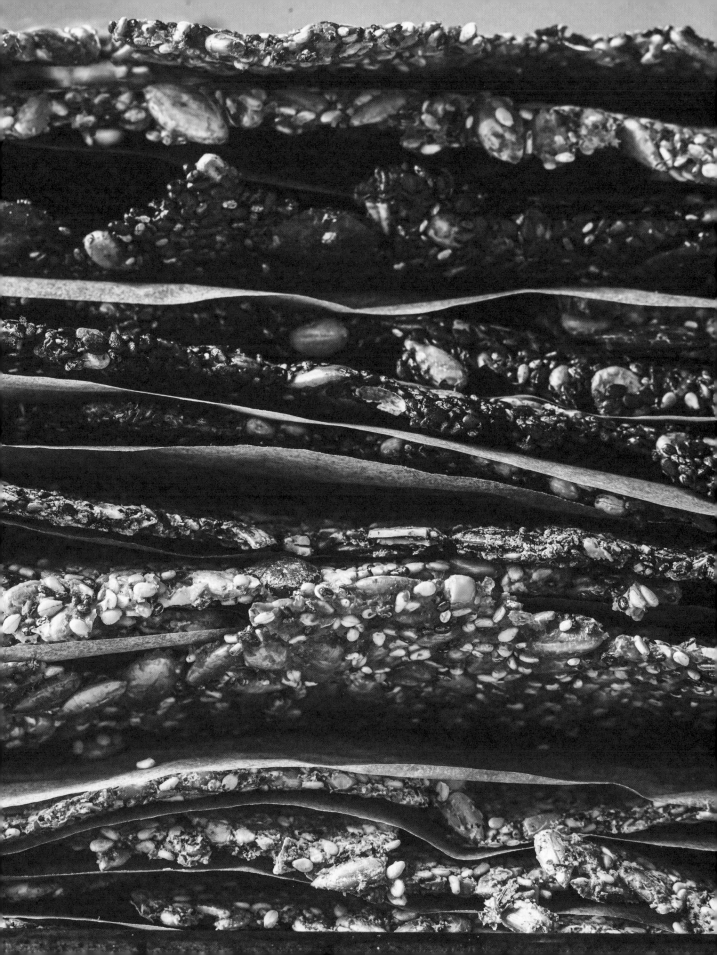

Grain-Free Seeded Crackers

MAKES 2 LARGE BAKING SHEETS

---

1 cup (5 ounces | 140 g) raw pumpkin seeds

1 cup (4½ ounces | 130 g) raw sunflower seeds

1 cup (4½ ounces | 130 g) raw unhulled sesame seeds

1 teaspoon flaky sea salt (or an additional ½ teaspoon fine sea salt)

1½ cups (8 ounces | 230 g) almond pulp, reserved from making almond milk (see page 71)

3 tablespoons (⅓ ounce | 10 g) psyllium husks

⅓ cup (80 ml) filtered water

2 tablespoons (30 ml) melted extra-virgin coconut oil

1 teaspoon fine sea salt

Position a rack in the middle of the oven and preheat the oven to 300°F (150°C). Have two large baking sheets ready.

Pulse the pumpkin seeds in a food processor until roughly chopped. Transfer to a medium bowl, add the sunflower seeds, sesame seeds, and flaky salt, and stir to combine; set aside.

Put the almond pulp, psyllium husks, water, oil, and fine sea salt in the food processor and process to combine. Scrape down the sides and blend again. Transfer to the bowl with the seed mixture and use your hands to mix well, squeezing the mixture through your fingers until thoroughly combined. At first it will seem as if there is not enough moisture, but just keep mixing and it will all come together. Gather the dough into a ball and divide it in half. Place one half in the center of a large sheet of parchment paper. Flatten the dough slightly, cover with a second sheet of parchment, and use a rolling pin to roll it out evenly into a rectangle slightly smaller than your baking sheets and about ⅛ inch (3 mm) thick; use extra pressure on the center of the dough so it is no thicker than the edges. Remove the top sheet of parchment paper (save it for rolling out the remaining dough) and slide the dough, still on the parchment, onto a baking sheet; the dough may tear slightly, but you can just press it back together. Bake for 20 minutes, or until set. Remove the pan from the oven, lift up one side of the parchment along with the cracker, and flip the cracker over onto the baking sheet; it's okay if it breaks a bit. Remove the parchment (save it for the remaining dough) and bake the crackers for another 15 to 20 minutes, until crisp. Remove from the oven and set on a rack to cool. Repeat with the remaining dough.

Meanwhile, once the first batch of crackers is cool enough to handle, break into shards. (If the center of the cracker is not completely crisp, return that part to the oven for another 5 minutes or so, until crisp.) Store the cooled crackers in an airtight container for up to 3 weeks.

Fennel–Poppy Seed Crackers

MAKES 2 LARGE BAKING SHEETS

1 recipe Grain-Free Seeded Crackers, using raw black sesame seeds instead of the unhulled sesame seeds

2 tablespoons (½ ounce | 15 g) poppy seeds

4 teaspoons (⅙ ounce | 5 g) fennel seeds

1 teaspoon spirulina powder

Make the crackers following the instructions for the base recipe, combining the poppy and fennel seeds with the other seeds and adding the spirulina to the processor along with the almond pulp. Continue with the recipe as directed.

Carrot-Sumac Crackers

MAKES 2 LARGE BAKING SHEETS

1 recipe Grain-Free Seeded Crackers, using 2 tablespoons (30 ml) water

¼ cup (1 ounce | 30 g) ground sumac

1 large (5 ounces | 140 g) carrot, grated (2 cups)

Make the crackers following the instructions for the base recipe, adding the sumac to the seed mixture and mixing well. Add half the grated carrots to the food processor along with the almond pulp and blend until thoroughly combined. Continue as directed, adding the remaining grated carrots to the finished dough, mixing well with your hands.

Spicy Seaweed Crackers

MAKES 2 LARGE BAKING SHEETS

1 recipe Grain-Free Seeded Crackers

3 sheets toasted nori, crushed (see page 202)

1 tablespoon dulse flakes, store-bought or homemade (see page 201)

1 tablespoon cumin seeds

2 tablespoons (⅓ ounce | 10 g) nutritional yeast

1 teaspoon ground turmeric

½ teaspoon cayenne pepper, or more to taste

¼ teaspoon garlic powder

¼ teaspoon onion powder

Make the crackers following the instructions for the base recipe, combining the nori, dulse, and cumin seeds with the other seeds and adding the nutritional yeast, turmeric, cayenne, and garlic and onion powders to the food processor along with the almond pulp. Continue with the recipe as directed.

OPPOSITE, FROM LEFT TO RIGHT: (served with Pine Nut Chickpea Pâté with Rosemary, page 157) Oat Pecan Crackers with Rosemary and Raisins; Black Rice–Black Sesame Crackers; Golden Brown Rice Crackers; Fennel–Poppy Seed Crackers; Beet-Millet Crackers with Dill Seeds

Seeded Whole-Grain Crackers

MAKES 2 LARGE BAKING SHEETS

1½ cups (7½ ounces | 210 g) raw unhulled sesame seeds

1½ cups (6¾ ounces | 190 g) raw sunflower seeds

1 cup (5 ounces | 140 g) raw pumpkin seeds

⅓ cup (1¾ ounces | 50 g) chia seeds

1 teaspoon flaky sea salt (or an additional ½ teaspoon fine sea salt)

2 cups (9½ ounces | 270 g) lightly packed cooled cooked millet, short-grain brown rice, or black rice (see the chart on page 391), or 3 cups (10½ ounces | 300 g) uncooked rolled oats

3 tablespoons (⅓ ounce | 10 g) psyllium husks

3 tablespoons (45 ml) melted extra-virgin coconut oil

2 tablespoons (30 ml) filtered water unless using black rice or rolled oats

1 teaspoon fine sea salt

Position a rack in the middle of the oven and preheat the oven to 350°F (180°C). Have two large baking sheets ready.

Put the sesame, sunflower, pumpkin, and chia seeds and the flaky sea salt in a large bowl, stir to combine, and set aside.

Put the cooked whole grains, psyllium husks, oil, water (if using millet, brown rice, or oats), and fine sea salt in a food processor and blend well until the mixture is smooth and forms a ball. Transfer to the bowl with the seeds and use your hands to mix well; the dough will be sticky. Wash and dry your hands, then divide the dough in half; it should not stick heavily to your dry hands at this point, but if it does, set it aside for 10 minutes before continuing. Place a large sheet of parchment paper on your counter and crumble one half of the dough onto the parchment, forming a rectangular shape roughly 12 x 9 inches (30 x 23 cm). Cover with a second sheet of parchment and use a rolling pin to roll out the dough evenly to about ⅛ inch (3 mm) thick; use extra pressure on the center of the dough so it is no thicker than the edges. Remove the top sheet of parchment paper (save it for rolling out the remaining dough) and slide the dough, on the parchment, onto a baking sheet; the dough may tear slightly, but you can just press it back together. Bake for 20 minutes, or until set. Remove the pan from the oven, lift up one side of the parchment, and flip the crackers over onto the baking sheet. Remove the parchment and bake for another 8 to 12 minutes, until fragrant and crisp. Set on a rack to cool. Repeat with the remaining dough.

Once the crackers are cool enough to handle, break into shards. (If the center of the cracker is not crisp, return that part to the oven for another 5 to 10 minutes.) Store in an airtight container for up to 3 weeks.

VARIATION RECIPES

Black Rice–Black Sesame Crackers

MAKES 2 LARGE BAKING SHEETS

1 recipe Seeded Whole-Grain Crackers, using 2 cups (10 ounces | 280 g) raw black sesame seeds instead of the unhulled sesame seeds, 1 cup (4½ ounces | 130 g) raw sunflower seeds, 1 cup (5 ounces | 140 g) raw pumpkin seeds, and cooked black rice and omitting the water

Make the crackers following the instructions for the base recipe; when using black rice, you shouldn't need to use any water, but if the mixture does not come together, add a teaspoon or two of water and blend until it forms a ball. Then continue as directed. **Pictured on page 285**

Golden Brown Rice Crackers

MAKES 2 LARGE BAKING SHEETS

1 recipe Seeded Whole-Grain Crackers, using short-grain brown rice

1 cup (3½ ounces | 100 g) rolled oats

2 teaspoons ground turmeric

½ teaspoon freshly ground black pepper

Make the crackers following the instructions for the base recipe, adding the oats to the bowl of mixed seeds and the turmeric and pepper to the food processor along with the rice. Continue as directed. **Pictured on page 285**

Beet-Millet Crackers with Dill Seeds

MAKES 2 LARGE BAKING SHEETS

1 recipe Seeded Whole-Grain Crackers, using cooked millet

4 teaspoons (⅓ ounce | 10 g) dill seeds

1 small (3 ounces | 90 g) red beet, peeled and grated (about ¾ cup)

Make the crackers following the instructions for the base recipe, adding the dill seeds to the bowl of seeds and the grated beet to the food processor along with the millet. Blend until well combined and continue as directed.

Oat Pecan Crackers with Rosemary and Raisins

MAKES 2 LARGE BAKING SHEETS

2 cups (7 ounces | 200 g) raw pecans

1 recipe Seeded Whole-Grain Crackers, using 3 cups (10½ ounces | 300 g) rolled oats and 2 cups (9 ounces | 270 g) mixed raw seeds and increasing the water to 1 cup (240 ml)

3 tablespoons (⅓ ounce | 9 g) minced fresh rosemary

½ cup (2½ ounces | 75 g) golden raisins

Preheat the oven to 300°F (150°C).

Put the pecans in a food processor and pulse until chopped into pieces about the size of a large lentil. Transfer to a large bowl and set aside.

Make the crackers following the instructions for the base recipe, using 2 cups of the oats and adding the rosemary and raisins when blending the oats and water. Add the seeds from the base recipe to the bowl with the pecans along with the remaining cup of oats. Combine the mixture and continue with the recipe as directed. You won't be able to roll these crackers as thinly as the base recipe, and that's okay. After you flip them over, increase the bake time of the crackers to 15 to 20 minutes, or until deeply golden. Although slightly thicker, these crackers are more delicate than the other whole-grain variations and it's best to allow them to cool and set completely before breaking them up. **Pictured on page 285**

NOTE: Oats absorb water pretty quickly, so if the dough cracks when you're rolling it out, simply pat it down with wet hands a couple of times; or if the finished dough seems too dry to roll, add 2 teaspoons water to the dough before rolling it out. Please also note the decreased oven temperature for this variation.

OPPOSITE: Beet-Millet Crackers with Dill Seeds

Chia
Puddings

—

These low-sugar chia puddings are quick and healthy treats you can make year-round. They're 100 percent fruit-sweetened and an excellent way to celebrate the seasons—start with strawberries in the spring, then turn to juicy stone fruit, berries, and pears in the summer and fall; in winter, use frozen berries or coconut. Serve these as dessert or enjoy them as an afternoon pick-me-up. They taste great either plain or stirred together with an equal amount of thick coconut yogurt. Chia seeds are an ancient endurance food, making these puddings the ideal antidote to an energy slump. You could also include them in your breakfast by stirring a spoonful or two into porridges or adding a dollop on top of muesli or yogurt. Or blend into a smoothie for added protein and texture.

The recipes and variations here can be based on any fruit you like and tweaked endlessly with spices and extracts to suit your mood. They come together with very little effort, and once you have a flavorful, creamy base, the chia seeds do all the work for you. These puddings keep extremely well, and their texture actually improves overnight.

Notes

TEXTURE

The difference between a good chia pudding and a great one is its consistency. Blending nuts into the fruit bases of these puddings creates a rich, silky, and satisfying texture. Creamy nuts like raw cashews and macadamias work best, as they blend up completely smooth, with no fibrous pulp. When experimenting with different ingredients in the base recipes, make sure that after blending you have a thick and creamy mixture before adding the chia seeds; if you do not, add more nuts or coconut butter or nut butter and blend again. The general rule is 2 tablespoons (10 g) seeds per cup (240 ml) of fruit/nut puree, but the amount of chia can be reduced slightly if the base has the consistency of a superthick smoothie. And remember that for chia seeds to really work their magic, you need to give them enough time in the fridge. Although the puddings will be good to go once they are completely chilled, they will continue to thicken overnight.

It's best to use store-bought coconut butter rather than homemade for these puddings, as its texture is finer and smoother and will result in a silkier mouthfeel. If you're allergic to nuts, you can double the coconut butter in any of the base recipes or use fresh or thawed frozen raw young coconut meat in place of one-third of the fruit.

FLAVOR

Fruit and berries play the starring role in the delicately flavored base recipes. It's best to cook the fruit (with the exception of mango), because that not only stabilizes the consistency and flavor of the pudding but also gives it a longer shelf life.

You can also use any of the Simple Compotes (pages 96–105) in place of the fruit in these recipes. Use a full recipe of compote in place of the fruit and add ¼ to ½ cup (60 to 120 ml) juice, water, or nut milk to help the mixture blend properly. Most of these base recipes call for orange juice because of its tangy, bright flavor, but you can substitute part

water and apple or pear juice. Coconut water works well in the coconut base, because coconut meat is not very sweet. For the healthiest option, look for unpasteurized coconut water, often sold frozen.

If you'd like to add spices to any of the fruit puddings, stir them into the fruit as it cooks, then add more to taste if needed when blending the mixture.

ADD-INS

To add a nutrient boost to your chia pudding, try 1 to 2 teaspoons of reishi or chaga mushroom powder. They both pair well with any of the cacao-flavored puddings. Since these powders all have a slightly bitter flavor, start with a teaspoon and increase to taste. Rose water or orange blossom water is another easy addition to any of the base recipes. Or swirl crushed berries into the pear or coconut variation, as in the Nectarine-Raspberry Chia Pudding.

GARNISHES

The pretty jewel-like colors of these chia puddings can be enhanced with a sprinkling of berries, a few edible flowers, and/or a dusting of cacao powder, matcha, or crushed freeze-dried berries. You can use a garnish of the same flavor as the pudding or experiment with other complementary flavors.

STORING AND FREEZING

Most of these puddings keep well for at least 5 days stored in an airtight container in the refrigerator. For maximum shelf life, store individual portions in glass jars; this also makes them ready for a snack on the go. Freezing and then thawing the puddings is not recommended, as some variations become watery when defrosted, but they do make delicious frozen treats: Once the pudding is frozen solid, allow to thaw just until you can chop it up, then blend in a food processor until thick and creamy.

PUDDING FLAVORINGS

Made with seasonal fruit, creamy nuts, and chia seeds, these puddings need no added sweeteners or toppings for a refreshing and satisfying snack or dessert. To create your own custom flavor, try adding cacao, fresh ginger, vanilla bean, cardamom, or cinnamon to any of the base recipes. Find these recipes on the following pages:

TOP ROW

○ Strawberry Rose Chia Pudding (page 301)

MIDDLE ROW, FROM LEFT TO RIGHT

○ Nectarine–Raspberry Chia Pudding (page 303)

○ Mango Coconut Chia Pudding (page 305)

○ Matcha Coconut Chia Pudding (page 305)

○ Apricot–Orange Blossom Chia Pudding (page 303)

BOTTOM ROW, FROM LEFT TO RIGHT

○ Cacao Berry Chia Pudding with Ginger (page 301)

○ Nectarine-Raspberry Chia Pudding (page 303)

○ Plum-Vanilla Chia Pudding (page 303)

○ Pear-Citrus Chia Pudding with Turmeric (page 297)

Pear Chia Pudding

MAKES 3 CUPS | 720 ML | SERVES 6

3 (1½ pounds | 680 g) firm but ripe pears, peeled, cored, and cut into 1-inch (2.5 cm) dice (about 3½ cups)

½ cup (120 ml) freshly squeezed orange juice or ¼ cup (60 ml) filtered water

Pinch of fine sea salt

½ cup (2¼ ounces | 65 g) raw cashews or macadamia nuts

2 tablespoons (1 ounce | 30 g) coconut butter (store-bought is best here)

1 teaspoon vanilla extract

6 tablespoons (2 ounces | 60 g) chia seeds

Combine the pears, orange juice or water, and salt in a medium pot and bring to a boil over high heat. Cover, reduce the heat to low, and simmer for 8 to 10 minutes, until the pears have cooked through. Remove from the heat and allow to cool slightly.

Transfer the mixture to an upright blender, add the cashews, coconut butter, and vanilla, and blend until completely smooth. Pour into a widemouthed quart jar or a medium bowl, add the chia seeds, and whisk thoroughly, making sure there are no clumps of seeds hiding anywhere. Allow to sit for a few minutes and then whisk again. Leave the whisk in place and refrigerate for at least 1 hour, or until completely chilled, whisking every now and then to distribute the chia seeds evenly and to help cool the pudding quickly. The pudding will thicken further overnight; if it gets too thick, stir in a splash of water or nut milk. Store the pudding in an airtight glass jar or other container in the fridge for up to 5 days.

Pear-Citrus Chia Pudding with Turmeric

MAKES 3 CUPS | 720 ML | SERVES 6

1 recipe Pear Chia Pudding

1 tablespoon finely grated peeled fresh turmeric

2 tablespoons (30 ml) freshly squeezed lemon or lime juice

1 teaspoon grated orange zest

1 teaspoon grated lemon or lime zest

Make the pudding following the instructions for the base recipe, adding the turmeric to the pot along with the pears. Continue as directed, then add the lemon or lime juice to the blender when blending the mixture. Whisk in the citrus zest before whisking in the chia seeds and continue as directed. **Pictured on page 295**

Pear-Cacao Chia Pudding

MAKES 3 CUPS | 720 ML | SERVES 6

1 recipe Pear Chia Pudding, using 1 tablespoon vanilla extract

6 tablespoons (¾ ounce | 22 g) cacao powder (see the sidebar)

Make the pudding following the instructions for the base recipe, adding the cacao to the blender when blending the cooked pears. Continue as directed.

CACAO POWDER

In its natural state, cacao contains an abundance of antioxidants and essential minerals that support both mental and physical well-being. Unprocessed raw cacao has not been roasted, therefore none of the beneficial enzymes or nutrients are lost. Cacao powder is made by cold pressing fermented cacao beans to extract the fat (cacao butter) before grinding the beans into a fine powder. This process concentrates the nutrients and enriches the flavor of cacao. Cocoa powder is made from beans that have been roasted at high temperatures before being pressed and ground into a powder. If you don't have cacao powder, you can use an equal amount of cocoa powder in any recipe.

Berry Chia Pudding

MAKES ABOUT 3 CUPS | 720 ML | SERVES 6

4 cups fresh or frozen berries (about 1 pound | 455 g; weight depends on the berries used)

1½ cups (360 ml) freshly squeezed orange juice

Pinch of fine sea salt

½ cup (2¼ ounces | 65 g) raw cashews or macadamia nuts

2 tablespoons (1 ounce | 30 g) coconut butter (store-bought is best here)

2 teaspoons vanilla extract

6 tablespoons (2 ounces | 60 g) chia seeds

Combine the berries, orange juice, and salt in a medium pot and bring to a boil over high heat. Cover, reduce the heat to low, and simmer for 5 minutes, or until the berries have softened and released their juices. Remove from the heat and allow to cool slightly.

Transfer the mixture to an upright blender, add the cashews, coconut butter, and vanilla, and blend until completely smooth. Pour into a widemouthed quart jar or a medium bowl, add the chia seeds, and whisk thoroughly, making sure there are no clumps of seeds hiding anywhere. Allow to sit for a few minutes and then whisk again. Leave the whisk in place and refrigerate for at least 1 hour, or until completely chilled, whisking every now and then to distribute the chia seeds evenly and to help cool the pudding quickly. The pudding will thicken further overnight; if it gets too thick, stir in a splash of water or nut milk. Store the pudding in an airtight glass jar or other container in the fridge for up to 5 days.

OPPOSITE: Cacao Berry Chia Pudding with Ginger with fresh berries and crushed freeze-dried berries

Strawberry Rose Chia Pudding

MAKES ABOUT 3½ CUPS | 840 ML | SERVES 6

1 recipe Berry Chia Pudding, using 5 cups (1½ pounds | 680 g) strawberries, hulled and sliced, and ½ cup (2½ ounces | 80 g) chia seeds

½ cup (⅕ ounce | 6 g) organic fresh rose petals (see the sidebar)

2 teaspoons organic rose water (see the sidebar on page 37), or more to taste

Make the pudding following the instructions for the base recipe, adding the rose petals to the pot along with the berries and adding the rose water to the blender when blending the mixture. Add more rose water to taste. Continue as directed. **Pictured on page 295**

ROSE PETALS

It's important to seek out organic rose petals when using them in cooking as most commercially grown roses have been heavily sprayed with pesticides and are often dipped in chemicals before arriving at your local florist. The best place to look for fresh organic or unsprayed rose petals is a farmers' market or a local garden. If you can't find fresh rose petals, simply leave them out and add a little extra rose water to taste.

Cacao Berry Chia Pudding with Ginger

MAKES ABOUT 3 CUPS | 720 ML | SERVES 6

1 recipe Berry Chia Pudding, using a combination of blueberries, blackberries, and raspberries

¼ cup (½ ounce | 16 g) cacao powder (see the sidebar on page 297)

1 teaspoon fresh ginger juice (see the sidebar on page 239), or more to taste

Make the pudding following the instructions for the base recipe, adding the cacao and ginger to the blender when blending the berries. Add more ginger juice to taste. Continue as directed. **Pictured on page 299**

Stone Fruit Chia Pudding

MAKES ABOUT 3 CUPS | 720 ML | SERVES 6

1¼ pounds (565 g) stone fruit, such as plums, peaches, apricots, or nectarines, halved, pitted, and cut into 1-inch (2.5 cm) dice (about 3 cups)

¾ cup (180 ml) freshly squeezed orange juice or ½ cup (120 ml) filtered water

Pinch of fine sea salt

½ cup (2¼ ounces | 65 g) raw cashews or macadamia nuts

2 tablespoons (1 ounce | 30 g) coconut butter (store-bought is best here)

1 teaspoon vanilla extract

¼ cup (1¼ ounces | 40 g) chia seeds

Combine the fruit, orange juice, and salt in a medium pot and bring to a boil over high heat. Cover, reduce the heat to low, and simmer for 8 to 10 minutes, until the fruit has cooked through. Remove from the heat and allow to cool slightly.

Transfer the mixture to an upright blender, add the cashews, coconut butter, and vanilla, and blend until completely smooth. Pour into a widemouthed quart jar or a medium bowl, add the chia seeds, and whisk thoroughly, making sure there are no clumps of seeds hiding anywhere. Allow to sit for a few minutes and then whisk again. Leave the whisk in place and refrigerate for at least 1 hour, or until completely chilled, whisking every now and then to distribute the chia seeds evenly and to help cool the pudding quickly. The pudding will thicken further overnight; if it gets too thick, stir in a splash of water or nut milk. Store the pudding in an airtight glass jar or other container in the fridge for up to 5 days.

Apricot–Orange Blossom Chia Pudding

MAKES ABOUT 3 CUPS | 720 ML | SERVES 6

1 recipe Stone Fruit Chia Pudding, using 1 pound (455 g) apricots (about 8 medium), pitted and quartered

1 tablespoon orange blossom water

Make the pudding following the instructions for the base recipe, adding the orange blossom water to the blender when blending the fruit. Continue as directed. **Pictured on page 295**

Plum-Vanilla Chia Pudding

MAKES ABOUT 3 CUPS | 720 ML | SERVES 6

1 recipe Stone Fruit Chia Pudding, using plums (about 7 medium) and increasing the vanilla extract to 1 tablespoon

1 vanilla bean, split, seeds scraped out, seeds and pod reserved

2 tablespoons (30 ml) pure maple syrup if the plums are very sour

Make the pudding following the instructions for the base recipe, adding the vanilla seeds and pod to the pot along with the plums. Remove the pod before blending the plum mixture. Taste the mixture once it is blended and add maple syrup if it is too sour. Blend again and continue as directed. **Pictured on page 295**

Nectarine-Raspberry Chia Pudding

MAKES ABOUT 3 CUPS | 720 ML | SERVES 6

1 recipe Stone Fruit Chia Pudding, using nectarines (about 4 medium)

¾ cup (3 ounces | 100 g) fresh raspberries, plus more for garnish

Make the pudding following the instructions for the base recipe. When the pudding is chilled and ready to serve, wash and drain the raspberries, put them on a small plate, and gently crush with a fork. Carefully stir them into the chia pudding, stopping before completely combined to create a ribbon effect. Serve garnished with more raspberries. (The raspberries will bleed a little if you're storing the pudding. You can store the crushed raspberries separately and swirl a little into each portion if you like.) **Pictured on page 294**

Coconut Chia Pudding

MAKES ABOUT 3 CUPS | 720 ML | SERVES 6

1 pound (455 g) raw young coconut meat, defrosted if frozen, any liquid reserved

1¼ cups (300 ml) unpasteurized coconut water

1 tablespoon vanilla extract

6 tablespoons (2 ounces | 60 g) chia seeds

Put the coconut meat (and any liquid that accumulated as it defrosted, if frozen) in an upright blender. Add the coconut water and vanilla and blend on high speed until completely smooth. Pour into a widemouthed quart jar or a medium bowl, add the chia seeds, and whisk thoroughly, making sure there are no clumps of seeds hiding anywhere. Allow to sit for a few minutes and then whisk again. Leave the whisk in place and refrigerate for at least 1 hour, or until completely chilled, whisking every now and then to distribute the chia seeds evenly. The pudding will thicken further overnight; if it gets too thick, stir in a splash of water, coconut water, or nut milk. Store the pudding in an airtight glass jar or other container in the fridge for up to 3 days.

NOTES: Although young coconut meat is now widely used in smoothies and desserts, it's important to remember that unless you live by a coconut grove, it's a decadent ingredient due to the fact that it has usually traveled a long way. Fresh coconuts in the United States are irradiated when imported, so it's best to buy frozen organic coconut meat.

Coconut meat is not that sweet, which is why I add coconut water here. If you want a less sweet pudding (or you're adding fruit, as in the mango variation), you can use homemade almond milk (see page 71) in its place. Or use part coconut water and part almond milk to suit your taste.

Matcha Coconut Chia Pudding

MAKES ABOUT 3 CUPS | 720 ML | SERVES 6

1 recipe Coconut Chia Pudding

1 tablespoon ceremonial-grade matcha tea powder (see Resources, page 392)

Make the pudding following the instructions for the base recipe, adding the matcha to the blender when blending the coconut meat. Continue as directed.

Pictured on page 295

Mango Coconut Chia Pudding

MAKES ABOUT 3 CUPS | 720 ML | SERVES 6

1 recipe Coconut Chia Pudding, using 1 cup (8 ounces | 230 g) coconut meat, replacing the coconut water with almond milk (see page 71), and using 3 tablespoons (1 ounce | 30 g) chia seeds

1½ cups (9 ounces | 255 g) cubed ripe mango (½-inch | 1.25 cm cubes)

Make the pudding following the instructions for the base recipe, adding the mango to the blender when blending the coconut meat. Continue as directed.

Pictured on page 295

Muffins

Whether you're looking for a muffin recipe that's whole-grain, gluten-free, vegan, grain-free, or sugar-free, you'll find it in this chapter. I spent years developing the ideal vegan and gluten-free muffin that was also 100 percent whole-grain, experimenting with dozens of recipes, looking for the secret, and coming up empty-handed. Finally I found the right combination of ingredients to make a muffin that no one would know was gluten-free, let alone vegan. I discovered textural magic (and a gorgeous golden-colored crumb) with a combination of millet flour, oat flour, and almond flour. These flours, along with plenty of ground flax seeds, became a winning base from which an endless number of variations have stemmed.

In my quest to create vegan and gluten-free muffins, I was also looking for the perfect dairy- and gluten-free muffin using eggs, which is often requested by my clients. I found that the same combination of whole-grain flours also worked with eggs whisked into the batter. This chapter includes these two recipe bases and a grain-free muffin base that uses both ground coconut and sunflower seeds along with coconut flour—great for anyone cutting down on grains and wanting a tasty protein-packed treat. All of the variations can be made with any of the three base recipes, so you can mix and match as you like. And for sugar-free options, they can be made without maple syrup; see page 318.

Notes

TEXTURE

With all of these recipes, it is very important that you don't serve the muffins warm out of the oven. Letting them cool first allows the structure to set, resulting in a tender crumb and an appealing texture. Both of the non-vegan base recipes contain a small amount of coconut flour, which helps absorb the excess moisture from the natural sweeteners. The grain-free muffins have a completely different texture from those made with whole-grain flours; although they are mildly sweet, they are actually more like a moist flourless cake than a muffin—and they taste amazing halved and toasted. As with all baking recipes, I highly recommend weighing the dry ingredients. This will guarantee the best textural result.

FLAVOR

Changing up the fruits, berries, and spices in these recipes will give you the option of irresistible healthy muffin recipes year-round. You can use the same amount of diced seasonal fruits such as peaches, pears, nectarines, or plums in place of the berries in any of the berry muffin variations. Or swap the winter squash for mashed sweet potato in the Spiced Seeded Winter Squash Muffins. A teaspoon or two of ground cardamom is a lovely aromatic addition to the Matcha Berry Muffins.

You can also switch out the almond flour for ground coconut or another nut or seed flour in those recipes. And you can use any other nut or seed milk (see page 71) in place of the almond milk.

ABOUT THE YIELDS

The yields of these muffins depend on the variation and base you choose. I don't recommend making the base recipes alone as they all depend on add-ins for texture and flavor.

ADD-INS

You can add toasted nuts or seeds to any of these muffin recipes. Toasted walnuts or pecans are especially good in the Golden Carrot-Spice Muffins. Grated orange zest or lemon zest will brighten the flavor of any of the variations. Fresh or frozen berries are another great addition—toss a handful of your favorite berries into the batter for the Apple Poppy Seed Muffins. When making the vegan batter, use fresh rather than frozen berries; they tend not to sink as much.

GARNISHES

Some of these muffins have a topping baked right onto them, and that same technique can be used with all the variations: see the recipes for Matcha Berry Muffins, Spiced Seeded Winter Squash Muffins, and Apple Poppy Seed Muffins for ideas. The Any-Berry Muffins are lovely served with a scattering of fresh berries. Or, if you want the look of a dusting of sugar without an added sweetener, sift a little coconut flour over the top of any of the muffins.

STORING AND FREEZING

Like most baked goods, these muffins are best served the day they're made. However, they all keep well for a day or two stored in an airtight container in a cool place or for up to 4 days in the fridge. They can also be frozen, sealed airtight, for up to 3 months; defrost on the counter in their container. No matter how you store them, all of these muffins benefit from being rewarmed before serving, which helps lighten their texture (coconut oil solidifies at room temperature). Reheat in a 375°F (190°C) oven for about 10 minutes or halve and toast.

Gluten-Free Vegan Muffins

MAKES ABOUT 10 MUFFINS

¼ cup (¾ ounce | 22 g) ground flax seeds

1 cup (240 ml) almond milk (see page 71)

1 cup (4½ ounces | 130 g) millet flour

½ cup (1½ ounces | 45 g) gluten-free oat flour

1 tablespoon aluminum-free baking powder

½ cup (1½ ounces | 45 g) almond flour

⅓ cup (80 ml) melted extra-virgin coconut oil (see Note)

¼ cup (60 ml) pure maple syrup

¼ cup (60 ml) freshly squeezed orange juice

1 tablespoon vanilla extract

½ teaspoon fine sea salt

Fruit, berries, or vegetables; see variations

Preheat the oven to 375°F (190°C). Line a standard muffin pan with 10 paper liners and set aside.

Combine the ground flax seeds and almond milk in a small bowl and set aside for 10 to 15 minutes to thicken.

Sift the millet flour, oat flour, and baking powder into a medium bowl. Add the almond flour and whisk to combine, breaking up any clumps of almond flour. Whisk together the coconut oil, maple syrup, orange juice, vanilla, and salt in another medium bowl. Add the flax–almond milk mixture and whisk to combine. Add the flour mixture and stir with a rubber spatula until just combined, adding any flavorings, such as fruit, berries, or vegetables, from the variations.

Spoon the batter into the muffin cups and bake for 35 minutes, or until a toothpick inserted in the center of a muffin comes out clean. Remove from the oven and allow the muffins to sit for 5 minutes before transferring them to a wire rack to cool. Be sure to cool completely before serving. Store leftovers in an airtight container at cool room temperature for up to 2 days or in the fridge for up to 4 days; bring to room temperature, warm in the oven, or halve and toast before serving. The muffins can be frozen in an airtight container for up to 3 months. Thaw at room temperature in the container they were frozen in.

NOTE: If melted coconut oil is added to cold ingredients, it will clump and harden. If your wet ingredients are cold, not at room temperature, don't add the coconut oil until right before combining the wet and dry ingredients.

BASE RECIPE

Gluten-Free Muffins

MAKES ABOUT 10 MUFFINS

1 cup (4½ ounces | 130 g) millet flour

½ cup (1½ ounces | 45 g) gluten-free oat flour

2 tablespoons (⅓ ounce | 10 g) coconut flour

2 teaspoons aluminum-free baking powder

½ cup (1½ ounces | 45 g) almond flour

2 medium eggs

½ cup (120 ml) almond milk (see page 71)

¼ cup (60 ml) pure maple syrup

¼ cup (60 ml) freshly squeezed orange juice

⅓ cup (80 ml) melted extra-virgin coconut oil (see Note, above)

1 tablespoon vanilla extract

½ teaspoon fine sea salt

Fruit, berries, or vegetables; see variations

Preheat the oven to 375°F (190°C). Line a standard muffin pan with 10 paper liners and set aside.

(continued)

Sift the millet flour, oat flour, coconut flour, and baking powder into a medium bowl. Add the almond flour and whisk to combine, breaking up any clumps of almond flour. Break the eggs into another medium bowl and whisk thoroughly, then add the almond milk, maple syrup, orange juice, coconut oil, vanilla, and salt and whisk to combine. Add the flour mixture and stir with a rubber spatula until just combined.

Spoon the batter into the muffin cups and bake for 30 to 35 minutes, until a toothpick inserted in a muffin comes out clean. Remove from the oven and allow the muffins to sit for 5 minutes before transferring them to a wire rack to cool. Be sure to cool completely before serving. Store leftovers in an airtight container at cool room temperature for up to 2 days or in the fridge for up to 4 days; bring to room temperature, warm in the oven, or halve and toast before serving. The muffins can be frozen in an airtight container for up to 3 months. Thaw at room temperature in the container they were frozen in.

Grain-Free Muffins

1 cup (3 ounces | 85 g) unsweetened shredded dried coconut

1 cup (4½ ounces | 130 g) raw sunflower seeds

1 cup (3 ounces | 85 g) almond flour

¼ cup (⅔ ounce | 20 g) coconut flour

2 teaspoons aluminum-free baking powder

2 medium eggs

¼ cup (60 ml) almond milk (see page 71)

¼ cup (60 ml) pure maple syrup

¼ cup (60 ml) freshly squeezed orange juice

¼ cup (60 ml) melted extra-virgin coconut oil (see Note, page 311)

1 tablespoon vanilla extract

¼ teaspoon fine sea salt

Fruit, berries, or vegetables; see variations

Preheat the oven to 375°F (190°C). Line a standard muffin pan with 10 paper liners and set aside.

Put the shredded coconut and sunflower seeds in a food processor and grind until fine; the mixture should be starting to clump in the corners of the processor bowl but still have a flour-like texture—if it is blended for too long, the coconut and seeds will release oil and be too wet to use. Transfer to a medium bowl and add the almond flour. Add the coconut flour and baking powder and stir well with a whisk, breaking up any clumps of almond flour.

Break the eggs into another medium bowl and whisk thoroughly. Add the almond milk, maple syrup, orange juice, coconut oil, vanilla, and salt and whisk to combine. Add the flour mixture and stir with a rubber spatula until just combined.

Spoon the batter into the muffin cups and bake for 30 to 35 minutes, until a toothpick inserted in a muffin comes out clean. Remove from the oven

and allow the muffins to sit for 5 minutes before transferring them to a wire rack to cool completely. Store leftovers in an airtight container at cool room temperature for up to 2 days or in the fridge for up to 4 days; bring to room temperature, warm in the oven, or halve and toast before serving. The muffins can be frozen in an airtight container for up to 3 months. Thaw at room temperature in the container they were frozen in.

VARIATION RECIPES

Zucchini, Lemon, and Walnut Muffins

MAKES 10 MUFFINS

2 small-medium (10 ounces | 285 g) zucchini, grated (3 cups)

1 recipe muffin base of your choice

3 tablespoons (½ ounce | 12 g) grated lemon zest

¾ cup (2½ ounces | 70 g) raw walnuts, chopped

Put the grated zucchini on a clean kitchen towel or in a nut-milk bag and squeeze out as much liquid as possible (you should get at least ¼ cup | 60 ml; discard the liquid). Make the batter following the instructions for the base recipe, stirring the zucchini and lemon zest into the wet mixture. Continue as directed, then stir about two-thirds of the walnuts into the finished batter. Once the batter is divided among the muffin cups, sprinkle with the remaining walnuts and lightly press them into the batter. Bake as directed. **Pictured on page 306 (center left)**

Apple Poppy Seed Muffins

MAKES ABOUT 9 MUFFINS

2 medium (12 ounces | 340 g) apples

1 recipe muffin base of your choice

2 tablespoons (½ ounce | 15 g) poppy seeds, plus more for sprinkling

1 teaspoon freshly grated nutmeg (see the sidebar on page 43)

1 teaspoon ground cinnamon

Core and thinly slice one apple. Grate the other apple on the largest holes of a box grater. Make the batter following the instructions for the base recipe, stirring the poppy seeds, nutmeg, and cinnamon into the dry mixture and adding the grated apple to the wet mixture. Continue as directed, then scoop the batter into the muffin cups, arrange the apple slices over the top of the muffins, and sprinkle with poppy seeds. Bake as directed. **Pictured on page 306 (center right)**

OPPOSITE: Grain-Free Muffins dry mixture

Spiced Seeded Winter Squash Muffins

MAKES 10 MUFFINS

1 recipe muffin base of your choice (see Notes)

1 teaspoon freshly grated nutmeg (see the sidebar on page 43)

1 teaspoon ground cinnamon

1 teaspoon ground ginger

1 teaspoon ground cardamom

¼ teaspoon ground allspice

1½ cups (11¾ ounces | 315 g) mashed squash (see page 73)

½ cup (2½ ounces | 70 g) raw mixed pumpkin, sunflower, and unhulled sesame seeds, toasted (see Notes) and coarsely chopped

Make the batter following the instructions for the base recipe, sifting the nutmeg, cinnamon, ginger, cardamom, and allspice into the bowl along with the flours and baking powder. Whisk the mashed squash into the wet mixture and continue as directed. Stir half the mixed seeds into the finished batter. Scoop the batter into the muffin cups and sprinkle the remaining seeds over the top of the muffins. Bake as directed. **Pictured on page 306 (top)**

NOTES: If you use the Gluten-Free Vegan Muffins base recipe, reduce the ground flax seeds and almond milk by half. If using the Grain-Free Muffin base recipe, increase the coconut flour to ½ cup (1⅓ ounces | 40 g) and omit the orange juice.

You can toast all three seeds together. Place the seeds in a medium skillet over medium heat and toast, stirring frequently, for 5 minutes, or until golden. Remove from the pan and set aside.

Golden Carrot-Spice Muffins

MAKES 10 MUFFINS

1 recipe muffin base of your choice

2 teaspoons ground cardamom

2 teaspoons ground ginger

2 teaspoons ground turmeric

1 teaspoon freshly grated nutmeg (see the sidebar on page 43)

1 teaspoon ground cinnamon

2 large (8 ounces | 230 g) carrots, grated (3 cups)

Make the batter following the instructions for the base recipe, sifting the cardamom, ginger, turmeric, nutmeg, and cinnamon into the bowl along with the flours and baking powder. Stir the grated carrots into the wet mixture and continue as directed.

Any-Berry Muffins

MAKES 10 MUFFINS

1 recipe muffin base of your choice

1 tablespoon grated orange zest or lemon zest (optional)

1½ cups (6 ounces | 170 g) fresh or frozen blueberries, raspberries, or blackberries, or a combination

Make the batter following the instructions for the base recipe, adding the citrus zest, if using, to the wet mixture and the berries to the finished batter. Bake as directed. **Pictured on page 319 (top)**

OPPOSITE: Golden Carrot-Spice Muffin

Matcha Berry Muffins

MAKES 10 MUFFINS

⅓ cup (1½ ounces | 45 g) raw pumpkin seeds, coarsely chopped

2 tablespoons plus ½ teaspoon (½ ounce | 13 g) ceremonial-grade matcha tea powder (see Resources, page 392)

1 recipe muffin base of your choice

1½ cups (6 ounces | 170 g) fresh or frozen berries

Combine the pumpkin seeds and ½ teaspoon matcha in a small bowl and set aside.

Make the batter following the instructions for the base recipe, sifting the 2 tablespoons matcha into the bowl along with the flours and baking powder. Continue as directed, stirring the berries into the finished batter. Scoop the batter into the muffin cups and sprinkle the pumpkin seed mixture over the top of the muffins. Bake as directed.

NUT-FREE MUFFINS

To make the Gluten-Free Vegan Muffins or the Gluten-Free Muffins without nuts, replace the almond flour with finely ground coconut: Grind ½ cup (1½ ounces | 45 g) unsweetened shredded dried coconut in a food processor until fine. The coconut will start to clump in the corner but will still have a flour-like texture—if blended too long, it will release oil and be too wet to use.

To make the Grain-Free Muffins without nuts, increase the unsweetened shredded dried coconut to 2 cups (6 ounces | 170 g) and omit the almond flour.

SUGAR-FREE OR REDUCED-SUGAR MUFFINS

The sugar content of these muffins is much lower than that of most healthy muffins. But you can make the muffin base recipes sugar-free (or with reduced sugar) by omitting the maple syrup and increasing the orange juice to ½ cup (120 ml). For no added sugar whatsoever, use ½ cup (120 ml) of almond milk in place of the maple syrup and orange juice. But note that without the sweetness, you will taste the grains or nuts and seeds and baking powder more, so it's a good idea to add some other flavorings like grated citrus zest and spices such as cinnamon, cardamom, or ginger. Or add berries to the finished batter for natural sweetness.

OPPOSITE, FROM TOP TO BOTTOM: Any-Berry Muffins; Matcha Berry Muffins; Golden Carrot-Spice Muffins

Easy Cakes

—

If you want to throw together a quick, fuss-free cake using pantry staples you probably already have on hand (no special gluten-free flours or other unusual ingredients required), you'll find it in this chapter. There are two base recipes, one made with almonds and one with hazelnuts. You can also add other ground nuts or seeds. Black sesame seeds will give the cake an unusual look and a rich, nutty flavor—see the Black Sesame Plum Cake. The Peach Almond Cake is a beautiful crowd-pleasing summer cake, as is the Fig Almond Cake with Fennel; it's easy to replace the peaches or figs for any ripe summer fruit. There are infinite ways you can go just by switching the cake base, changing the fruit, and/or adding spices or citrus zest to the batter.

Notes

TEXTURE

The moist, light, and "moreish" texture of these cakes comes from a combination of almond or hazelnut flour, a little oat or buckwheat flour, and a couple of eggs. These ingredients, along with oil and maple syrup, give the cake its structure and lift. If you top the batter with super-juicy fruit, the cake may need more time to bake because of the extra moisture. Simply test it with a toothpick every 10 minutes after the given baking time until it's done.

FLAVOR

Varying the fruit toppings in these recipes will give you endless options for different cakes that can reflect any season. When it comes to changing the flavor of the cake itself, there are many directions you can take. One of the easiest ways is to sift in ½ cup (1 ounce | 32 g) cacao powder when mixing the batter. Or open your spice drawer and add a teaspoon or two (depending on its strength) of your favorite spice. You can also add ¼ to ½ teaspoon of an extract such as almond or orange. Or stir in a tablespoon of grated orange zest or lemon zest or a teaspoon of rose or orange blossom water. Once you're confident about making these batters, you can try replacing some of the almond or hazelnut flour with ground pistachios, walnuts, or pecans. See the Black Sesame Plum Cake recipe for guidance.

ADD-INS

Berries can be added to the batter for either base recipe, and the result looks lovely, especially if the cake is topped with more fresh berries before serving. See the Berry Hazelnut Cake.

GARNISHES

One of the reasons these cakes are so easy is that they can be served just as they are—no need for a frosting, filling, or additional topping. The glistening, caramelized fruit baked on top makes the ideal rustic garnish. Serving slices with a dollop of thick yogurt is a lovely way to give them a festive look.

STORING AND FREEZING

These cakes keep very well and taste just as good even a day or two after they're baked. If it's cool, you can store them out of the fridge in an airtight container for a day or so. Most of them can be kept for at least 4 days in the fridge, though cakes topped with very juicy fruit won't keep for as long. Bring refrigerated cakes to room temperature before serving.

MAKING THESE CAKES VEGAN

Making a successful gluten-free cake is much more difficult when you are avoiding eggs. Follow these steps for a good result:

○ Replace the eggs with ½ cup (120 ml) filtered water combined with 3 tablespoons (½ ounce | 15 g) ground flax seeds.

○ Increase the baking powder to 1 tablespoon.

○ Add ¼ cup (1 ounce | 30 g) brown rice flour along with the oat flour.

○ When making the berry cake vegan, reduce the berries by half and bake for an extra 20 to 30 minutes, until a toothpick inserted into the center comes out clean.

Almond Cake

MAKES ONE 13 x 4-INCH (33 x 10 CM) RECTANGULAR OR
9-INCH (23 CM) ROUND CAKE | SERVES 8

2½ cups (7½ ounces | 215 g) almond flour

¼ cup (¾ ounce | 22 g) gluten-free oat flour

1 teaspoon aluminum-free baking powder

2 large eggs, at room temperature

½ cup (120 ml) pure maple syrup

¼ cup (60 ml) melted extra-virgin coconut oil

1 tablespoon vanilla extract

¼ teaspoon almond extract (optional)

½ teaspoon fine sea salt

Fresh or roasted fruit or berries of your choice; see the variations

Preheat the oven to 350°F (180°C). Line your pan of choice with parchment paper, creasing the paper against the sides of the pan as necessary.

Put the almond flour in a medium bowl and use your fingertips to work out any lumps. Sift in the oat flour and baking powder and whisk to combine; set aside. Beat the eggs in another medium bowl. Add the maple syrup, coconut oil, vanilla, almond extract, if using, and salt and whisk to combine. Pour into the almond flour mixture and stir with a rubber spatula until just combined.

Pour the batter into the prepared pan and spread it out evenly with a rubber spatula. Add the fruit or berries of your choice. Bake for 35 to 40 minutes, until the cake is golden on top and a toothpick inserted into the center comes out clean (some of the variations may take a bit more time to bake). Remove from the oven and set on a rack to cool for at least 10 minutes before removing from the pan. Serve slightly warm or at room temperature. Cover any leftover cake and store for 1 day at cool room temperature or up to 4 days in the fridge; allow to come to room temperature before serving.

OPPOSITE: Roasted Apple–Almond Cake with Cardamom

Roasted Apple–Almond Cake with Cardamom

MAKES ONE 13 x 4-INCH (33 x 10 CM) RECTANGULAR OR 9-INCH (23 CM) ROUND CAKE | SERVES 8

4 medium (1½ pounds | 680 g) apples, peeled, cored, and cut into 8 wedges each (see Note)

1 tablespoon melted extra-virgin coconut oil

1 tablespoon pure maple syrup

1 recipe Almond Cake, using the almond extract

2 teaspoons ground cardamom

¼ cup (1¼ ounces | 35 g) whole raw almonds, roughly chopped

Roast the apples: Preheat the oven to 400°F (200°C). Line a rimmed baking sheet with parchment paper and put the apples on it. Drizzle with the coconut oil and maple syrup and toss well to evenly coat. Spread out evenly and roast for 20 minutes. Remove the pan from the oven and gently turn the fruit over. Return to the oven and roast for another 10 minutes, or until the apples are golden brown and tender. Remove from the oven, slide the apples off the parchment onto a plate (they will stick if left to cool on the parchment), and set aside while you prepare the cake. Reduce the oven temperature to 350°F (180°C).

Make the batter following the instructions for the base recipe, sifting the cardamom into the bowl along with the oat flour and baking powder. Continue as directed. After you spread the batter in the pan, arrange the apples over the top and sprinkle with chopped almonds. Bake as directed. **Pictured on page 324**

NOTE: If you are using a rectangular pan, you may not need all the roasted apples, but they're delicious to snack on.

Peach Almond Cake

MAKES ONE 13 x 4-INCH (33 x 10 CM) RECTANGULAR OR ONE 9-INCH (23 CM) ROUND CAKE | SERVES 8

1 recipe Almond Cake, using the almond extract

4 teaspoons (⅕ ounce | 6 g) grated lemon zest

2 medium (12 ounces | 340 g) ripe peaches, halved, pitted, and cut into ¾-inch (2 cm) wedges

Make the batter following the instructions for the base recipe, whisking in the lemon zest along with the vanilla. Continue as directed. After you spread the batter in the pan, arrange the peach wedges, skin side down, over the top. Bake for 50 to 60 minutes, until the cake is golden on top and a toothpick inserted into the center comes out clean (the exact time may vary depending on the juiciness of your peaches).

OPPOSITE: Peach Almond Cake

ABOVE: Black Sesame Plum Cake; OPPOSITE: Fig Almond Cake with Fennel

Black Sesame Plum Cake

MAKES ONE 13 x 4-INCH (33 x 10 CM) RECTANGULAR OR
ONE 9-INCH (23 CM) ROUND CAKE | SERVES 8

1 cup (4½ ounces | 130 g) raw black sesame seeds

1 recipe Almond Cake, using 1½ cups
(4½ ounces | 130 g) almond flour

2 teaspoons grated orange zest

12 ounces (340 g) plums, about 6 small-medium
plums, halved, pitted, and cut into 1¼-inch (3 cm)
wedges

Put the sesame seeds in a food processor and grind
until fine, being careful that the seeds don't start
turning into tahini; set aside. Make the batter
following the instructions for the base recipe, adding
the ground sesame seeds to the bowl along with the
almond flour and adding the orange zest to the wet
ingredients. Continue as directed. After you spread
the batter in the pan, arrange the plums, cut side up,
over the top. Bake as directed. **Pictured on page 328**

Fig Almond Cake with Fennel

MAKES ONE 13 x 4-INCH (33 x 10 CM) RECTANGULAR OR
ONE 9-INCH (23 CM) ROUND CAKE | SERVES 8

1 tablespoon fennel seeds, plus more for sprinkling

1 recipe Almond Cake

10 (10 ounces | 285 g) ripe figs, stemmed and
cut in half lengthwise

Grind the fennel seeds in a spice grinder until fine.
Make the batter following the instructions for the
base recipe, adding the ground fennel to the bowl
along with the almond flour. Continue as directed.
After you spread the batter in the pan, arrange the
figs, cut side up, over the top and sprinkle with
fennel seeds. Bake as directed. **Pictured on the
preceding page**

Hazelnut Cake

**MAKES ONE 13 x 4-INCH (33 x 10 CM) RECTANGULAR OR
ONE 9-INCH (23 CM) ROUND CAKE | SERVES 8**

2½ cups (7¼ ounces | 110 g) hazelnut flour

¼ cup (1 ounce | 30 g) buckwheat flour

1 teaspoon aluminum-free baking powder

2 large eggs, at room temperature

½ cup (120 ml) pure maple syrup

¼ cup (60 ml) melted extra-virgin coconut oil

1 tablespoon vanilla extract

½ teaspoon fine sea salt

Fresh fruit or berries of your choice; see the variations

Preheat the oven to 350°F (180°C). Line your pan of choice with parchment paper, creasing the paper against the sides of the pan as necessary.

Put the hazelnut flour in a medium bowl and use your fingertips to work out any lumps. Sift in the buckwheat flour and baking powder and whisk to combine; set aside. Beat the eggs in another medium bowl. Add the maple syrup, coconut oil, vanilla, and salt and whisk to combine. Pour into the buckwheat flour mixture and stir with a rubber spatula until just combined.

Pour the batter into the prepared pan and spread it out evenly with a rubber spatula. Add the fruit or berries of your choice. Bake for 35 to 40 minutes, until a toothpick inserted into the center of the cake comes out clean. Remove from the oven and set on a rack to cool for at least 10 minutes before removing from the pan. Serve slightly warm or at room temperature. The cake will keep, covered, for a day at cool room temperature or up to 4 days in the fridge; allow to come to room temperature before serving.

Cacao-Pear Hazelnut Cake

MAKES ONE 13 x 4-INCH (33 x 10 CM) RECTANGULAR
OR ONE 9-INCH (23 CM) ROUND CAKE | SERVES 8

1 recipe Hazelnut Cake

½ cup (1 ounce | 32 g) cacao powder (see the
sidebar on page 297)

2 medium (12 ounces | 340 g) pears, peeled,
quartered, cored, and cut into ¾-inch (2 cm)
wedges

¼ cup (1 ounce | 30 g) hazelnuts, toasted
(see page 390), skins removed, and roughly
chopped

Make the batter following the instructions for the
base recipe, sifting the cacao powder into the bowl
along with the buckwheat flour. Continue as directed.
After you spread the batter in the pan, arrange
the pears over the top and sprinkle with chopped
hazelnuts. Bake as directed. **Pictured on page 320 (top)**

Berry Hazelnut Cake

MAKES ONE 13 x 4-INCH (33 x 10 CM) CAKE | SERVES 8

1 cup (4 ounces | 115 g) fresh or frozen blueberries

1 cup (4 ounces | 115 g) fresh or frozen blackberries

1 cup (4 ounces | 115 g) fresh or frozen raspberries

1 recipe Hazelnut Cake, using ½ cup (2 ounces | 60 g)
buckwheat flour

Grated zest of 1 orange

If using fresh berries, gently rinse them and drain
well, then combine in a bowl; set aside. If using
frozen berries, leave them in the freezer while you
prepare the batter. Make the batter following the
instructions for the base recipe, adding the orange
zest to the wet mixture. Continue as directed,
then gently stir half the berries into the finished
batter. Pour the batter into the pan and spread it
evenly with a rubber spatula. Cover the top of the
cake with the remaining berries. Bake for 40 to
45 minutes, or a few minutes longer if you're using
frozen berries. Because of the large amount of
berries, the cake needs to be stored in the fridge.

NOTE: The berries create extra moisture in
this batter, which is why it's best to bake it in
a rectangular pan.

OPPOSITE: Berry Hazelnut Cake

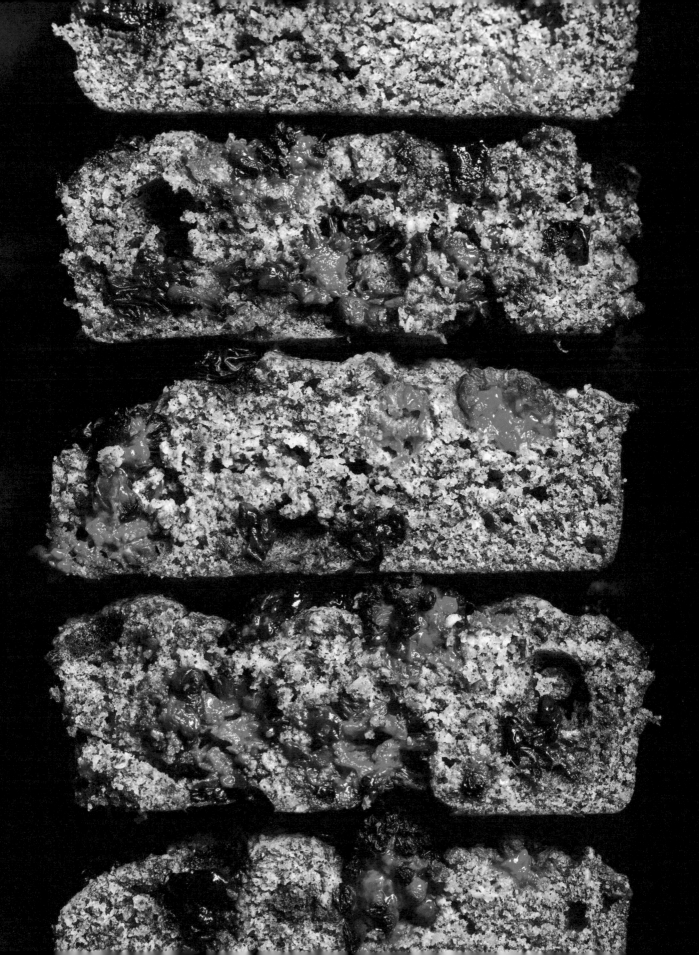

Seeded Bars

These bars can be a lifesaver. Whether you're on a long trip, running around all day with no time to stop, or at your desk with a midafternoon craving, any of the bars in this chapter make the ideal energizing snack.

Not only are the bars a cinch to pull together, they also keep very well—for a month or longer. They're made with whole and ground toasted seeds and coconut combined with brown rice syrup or yacon syrup, vanilla, and salt. The mixture is simply pressed into the pan to set in the fridge or freezer—no baking required.

The base recipe resulted from my ongoing desire for a really good bar: satisfying, barely sweet, high in protein, and not based on grains, as most energy bars are. The base recipe, which uses equal parts pumpkin, sunflower, and sesame seeds, is easily adaptable, and there are six different variations here. The Hazelnut Dukkah Bars, which have a salty, spicy kick, teeter between savory and sweet, as do the Super-Green Bars, which include nori, matcha, dried nettle leaves, and hemp seeds. The Sesame Date Bars and the Salted Almond Cacao Bars with Raspberries are on the sweeter side and are crowd-pleasers. Once you've made the base recipe or a variation or two, you'll be ready to customize the recipe and make it your own.

You can make the bars completely grain-free if you use yacon syrup, a mild sweetener made from a Peruvian root vegetable of the same name. The syrup has a slightly fruity, almost tropical flavor. However, I call for brown rice syrup as the first option in the base recipe because it is more readily available, a lot less expensive, and a good way of cutting back on sugar.

Notes

TEXTURE

The hearty texture of these bars comes from grinding the toasted seeds, nuts, and coconut flakes until a butter forms, then combining it with brown rice syrup (or yacon syrup) and folding in whole seeds or chopped nuts. They are both crisp and chewy at once and excellent with a cup of tea any time of year.

FLAVOR

Freshly toasted seeds, nuts, and coconut are always delicious, but these bars, with a touch of salt, vanilla, and the subtle sweetness of brown rice syrup or yacon syrup, elevate that combination to a whole new level. The flavor, of course, depends on the seeds and/or nuts you use, but you can't go wrong. The amount of sweetener in the base recipe and most of the variations is minimal, and when made with ingredients like nori or dukkah, the bars have a slightly savory and very satisfying flavor. The Salted Almond Cacao Bars with Raspberries include a little maple syrup, and if you'd like things sweeter, you can add a tablespoon or so of maple syrup to any of the variations.

In addition to or instead of the different flavorings used in the variations, you can add other dried herbs, spices, or extracts you like. If you want to flavor the bars with powders like matcha, freeze-dried berries, or cacao, wait until the seed mixture is smooth and liquid before adding them, or the powder will absorb some of the oil in the mix, resulting in crumbly bars.

ADD-INS

If you want to add grated ginger or citrus zest, wait until the seed mixture is smooth and liquid, or, again, the bars may be crumbly. For a different look, switch out some of the regular pumpkin seeds with Austrian pumpkin seeds (see Resources, page 393), which have a deep green color.

GARNISHES

These bars look vibrant and dramatic as they are, but for even more flavor and a dash of color, garnish them with freeze-dried berries as with the Salted Almond Cacao Bars with Raspberries. Any of the variations can be dusted with a berry or superfood powder.

STORING AND FREEZING

These bars should be stored in airtight containers at cool room temperature or in the fridge, where they will keep for at least a month. Some of the variations may become oily in warmer weather; if that starts to happen, keep them in the fridge instead. The bars can also be frozen for up to 3 months.

CHOOSING YOUR PAN

You can use almost any pan you have on hand for these bars. Using different-shaped pans keeps things interesting—somehow these feel like completely different recipes when the bars are cut into different shapes. Here are the pans I like to use and the yields they will give you:

o 8-inch (20 cm) round cake pan: twenty 1-inch (2.5 cm) wedges

o 8-inch (20 cm) square cake pan: sixteen 1¾-inch (4.5 cm) squares

o 5 x 9½-inch (13 x 24 cm) loaf pan: eighteen ½-inch (1.25 cm) slices

o 13 x 4-inch (33 x 10 cm) rectangular tart pan: eighteen 1½-inch (3.75 cm) wedges

Seeded Bars

MAKES 16 TO 20 BARS, DEPENDING ON THE PAN YOU USE (SEE THE PRECEDING PAGE)

1 cup (4½ ounces | 130 g) raw
sunflower seeds

1 cup (5 ounces | 140 g) raw
pumpkin seeds

1 cup (5 ounces | 140 g) raw
unhulled sesame seeds

2 cups (3½ ounces | 100 g)
unsweetened flaked dried coconut

½ teaspoon fine sea salt, plus more
to taste

⅓ cup (80 ml) brown rice syrup or
yacon syrup

1 teaspoon vanilla extract

Preheat the oven to 300°F (150°C). Choose your pan (see the preceding page) and line the bottom and sides with parchment paper.

Put the sunflower, pumpkin, and sesame seeds in a large strainer and rinse well under cold running water, then drain and set over a bowl to drain thoroughly while the oven heats.

Line a rimmed baking sheet with parchment paper and spread out the seeds. Toast for 15 minutes. Remove the pan from the oven and sprinkle the coconut over top. Return to the oven for another 8 minutes, or until the coconut is browning and the seeds are toasted. Transfer the mixture to a bowl, add the salt, and mix well. Transfer 2 cups (3½ ounces | 100 g) of the mixture to a food processor and process, scraping the sides as necessary, until the mixture is smooth and liquid; set aside.

If using rice syrup, bring it to a simmer in a small saucepan over medium heat. Stir in the vanilla and remove from the heat. If using yacon syrup, just combine it with the vanilla in a medium bowl. Add the ground seed mixture to the syrup mixture and stir until smooth. Pour into the bowl with the remaining toasted seeds and coconut and stir until thoroughly combined; you may need to use your hands to do this. Using clean, damp hands, press the mixture firmly and evenly into the parchment-lined pan.

Put the bars in the fridge for 1 hour or in the freezer for 30 minutes, or until thoroughly chilled and set. Cut into wedges, slices, or squares, depending on the pan, and store in an airtight container at cool room temperature for up to 4 weeks; in warmer weather, store in the fridge. The bars can be frozen for up to 3 months.

VARIATION RECIPES

Hazelnut Dukkah Bars

MAKES 16 TO 20 BARS, DEPENDING ON THE PAN YOU USE

1 recipe Seeded Bars, using ½ cup (2½ ounces | 70 g) raw unhulled sesame seeds, omitting the sunflower seeds, and increasing the brown rice syrup or yacon syrup to ½ cup (120 ml)

1 cup (4½ ounces | 130 g) raw hazelnuts, toasted (see page 390) and skinned, coarsely chopped

½ cup (1¾ ounces | 50 g) Hazelnut Dukkah (page 153)

Make the bars following the instructions for the base recipe, adding the hazelnuts and dukkah to the bowl of toasted seeds and coconut and stirring to combine. Continue as directed. **Pictured on page 341**

ABOVE: Ingredients for Salted Almond Cacao Bars with Raspberries; OPPOSITE: Hazelnut Dukkah Bars

Salted Almond Cacao Bars with Raspberries

MAKES 16 TO 20 BARS, DEPENDING ON THE PAN YOU USE

1 recipe Seeded Bars, using 3 cups (15 ounces | 420 g) whole raw almonds in place of the seeds (no need to rinse the almonds)

1 teaspoon flaky sea salt

¼ cup (½ ounce | 16 g) cacao powder (see the sidebar on page 297)

2 tablespoons (30 ml) pure maple syrup

½ cup (½ ounce | 15 g) freeze-dried raspberries, crushed

Make the bars following the instructions for the base recipe. After toasting the almonds and coconut, toss to combine, then remove 2 cups (7 ounces | 200 g) of the mixture and set aside. Pulse the remaining almonds and coconut in a food processor until they are chopped and no whole almonds remain, about 15 times. Transfer to a bowl and stir in the flaky salt; set aside.

Process the reserved almonds and coconut as directed until smooth and liquid. Add the cacao and blend until smooth. Warm the maple syrup with the rice syrup; remove from the heat and add the vanilla. (Or, if using yacon syrup, just combine the maple syrup, yacon syrup, and vanilla in a small bowl.) Continue with the recipe as directed. Once the mixture is in the pan, press the freeze-dried raspberries onto the top. Chill as directed. **Pictured on page 334 (bottom left)**

Super-Green Bars

MAKES 16 TO 20 BARS, DEPENDING ON THE PAN YOU USE

1 recipe Seeded Bars, omitting the sesame seeds and using 1½ cups (7½ ounces | 215 g) raw pumpkin seeds and 1½ cups (7½ ounces | 215 g) raw Austrian pumpkin seeds (see Note)

3 tablespoons (¾ ounce | 22 g) hemp seeds

2 tablespoons (1 g) dried nettle leaves (see Resources, page 392)

2 teaspoons ceremonial-grade matcha tea powder (see Resources, page 393)

1 sheet nori, toasted and crushed (see page 202)

1 teaspoon flaky sea salt

Make the bars following the instructions for the base recipe. After removing 2 cups (3½ ounces | 100 g) of seeds and coconut to blend, add the hemp seeds, nettle, matcha, nori, and flaky salt to the bowl with the toasted pumpkin seeds and coconut mixture and stir well to combine. Continue with the recipe as directed.

NOTE: If you don't have Austrian pumpkin seeds (see Resources, page 393), you can make this with all regular pumpkin seeds or use sunflower seeds instead of the Austrian seeds.

OPPOSITE: Super-Green Bars

Black Sesame Bars

MAKES 16 TO 20 BARS, DEPENDING ON THE PAN YOU USE

1 recipe Seeded Bars, using 3 cups (15 ounces | 425 g) raw black sesame seeds in place of the other seeds

Grated zest of 1 orange

Make the bars following the instructions for the base recipe, adding the orange zest to the blended seed and coconut mixture and pulsing to combine. Continue as directed.

Sesame Date Bars

MAKES 16 TO 20 BARS, DEPENDING ON THE PAN YOU USE

1 recipe Seeded Bars, using 2 cups (10 ounces | 280 g) raw unhulled sesame seeds and omitting the pumpkin seeds

1½ teaspoons finely grated peeled fresh ginger

1 teaspoon flaky sea salt

6 Medjool dates, pitted and sliced

Make the bars following the instructions for the base recipe, adding the ginger once the blended seeds and coconut are smooth and liquid, then pulsing to combine. Stir the flaky salt into the remaining toasted seeds and coconut and toss to combine. Continue with the recipe as directed, adding the dates to the bowl of seeds and coconut along with the other ingredients and mixing well. Continue as directed. These bars are best stored in the fridge, as they become oily at room temperature. **Pictured on page 334 (top right)**

OPPOSITE: Black Sesame Bars

Matcha Pumpkin Seed Bars

MAKES 16 TO 20 BARS, DEPENDING ON THE PAN YOU USE

1 recipe Seeded Bars, using 3 cups (15 ounces | 425 g) pumpkin seeds in place of the other seeds

1 tablespoon ceremonial-grade matcha tea powder (see Resources, page 392)

1 teaspoon flaky sea salt

Make the bars following the instructions for the base recipe. After processing the seeds and coconut until smooth and liquid, add 1 teaspoon of the matcha and process to combine. Add the remaining 2 teaspoons matcha and the flaky salt to the bowl with the toasted pumpkin seeds and coconut and toss well to coat evenly. Continue as directed. **Pictured on page 334 (top left)**

Granola

———

Granola's reputation as an efficient make-ahead meal is spot on: Invest the time to make a batch, and you will enjoy the gift of zero-fuss breakfasts for weeks to come. It also doubles as a snack, travels well, makes a lovely gift, and is adored by just about everyone. The downside is that even "healthy" granolas tend to be high in sugar (such as maple syrup, brown sugar, or honey), and they're usually made with refined oils (grapeseed, canola, or regular olive oil). The base recipe in this chapter uses brown rice syrup or yacon syrup, which are two of the healthiest natural sweeteners. Brown rice syrup is 50 percent maltose, a slow-digesting carbohydrate that enters the bloodstream gradually, and yacon syrup is a low-glycemic sweetener (yacon is harder to source and more expensive than brown rice syrup, but it's necessary for the grain-free variation). Both of these mild sweeteners add a lovely malty flavor to the granola. Of course, adding dried fruit to your granola after baking will also make it sweeter.

There's also a sugar-free variation made with berries and mesquite powder, which you might actually prefer for your daily breakfast. You'll also find interesting variations enhanced with turmeric and squash, cacao, matcha, and other superfoods. And the Flower and Berry Granola may be the prettiest breakfast you'll ever see. Make it to give as hostess, holiday, or birthday gifts or to serve as a treat when friends or family come to stay; it's lovely with the Rose Almond Milk (page 72). The Superfood Granola incorporates ground flax, maca, and hemp seeds, the same health-boosting ingredients you might sprinkle over a Genius Whole-Grain Porridge (pages 34–47) or Chia Bircher Bowl (pages 20–25).

With the base recipe and the eight variations in this chapter for inspiration, you'll be set to create your own favorite blend. And making a batch of granola is the perfect solution for those overlooked bags or too-tiny-for-anything-else leftover packages of rolled grains, nuts, seeds, and coconut in your pantry.

Serve any of these granolas with berries and coconut or dairy yogurt or homemade nut milk (see page 71); see Flavor, opposite, for some ways to mix and match flavors and colors.

Notes

TEXTURE

Snacking on clumps of granola is probably what most people love about having a jar of it on hand. In the base recipe, the mixture is stirred during baking, which results in some clumping. The way to achieve larger clumps and more of them is to not stir the mixture at all, just be sure to rotate the trays and switch the top one with the bottom one halfway through baking. To make sure the granola is ready, you can check that the bottom is golden by flipping over a clump. Allow it to cool completely, without stirring. Be sure the granola is completely cool before gently transferring it to jars or bags. The granola will crumble a bit when handled, as the clumps are not as sturdy as those in granolas made with larger amounts of sweeteners to bind them, but it maintains a pleasing texture. (If your granola does not seem crisp after the stated baking time, keep in mind that it will crisp up further as it cools; be careful not to overbake it, which can happen in a matter of minutes.)

FLAVOR

Because they are low in sugar, these recipes are less sweet than your average granola, allowing you to taste the complex flavors of the nuts, seeds, whole grains, and any additions you incorporate. The different spices, cacao, matcha, and other superfoods in the variations boost the flavor without increasing the sweetener. If you do want a sweeter granola, you can add up to ½ cup (120 ml) pure maple syrup along with the brown rice syrup or yacon syrup. Serve the granola with any of the flavored nut milks (see pages 72–77). Try the Matcha–Black Sesame Granola with Matcha Almond Milk (page 72), the Date-Sweetened Cacao Granola with Rose Almond Milk (page 72), or the Turmeric–Pumpkin Spice Granola with Golden Milk (page 88).

ADD-INS

There may not be another chapter in this book better suited to "add-ins." Before baking the granola, you can stir in any of your favorite nuts and seeds (except ground flax or hemp seeds, which shouldn't be cooked, so add them after baking). After baking, you can add dried berries or fruits and/or superfood powders such as pomegranate, goji, acai, lucuma, and maca. If using dried fruit, stir it in while the granola is still warm, as this helps soften it up a bit. Adding the powders will take the sheen off your granola, but a matte look is cool too. Although it's nice to serve the granola with fresh berries, when they are not in season, you can stir freeze-dried strawberries, raspberries, or blueberries (see Resources, page 392) into the finished granola.

GARNISHES

Any of these recipes would be good with a garnish of fresh berries or sliced peaches or nectarines in summer. For something more delicate, edible fresh flowers will elevate your breakfast experience. But even a pinch of dried flowers or freeze-dried berries looks beautiful.

STORING

This granola keeps well and tastes fresh for 6 weeks and sometimes longer. Be sure to cool it completely before storing it in airtight glass jars or other containers. Most of the granolas keep well at cool room temperature, but if you add ground flax seeds, store that batch in the fridge to preserve the delicate omega-3–rich oils. Since the granola keeps so well at room temperature, there is no need to freeze it.

GRANOLA FLAVORS

From turmeric and flowers to matcha and mesquite, you may be surprised by how many different ways you can flavor granola. Try some of these recipes (pictured from left to right) or create your own.

- Flower and Berry Granola (page 355)

- Turmeric–Pumpkin Spice Granola (page 355)

- Matcha–Black Sesame Granola (page 353)

- Superfood Granola (page 355)

- Grain-Free Granola (page 358)

- Puffed Millet Granola with Ginger and Cardamom (page 358)

- Date-Sweetened Cacao Granola (page 358)

- Sugar-Free Granola with Berries and Mesquite (page 353)

Granola

MAKES ABOUT 15 CUPS | 3 POUNDS, 6 OUNCES | 1.5 KG

4 cups (14 ounces | 400 g) rolled oats

2 cups (11 ounces | 320 g) raw buckwheat groats

4 cups (7 ounces | 200 g) unsweetened flaked dried coconut

1 cup (5 ounces | 140 g) whole raw almonds

1 cup raw nuts, such as walnuts, hazelnuts, pecans, or pistachios (weight depends on the nuts used; see the variations for measures), roughly chopped

1 cup (5 ounces | 140 g) raw pumpkin seeds

½ cup (2¼ ounces | 65 g) raw sunflower seeds

½ cup (2½ ounces | 70 g) raw unhulled sesame seeds

¼ cup (1¼ ounces | 40 g) chia seeds

1 teaspoon fine sea salt

1 teaspoon ground cinnamon

¾ cup (160 ml) brown rice syrup or yacon syrup

½ cup (120 ml) melted extra-virgin coconut oil

1 tablespoon vanilla extract

Preheat the oven to 300°F (150°C). Line two rimmed baking sheets with parchment paper and set aside.

Combine the oats, buckwheat, coconut, almonds, raw nuts, pumpkin seeds, sunflower seeds, sesame seeds, chia seeds, salt, and cinnamon in a large bowl; stir well and set aside. If using brown rice syrup, combine it with the coconut oil in a small saucepan and gently warm over low heat, stirring until smooth. Then add the vanilla and stir again. Or, if using yacon syrup, just stir the syrup and oil together in a small bowl, then stir in the vanilla. Pour the syrup mixture over the oat-nut mixture and mix well to combine.

Divide the mixture between the baking sheets and spread out evenly. Bake for 15 minutes, then stir, rotate the trays, and return to the oven for another 15 minutes, or until the granola is golden and fragrant. (You may need to bake the granola for another couple of minutes, but be careful, as it can easily burn; and keep in mind that it will crisp up further as it cools.) Remove from the oven and let cool completely. Store the granola in airtight jars for up to 6 weeks.

Sugar-Free Granola with Berries and Mesquite

MAKES 14 CUPS | 3 POUNDS, 4½ OUNCES | 1.5 KG

1 recipe Granola, using 1 cup (4½ ounces | 130 g) raw hazelnuts, omitting the brown rice syrup or yacon syrup, and using 2 tablespoons (30 ml) vanilla extract

½ cup (1½ ounces | 45 g) mesquite powder (see the sidebar on page 23)

½ cup (1¾ ounces | 50 g) dried goji berries

½ cup (1¾ ounces | 50 g) dried golden mulberries

2 cups (2 ounces | 60 g) mixed freeze-dried berries, such as raspberries, blueberries, and strawberries

Make the granola following the instructions for the base recipe, adding the mesquite powder to the oat-nut mixture along with the cinnamon. Combine the oil and vanilla, pour over the dry oat-nut mixture, and stir well to combine, then continue as directed. After you remove the granola from the oven, sprinkle the goji berries and mulberries over it. Let cool, then transfer to a large bowl and toss with the freeze-dried berries. Store as directed. **Pictured on page 351**

Matcha–Black Sesame Granola

MAKES ABOUT 15 CUPS | 3 POUNDS, 6 OUNCES | 1.5 KG

1 recipe Granola, using brown rice syrup, 1 cup (4½ ounces | 130 g) raw black sesame seeds in place of the unhulled sesame seeds and sunflower seeds, and 1 cup (4½ ounces | 130 g) raw pistachios and omitting the cinnamon

¼ cup (⅔ ounce | 20 g) culinary-grade matcha tea powder (see Resources, page 392)

Make the granola following the instructions for the base recipe, adding the matcha to the dry oat-nut mixture and tossing well to combine. Continue as directed. **Pictured on page 359**

Flower and Berry Granola

MAKES ABOUT 16 CUPS | 3 POUNDS, 6 OUNCES | 1.5 KG

1 recipe Granola

½ cup (1¾ ounces | 50 g) dried goji berries

2 tablespoons (1 g) dried organic rose petals (see the sidebar on page 301)

2 tablespoons (1 g) dried organic cornflower petals

2 tablespoons (1 g) dried organic calendula petals (see Resources, page 392)

1½ cups (1½ ounces | 45 g) freeze-dried raspberries

½ cup (½ ounce | 14 g) freeze-dried blueberries

Make the granola following the instructions for the base recipe. After you remove the granola from the oven, sprinkle the goji berries over it. Once the granola has cooled, transfer it to a bowl and add the rose, cornflower, and calendula petals. Crush half the freeze-dried raspberries, add to the bowl along with the remaining whole raspberries and the blueberries, and gently toss to combine. Store as directed.

Superfood Granola

MAKES ABOUT 16½ CUPS | 4 POUNDS, 2 OUNCES | 1.9 KG

1 recipe Granola, using yacon syrup

½ cup (1¾ ounces | 50 g) dried goji berries

½ cup (1¾ ounces | 50 g) dried mulberries

½ cup (2¼ ounces | 65 g) golden berries, coarsely chopped

½ cup (2¼ ounces | 65 g) hemp seeds

½ cup (2 ounces | 60 g) ground flax seeds

OPPOSITE: Flower and Berry Granola

6 tablespoons (1½ ounces | 45 g) pomegranate powder (see Resources, page 393)

¼ cup (1 ounce | 30 g) gelatinized maca powder (see Resources, page 393)

Make the granola following the instructions for the base recipe. After you remove the granola from the oven, sprinkle the goji berries, mulberries, and golden berries over it. Transfer the cooled granola to a bowl, add the hemp seeds, ground flax seeds, pomegranate powder, and maca, and combine. Because of the ground flax seeds, it's best to store this granola in the fridge. **Pictured on page 351**

Turmeric–Pumpkin Spice Granola

MAKES ABOUT 15 CUPS | 3 POUNDS, 6 OUNCES | 1.5 KG

1 recipe Granola, using 2 teaspoons cinnamon

4 teaspoons (¼ ounce | 8 g) ground turmeric

2 teaspoons ground ginger

2 teaspoons ground cardamom

2 teaspoons freshly grated nutmeg (see the sidebar on page 43)

½ teaspoon ground allspice

2 cups (15 ounces | 425 g) mashed squash (see page 73)

Make the granola following the instructions for the base recipe, adding the turmeric, ginger, cardamom, nutmeg, and allspice to the bowl along with the cinnamon. Whisk the mashed squash into the oil, rice syrup (or yacon syrup), and vanilla mixture until smooth, then add to the dry oat-nut mixture and stir well. Continue as directed. (You will need to bake this granola longer because of the moisture from the squash.) Bake for 20 minutes, then stir, rotate the sheets, and return to the oven for another 20 minutes, or until the granola is golden and fragrant. Store as directed. **Pictured on page 350**

ABOVE AND OPPOSITE: Matcha–Black Sesame Granola

Puffed Millet Granola with Ginger and Cardamom

MAKES ABOUT 16½ CUPS | 2 POUNDS, 6 OUNCES | 1.1 KG
---

1 recipe Granola, using 6 cups (3½ ounces | 100 g) puffed millet in place of the oats and buckwheat and omitting the cinnamon

2 teaspoons ground ginger

2 teaspoons ground cardamom

Make the granola following the instructions for the base recipe, adding the ginger and cardamom to the puffed millet and nut mixture. (You will need to reduce the baking time for this recipe because puffed millet cooks faster than oats and buckwheat.) Bake for 10 minutes, then stir, rotate the sheets, and return to the oven for another 10 to 15 minutes, until the granola is light golden and fragrant. Store as directed. **Pictured on page 351**

Grain-Free Granola

MAKES 10 CUPS | 2 POUNDS, 1 OUNCE | 950 G
---

1 recipe Granola, omitting the oats and buckwheat and using an extra 4 cups (7 ounces | 400 g) coconut, an extra 1 cup (4½ ounces | 130 g) raw sunflower seeds, ½ teaspoon salt, 6 tablespoons (90 ml) yacon syrup, and ¼ cup (60 ml) coconut oil

¼ cup (1¼ ounces | 35 g) whole flax seeds

1 teaspoon freshly grated nutmeg (optional; see the sidebar on page 43)

Grated zest of 1 orange (optional)

Make the granola following the instructions for the base recipe, adding the flax seeds and the nutmeg and orange zest, if using, to the bowl along with the nut, seed, and coconut mixture. Continue as directed. Bake for 10 minutes, then stir, rotate the baking sheets, and return to the oven for another 10 to 15 minutes, until the granola is golden and fragrant. Store as directed. **Pictured on page 351**

Date-Sweetened Cacao Granola

MAKES ABOUT 16 CUPS | 3 POUNDS, 6 OUNCES | 1.5 KG
---

2 cups (9 ounces | 255 g) pitted dates

1 recipe Granola, omitting the brown rice syrup or yacon syrup

½ cup (1 ounce | 32 g) cacao powder (see the sidebar on page 297)

Grated zest of 2 oranges

6 tablespoons (1½ ounces | 45 g) cacao nibs (optional)

Put the dates in a bowl and cover with boiling water. Soak for 10 minutes, then pour into a strainer set over a bowl and set aside to drain thoroughly.

Make the granola following the instructions for the base recipe, adding the cacao powder to the oat mixture along with the cinnamon. Put the dates, coconut oil, and vanilla in a food processor and blend until smooth. Add the orange zest and pulse to combine. Add the date mixture to the oat-nut mixture and mix well.

Bake for 20 minutes, then stir, rotate the sheets, and return to the oven for another 20 minutes, or until the granola is fragrant. Transfer the cooled granola to a bowl and stir in the cacao nibs, if using. Store as directed.

OPPOSITE, FROM TOP TO BOTTOM: Date-Sweetened Cacao Granola with Rose Almond Milk (page 72); Matcha–Black Sesame Granola with Matcha Almond Milk (page 72); Flower and Berry Granola

Waffles

—

Who says waffles are for weekends only? Make a batch of these whole-grain, gluten-free, sugar- and dairy-free waffles on Sunday morning, enjoy some of them fresh, and store the rest in the freezer, ready for quick, healthy breakfasts during the week. Warm them up in the toaster and top them with thick yogurt and a berry compote (see pages 96–97), or enjoy them with butter. Waffles are a great alternative to toast, and the recipes for both vegan and non-vegan gluten-free waffles in this chapter mean everyone can delight in them.

Most waffles are quite plain because they are intended as a vehicle for lashings of maple syrup or other indulgent, dessert-worthy toppings. But the nourishing waffles you'll find here are so tasty they don't even need an added sweetener. When you cut sugar from a recipe (and from your diet in general), adding spices, citrus zest, and/or other flavorings, as in the variations here, amps up the taste and provides enough interest to keep you satisfied.

These waffles are good served on their own with a cup of tea or a Nut Milk Latte (pages 79–87), but you can top them with fresh fruit or berries or a Simple Compote (pages 96–105), thick coconut or whole-milk yogurt, a drizzle of Coconut Butter (page 115) or pure maple syrup, or any of your own favorite toppings.

Notes

TEXTURE

Whole-grain waffles that are gluten- and dairy-free rely on eggs to both bind the batter and keep them light. Separating the eggs and then folding the beaten egg whites into the batter just before cooking is the difference between a good and a great waffle. For vegan gluten-free waffles, you need a thickener, like mashed banana, along with flax seeds to help bind the batter; a splash of apple cider vinegar keeps these tender. All of these recipes result in waffles with crisp edges, but because they are gluten-free, they will soften as they cool. Reheating them in a toaster, a waffle iron, or the oven will crisp them up again. As with all baking recipes, it's best to weigh your dry ingredients to guarantee the best texture.

FLAVOR

The gluten- and dairy-free base recipe here includes subtle notes of orange, vanilla, and coconut. There are two or three variations for each of the bases, but they can be flavored in almost any way you like. Serving the waffles with any of the Simple Compotes (pages 96–105) will change the flavor profile, of course, as will the Nut, Seed, and Coconut Butters (pages 112–116). Traditional toppings like maple syrup or honey, as well as fresh fruit or a squeeze of lemon or lime, are also delicious here. Offer a variety of toppings and let everyone customize their own waffles. Depending on what you choose as a thickener for the vegan base recipe—mashed banana, apple compote, or mashed squash—you'll get a hint of but not a strong flavor coming through.

ADD-INS

Everything from chopped nuts or seeds to citrus zest and spices to matcha and cacao can easily be added to these waffle batters. Use the variations as a guide for creating your own custom flavors. You can replace the banana in the vegan version with another homemade puree or mash, such as squash, sweet potato, or carrot. (The extra moisture in store-bought applesauce or canned pumpkin puree will throw off the balance.) As good as berries are with waffles, they are actually best served as a topping rather than added to the batter, unless you have wild blueberries or other tiny berries. Most waffle irons don't allow much room for juicy berries, and the berries can stick to the iron and burn.

GARNISHES

Garnishing these waffles is optional but fun. Berries and seasonal fruits are always good, as are the colorful Coconut Butters (pages 115–116). In winter, top them with freeze-dried berries and yogurt, and in summer, if you want to get fancy, scatter some edible flowers over them. You can dust the variations made with cacao or matcha with more of the same powder or a freeze-dried berry powder. If you've cut out sugar but want the look of a shower of powdered sugar, dust the waffles with a little coconut flour. Or if you just want a healthier alternative to the white stuff, grind maple sugar in a spice grinder and sift a little over the warm waffles.

STORING AND FREEZING

Leftover waffles (if you have any!) keep very well. Once they are cool, you can store them in an airtight container in the fridge for up to 3 days or freeze them for up to 3 months. Either way, they reheat beautifully in a toaster or a waffle iron set on low, or in the oven.

Gluten-Free, Dairy-Free Waffles

MAKES 12 WAFFLES

2 cups (6 ounces | 170 g) almond flour

1½ cups (6¾ ounces | 190 g) millet flour

1 cup (3 ounces | 85 g) gluten-free oat flour

1 teaspoon aluminum-free baking powder

4 medium eggs, separated

1 cup (240 ml) almond milk (see page 71)

1 cup (240 ml) freshly squeezed orange juice

½ cup (120 ml) melted extra-virgin coconut oil (see Note, page 311), plus more for the waffle iron

1 tablespoon vanilla extract

Preheat the waffle iron. Meanwhile, put the almond flour in a medium bowl and break up any lumps with your fingertips. Sift in the millet flour, oat flour, and baking powder and whisk to combine; set aside. Put the egg yolks in another medium bowl and whisk to break them up, then add the almond milk, orange juice, oil, and vanilla and whisk to combine. Beat the egg whites until stiff peaks form. Pour the flour mixture into the egg yolk mixture and stir with a rubber spatula until just combined, then gently fold in the egg whites.

Lightly brush the waffle iron with oil and scoop about a scant ½ cup (120 ml) batter (the exact amount will depend on your iron) onto the iron. Cook according to the manufacturer's instructions until golden. Remove the waffles and serve immediately with any of the toppings suggested on the preceding page, or place on a rack to cool if you are making them ahead. Repeat with the remaining batter. To keep the waffles warm, see the Note on page 369. To store, once the waffles are cool, transfer to airtight containers and refrigerate for up to 3 days or freeze for up to 3 months.

Matcha Cardamom Waffles

MAKES 12 WAFFLES

1 recipe Gluten-Free, Dairy-Free Waffles

1 tablespoon ceremonial-grade matcha tea powder (see Resources, page 392)

2 teaspoons ground cardamom

Make the batter following the instructions for the base recipe, sifting in the matcha and cardamom along with the flours. Continue with the recipe as directed. **Pictured on the following page**

Orange Blossom Waffles

MAKES 12 WAFFLES

1 recipe Gluten-Free, Dairy-Free Waffles

2 tablespoons (⅓ ounce | 10 g) grated orange zest (zest the oranges before you juice them for the batter)

2 tablespoons (30 ml) orange blossom water

Make the batter following the instructions for the base recipe, adding the orange zest and orange blossom water along with the vanilla. Continue with the recipe as directed.

Buckwheat Pecan Spice Waffles

MAKES 12 WAFFLES

1 recipe Gluten-Free, Dairy-Free Waffles, using 1½ cups (6 ounces | 170 g) buckwheat flour in place of the millet flour

2 teaspoons ground cinnamon

2 teaspoons freshly grated nutmeg (see the sidebar on page 43)

2 teaspoons ground ginger

2 teaspoons cardamom

2 tablespoons (⅓ ounce | 10 g) grated orange zest (zest the oranges before you juice them for the batter)

1 cup (3½ ounces | 100 g) raw pecans, finely chopped

Make the batter following the instructions for the base recipe, sifting in the cinnamon, nutmeg, ginger, and cardamom along with the flours and whisking the orange zest into the wet mixture. Fold in the pecans along with the beaten egg whites. Continue with the recipe as directed.

ABOVE: Matcha Cardamom Waffles with coconut yogurt and Cherry Vanilla Compote (page 101)
OPPOSITE, FROM LEFT TO RIGHT: Gluten-Free Vegan Waffles using squash, Matcha Cardamom Waffles, Banana-Cacao Waffles with Walnuts, Rose Sesame Waffles

Gluten-Free Vegan Waffles

MAKES 8 WAFFLES

1¼ cups (300 ml) almond milk (see page 71)

2 tablespoons plus 2 teaspoons (½ ounce | 16 g) ground flax seeds

½ cup (1½ ounces | 45 g) almond flour

1 cup (3 ounces | 85 g) gluten-free oat flour

½ cup (2¼ ounces | 65 g) millet flour

¼ cup (1 ounce | 30 g) brown rice flour

1 tablespoon aluminum-free baking powder

½ cup (120 ml) mashed bananas or ½ cup (3¾ ounces | 105 g) mashed squash (see page 73)

¼ cup (60 ml) melted extra-virgin coconut oil (see Note, page 311), plus more for the waffle iron

1 tablespoon vanilla extract

1 teaspoon raw apple cider vinegar

Whisk the almond milk and ground flax seeds together in a medium bowl. Set aside for at least 10 minutes to thicken.

Preheat the waffle iron. Meanwhile, put the almond flour in a medium bowl and break up any lumps with your fingertips. Sift in the oat flour, millet flour, brown rice flour, and baking powder and whisk to combine; set aside. Whisk the flax mixture again, add the bananas or squash, oil, vanilla, and vinegar, and stir well. Add the flour mixture and stir with a rubber spatula until just combined.

Lightly brush the waffle iron with oil and scoop about a scant ½ cup (120 ml) batter (the exact amount will depend on your iron) onto the iron. Cook according to the manufacturer's instructions, or slightly longer, until golden; vegan waffles usually need to cook for a few minutes longer than suggested for regular waffles. Remove the waffles and serve immediately with any of the toppings suggested on page 363, or place on a rack to cool if you are making them ahead. Repeat with the remaining batter. To store, once the waffles are cool, transfer to airtight containers and refrigerate for up to 3 days or freeze for up to 3 months. **Pictured on page 367 (far left, using mashed squash)**

NOTE: If you want to make and serve these waffles all at once, you can keep the first batches warm in a 200°F (95°C).

VARIATION RECIPES

Banana-Cacao Waffles with Walnuts

MAKES 8 WAFFLES

1 recipe Gluten-Free Vegan Waffles, using mashed bananas

¼ cup (60 ml) filtered water

⅓ cup (¾ ounce | 22 g) cacao powder (see the sidebar on page 297)

¼ teaspoon ground cinnamon

½ cup (1¾ ounces | 50 g) raw walnuts, finely chopped

Make the batter following the instructions for the base recipe, adding the water to the wet mixture along with the mashed bananas, sifting in the cacao and cinnamon along with the flours, and stirring the walnuts into the finished batter. Continue as directed. **Pictured on page 367 (center right)**

Rose Sesame Waffles

MAKES 8 WAFFLES

1 recipe Gluten-Free Vegan Waffles, using ½ cup (4¼ ounces | 120 g) Fall Fruit Compote made with apples (page 104) in place of the banana or squash

1 tablespoon organic rose water (see the sidebar on page 37)

⅓ cup (1½ ounces | 45 g) raw sesame seeds, toasted (see page 390)

Organic fresh or dried rose petals for garnish (optional; see the sidebar on page 301)

Make the batter following the instructions for the base recipe, adding the rose water along with the vanilla and stirring the sesame seeds into the finished batter just until incorporated. Continue as directed. If desired, sprinkle the waffles with rose petals before serving. **Pictured on page 367 (far right)**

Meal Prep

Although it can seem like an impossible luxury to be able to set aside time to prep and cook meals in advance, once you've tried it and experienced the pleasure and sense of calm you feel around mealtime, you'll be sold. You will be rewarded handsomely with a stock of instant, delicious, and healthy meals (and snacks), and you won't have to waste a moment wondering what to eat. This is really the best way to take control of your health and to assure you have nutritious food options when you have a busy schedule. And if you're buying local and organic, it's also a good way to nourish your family and the greater community as a whole. Plus all the scraps from these make-ahead cooking sessions can be returned to the earth via composting to feed the soil, keeping the cycle continuous. Cooking responsibly is no small act!

Cooking and coordinating multiple recipes at once is an intense mental exercise. But if you can stay focused on the task for a couple of hours, you will get a lot done. And you don't need a big fancy kitchen for these meal prep sessions—I've put these menus together with a work space the size of a large cutting board.

The steps in each plan are ordered to guarantee the most productive results. Getting easy things like beans on to cook immediately, even before unpacking all the groceries, gives you a jump-start. While the beans come up to a boil, you can scrub vegetables and wash greens and herbs. Using these prep lists as guidelines, you will create your own rhythm and discover what works best in your kitchen.

Because most people can't dedicate a whole day to cooking ahead for every meal of the week, I offer seven different options here, including breakfast, boxed lunches, two dinner menus, snacks, and a cleanse, as well as what to do when you're caught out on a Sunday night. You can pick and choose the meal prep plans that best suit your lifestyle. And preparing even just a few recipes from a plan will lighten your week, so don't be discouraged if you don't have much time to devote to prepping ahead.

Meal Prep Tips

Although many of these tips refer specifically to the prepping of the weekly meal plans in this chapter, some of them are general suggestions that will make your time in the kitchen more efficient, productive, and enjoyable.

o No matter what size your kitchen is, it's important to stop from time to time to do dishes, clean the counters, and clear your mind.

- Make a physical list—write down what you need to do in rough order so you can glance at the list if you get distracted; plus, crossing items off as you go is a true joy!

- Also create mental lists—give yourself mini challenges, such as making the dressing and a quick pickle before the soup timer goes off, to help you stay on track timewise.

- Fill the largest bowl you have (or a clean sink) with water for washing your produce. Start with the cleanest vegetables and fruits: fennel, cabbage, apples, pears, and so on—anything that only needs to be dunked in and out. Use the same water to wash anything gritty, like cilantro or greens, and then change the water to wash the greens or herbs a second time. Be sure to wash anything that will touch your cutting board, including onions, lemons or other citrus, and anything else you plan to peel.

- When you don't know where to start, put the kettle on to boil. You can use boiling water to infuse flavorings for nut milks, make a batch of dandelion coffee, and speed up soup making, among other tasks.

- You only need to give the blender a good rinse between batches of nut milks or dressings. If, however, you go from savory to sweet, wash it with soap and give it a sniff—the last thing you want is a hint of garlic from a marinade in your nut milk!

- Use every moment in the kitchen wisely. If you're waiting for soup or beans to come to a boil, for example, you can pluck herbs, squeeze out the last drops of milk from the nut-milk bag, or do the dishes.

- Be sure that grains, beans, baked tempeh, soups, and other dishes are cool before sealing the containers and refrigerating them. If your kitchen is warm, you might want to let them cool elsewhere; or place them in the fridge once they have stopped steaming, then seal them once cool.

- Be sure to get soups, grains, and the like out of the pots they were cooked in, and always remove them from the stove if your oven is on. Grains, for example, can ferment and spoil if they're left in a warm place for an extended period of time.

- Prepped dressings, nut milks, and garnishes should be put in the fridge immediately to maximize shelf life; this also helps keep your work space clear.

- Although the recipes for chia Bircher bowls, porridges, chia puddings, and many other dishes state that they will keep for 4 days when stored properly, they actually are often good for a day or two longer. So, carefully evaluate and smell food that you still have after 4 days; don't just automatically throw it away (and please be sure to compost anything that has gone bad—at least the worms can eat it!).

- If the oven is on and you have a few extra minutes, toast some nuts or seeds. These can be added to many dishes, and of course they make the perfect snack.

- If your plans change and you know you won't get to all the portions of any particular dish, freeze the extras as soon as possible. (You'll find specific freezing instructions in each recipe chapter.) And once you get into a routine of cooking for the week, you'll build up a healthy stock in your freezer and be able to fill in meal gaps without any planning.

- Be sure to check out the Essential Garnishes on page 384. These tasty pops of flavor do far more than just make your simple meals look more inviting; they are an integral part of making simple food taste great. These garnishes can be added to savory porridges or bean or grain bowls, sprinkled over toast, and used in Instant Miso Soup (see page 383).

MEAL PREP INSPIRATION

Glass jars are the best choice for storing items in these meal plans. Seeing all the colorful food will spark ideas for making a quick lunch, planning dinner, or mixing and matching breakfast items. Plus, seeing the food reminds you to use everything you have. Pictured here from left to right, top to bottom:

- Black Rice–Black Sesame Crackers (page 287)
- Quick Marinated Arame (page 204)
- Spring/Summer Steamed Vegetable Salad (page 173)
- Marinated Beans (page 148)
- Prepped kale
- Blueberry Compote with Cardamom and Orange (page 97)
- Berry–Rose Petal Compote (page 97)
- Fermented Carrots with Turmeric and Ginger (page 192)
- Golden Cashew Sauce with Chile and Lime (page 240)
- Grated ginger
- Broccoli Spinach Soup (page 128)
- Cooked chickpeas
- Toasted Seed and Nori Salad Topper (page 202)
- Beet-Millet Crackers with Dill Seeds (page 289)
- Chopped scallions
- Flower and Berry Granola (page 355)
- Tangy Beet-Cashew Dressing with Chile (page 223)
- Dulse Rose Za'atar (page 201)
- Radishes
- Almond milk (see page 71)
- Pear-Citrus Chia Pudding with Turmeric (page 297)

Before You Start

○ Inspect your pantry, freezer, and fridge; what you find will help inspire your decisions about the flavors you want to use in each recipe.

○ Check recipe portions and scale up accordingly if you want to make a larger quantity.

○ Check Always on the Shopping List (page 385) for ways to help you through the week or month.

○ Make sure you have enough containers and jars of various sizes; you will probably need more than you think. If you're planning on freezing some portions, be sure you have enough freezer containers on hand.

○ Soak any grains, beans, nuts, and seeds you need for each dish. Portion them out and label them if you're using the same nut or seed for multiple dishes.

○ Always read through the recipes to familiarize yourself with what they involve and the equipment you'll need.

○ See Vegetables: Land and Sea (beginning on page 165) for lunch box and simple dinner options.

MEAL PLANS

Make-Ahead Items for Inspired Snacks and Meals

I scatter the prep for these items throughout the month, making a couple of them when I have a little extra time or sometimes dedicating an afternoon to making my favorites. It's great to have these snacks on hand for "filling in the gaps," traveling, breakfasts, afternoon teas, and even last-minute meals. You can also buy some of these items to keep in the pantry or fridge.

○ Nut Butters (pages 112–114)

○ Toasted nuts and seeds (see page 390)

○ Seeded Crackers (pages 282–289)

○ Dulse Rose Za'atar (page 201)

○ Granola (pages 352–358)

○ Magic Mineral Dust (page 202)

○ Toasted Seed and Nori Salad Topper (page 202)

○ Seeded Bars (pages 338–345)

○ Easy Pine Nut Pasta Sauce (page 242)

○ Fermented Vegetables (pages 192–195)

○ Vegan Latte Mixes (pages 79, 82, 83, and 87)

Breakfast All Week

Eating a good breakfast sets the tone for the day. This plan provides one person with a chia Bircher bowl or porridge for breakfast for 4 or 5 days, plus bread for toast on the weekend and enough extra to freeze for the following week. In the warmer months, make a chia Bircher bowl, and in winter, one of the porridges. But if you need a breakfast to grab and go, the chia Bircher bowl is perfect at any time of year, as it can be refrigerated in individual portions, including the compote and nut milk. This plan also includes the option of making a vegan latte mix to have on hand as a lovely treat.

MENU

○ Chia Bircher Bowl (pages 20–25) or Genius Whole-Grain Porridge (pages 34–43)

○ Simple Compote (pages 96–105)

- Almond milk (see page 71) for lattes

- Nut Milk (pages 71–77); choose a flavor that pairs well with the chia Bircher bowl or porridge

- Gluten-Free Bread (pages 52–57)

- Vegan latte mix (see pages 79, 82, 83, and 87; optional)

MIX-AND-MATCH OPTIONS

- Pair the compote with thick coconut or dairy yogurt for a snack or dessert.

- Use the almond milk on granola, oatmeal, or muesli.

- The almond milk or flavored nut milk can be used in a smoothie for a breakfast or a snack.

- Serve a slice or two of the bread with avocado and a poached egg for a quick savory meal anytime.

- Toast a slice of the bread, drizzle with olive oil, rub with a clove of garlic, and serve with soup or salad for a quick dinner.

- Use the bread to make tartines or open-faced sandwiches, topped with sliced radishes and goat or nut cheese or a Bean Pâté (pages 152–157).

- Make a Matcha Latte (page 79) for the morning or a Turmeric Latte (page 86) for an afternoon snack or after-dinner treat.

DO-AHEAD

- Check the pantry, fridge, and freezer; make a list; and shop for ingredients.

- Soak the ingredients for the chia Bircher bowl or porridge.

- Soak the nuts for the two nut milks.

- Soak the grains and seeds for the bread.

PREP LIST

- Make the bread.

- Make the compote.

- Make the almond milk (no need to wash the blender).

- Make the flavored nut milk (no need to wash the blender).

- Make the chia bowl or porridge.

- Prepare the optional vegan latte mix (and make yourself a latte to drink while you wait for the bread to cool).

- Slice the bread and store in the freezer.

Packed Lunches for the Week

Having a nutritious lunch already prepared can help you stay focused throughout the morning and then fuel you for a productive afternoon. There's nothing better than opening up one of these box lunches, especially when it's been dressed up with colorful sprouts, microgreens, and/or vibrant garnishes. Since steamed greens won't keep well for 4 days, baby spinach or thinly sliced kale or another raw green works best with these. In winter, though, if you're eating at home, you could warm the beans in the steamer, throw in the prepped raw greens at the last minute, transfer to a bowl, and top with avocado or other garnishes.

MENU

- Plain beans (see pages 146–147) or marinated beans (see pages 148–149)

- Steamed squash (see page 171) or a steamed vegetable salad (see page 173)

- Whole grain (see page 391)

- Roasted vegetable or two (see pages 178–179)

- Dressing (pages 214–229) or Quick Tahini Sauce (pages 246–247)

CLOCKWISE FROM TOP RIGHT: Short-grain brown rice (see page 391) with toasted black sesame seeds (see page 390) and microgreens; herbed heirloom beans (see page 149); salad greens and shaved radishes; steamed sugar snap peas (see page 171); Quick Marinated Arame (page 204); roasted winter squash (see page 178); Artichoke–Meyer Lemon Dressing with Chives (page 221); **OPPOSITE:** Black Rice–Black Sesame Bread (page 53) topped with fresh goat cheese (use a creamy cashew cheese as a substitute), shaved radishes, and radish microgreens

- Quick Marinated Arame (page 204)

- Boiled eggs (see page 383; optional)

- Thinly sliced kale, baby spinach, or other greens

- Sliced raw vegetables, sliced avocado, and sprouts

- Fermented vegetables (store-bought) or a quick pickle (see pages 188–190)

- Essential Garnishes (page 384)

MIX-AND-MATCH OPTIONS

- Extra steamed squash can be used in the Leftover Steamed Vegetable Miso Bowl (page 174) or in muffins (see pages 310–318), or tossed into simple salads.

- Eat the grains (warm or at room temperature) for breakfast or dinner instead. Top with Toasted Seed and Nori Salad Topper (page 202), some of the garnishes, and avocado and/or a boiled egg.

- Make extra roasted vegetables and toss with salad greens and avocado or feta for dinner.

- The dressing recipe can be doubled and extra greens prepped for salads for dinner.

- Prep extra kale and other vegetables to steam fresh for dinner; serve drizzled with olive oil and tamari and top with some of the Essential Garnishes on page 384 and a poached or boiled egg.

- The avocado and fermented vegetables can be eaten as a snack on crackers (store-bought or homemade; see pages 282–289).

- Serve lunch with Instant Miso Soup (see page 383).

DO-AHEAD

- Check the pantry, fridge, and freezer; make a list; and shop for ingredients.

- Soak the beans.

- Soak the grains.

PREP LIST

- Cook the beans.

- Cook the grains.

- Soak the arame.

- Roast the vegetables.

- Drain and marinate the arame.

- Make the dressing or tahini sauce.

- Steam the squash or the vegetables for the steamed vegetable salad.

- Prep the garnishes, greens, and raw vegetables.

- Make a quick pickle if you don't have store-bought fermented vegetables on hand.

- Boil the eggs, if using.

- Once all the ingredients are cool, pack into lunch boxes.

- Add the raw greens, sprouts, garnishes, and egg, if using (keep boiled eggs unpeeled until ready to serve).

- If possible, store the dressing in a separate container; if not, add to the lunch box each morning.

Simple Dinner Options for a Busy Week

This plan gives you a few different options for when you want to be prepared but not tied down to a set meal. You can enjoy one of the soups when you're too tired to digest much else or warm up something more filling like a roasted sweet potato with a bean sauce and lots of tasty toppings. The Easy Pine Nut Pasta Sauce is perfect for a night when you just want the ease and comfort of pasta—or when you have impromptu company. If you don't get to it during the week, the extra sauce will keep for up to a month in the fridge. The soup recipe makes more than you'll need, so be sure to freeze what you won't eat.

MENU

- Simple and Healing Soup (pages 126–141)
- Salad greens
- Whole grain (see page 391)
- Quick Bean Sauce base recipe (page 158)
- Steamed vegetable (see pages 170–171)
- Roasted whole sweet potatoes (see page 179)
- Fermented vegetables (store-bought) or a quick pickle (see pages 188–190)
- Dressing (see pages 214–229)
- Easy Pine Nut Pasta Sauce (page 242) for a pasta dish of your choice
- Creamy Nut Sauce (pages 238–240)
- Essential Garnishes (page 384)

MIX-AND-MATCH OPTIONS

- Serve the soup with a green salad for a light meal.
- Stir some grains into the soup for a more substantial meal.
- Serve the bean sauce over steamed greens and top with sliced avocado or goat cheese.
- Split open the roasted sweet potato, stuff with the bean sauce, and top with cilantro leaves, fermented vegetables or a quick pickle, sliced avocado, scallions, and a drizzle of dressing.
- Warm the grains and bean sauce together and serve with the garnishes of your choice, a drizzle of olive oil, and a crumble of feta, goat cheese, or cashew cheese.
- Toss a green salad with fermented vegetables or some of the quick pickle and a drizzle of dressing or olive oil.
- Drizzle steamed vegetables and the roasted sweet potato with the creamy nut sauce.

- Make a grain salad with leftover grains, lots of chopped fresh herbs, vinegar, and olive oil. Serve with a poached or boiled egg and fermented vegetables.
- Make pasta and a salad.

DO-AHEAD

- Check the pantry, fridge, and freezer; make a list; and shop for ingredients.
- Soak the beans.
- Soak the grains.

PREP LIST

- Cook the beans.
- Cook the grains.
- Make the soup.
- Roast the sweet potatoes.
- Prep the steamed vegetables.
- Prep the salad greens.
- Make the pine nut sauce and prep any herbs needed for the pasta.
- Make the dressing (rinse out the blender).
- Blend the soup (rinse out the blender).
- Make the nut sauce.
- Make the bean sauce.
- Make the quick pickle.
- Prep the garnishes.

Comforting Dinners

Sometimes you want a complete meal to look forward to at the end of the day, especially during the cold winter months. This plan is for those weeks when you know you'll be nesting at home in the evening. Because most of the cauliflower bakes are complete meals, there aren't any mix-and-match suggestions with this plan. If you choose the Leek and Greens Cauliflower Bake, though, you might like to serve it topped with a poached egg to add protein or make some marinated beans to serve alongside it. The menu also includes the instant miso soup, because it's a lovely light and warming beginning to the meal. (Be sure to freeze any extra bake you won't get to within 4 days.)

MENU

- Cauliflower Bake (pages 268–274)
- Instant Miso Soup (see page 383)
- Green salad with your choice of dressing (see pages 214–229)
- Fermented vegetables (store-bought) or a quick pickle (see pages 188–190)
- Essential Garnishes (page 384)

DO-AHEAD

- Check the pantry, fridge, and freezer; make a list; and shop for ingredients.
- Soak the beans or lentils for the bake (and for the marinated beans if making them).

PREP LIST

- Cook the beans and/or lentils.
- Make the bake filling.
- Make the dressing (rinse out the blender).
- Divide the bake filling among individual containers.
- Make the cauliflower topping and top the filling.
- Prep the salad greens.
- Make a quick pickle.
- Prep the garnishes for the miso soup.

Snacks All Week (and Beyond)

This plan gives you plenty of snacking options, like Seeded Crackers (pages 282–289), bean pâté (see pages 152–157), toasted nuts and seeds (see the chart on page 390), and more. These items are all handy when you're traveling or you're just out and about and want a nutritious snack to get you through the day. If you crave something on the sweeter side, the Seeded Bars (pages 338–345) will hit the spot, and they also travel well. Chia Pudding (pages 296–305) is an energizing high-protein snack that can be portioned into small jars for individual servings.

The Instant Miso Soup (see page 383) is also included here, because it is an excellent grounding drink to support your immune system when you're on the go. Keep a jar of miso in your fridge at work, or spoon the ingredients for the soup into a jar and pop it into your bag, so all you need to do is add boiling water, stir, and enjoy, wherever you are.

The Essential Garnishes on page 384 are also listed here, because they can transform simple meals in an instant. Try scattering scallions and turmeric, for example, over a poached egg and steamed greens, or sprinkle them into a split roasted sweet potato and add sliced avocado, cilantro, and a squeeze of lime.

MENU

- Seeded Crackers (pages 282–289)
- Bean pâté (see pages 152–157)
- Nut or Seed Butter (pages 112–114)
- Raw vegetables for the pâté (such as radishes, celery, daikon, and/or carrots)
- Toasted nuts and seeds (see page 390)
- Chia Puddings (pages 296–305)
- Seeded Bars (pages 338–345)
- Instant Miso Soup (see page 383)
- Essential Garnishes (page 384)

MIX-AND-MATCH OPTIONS

○ The crackers can be eaten plain or smeared with the bean pâté or nut butter.

○ Nut butter can be served with sliced fruit or the prepped raw vegetables, or stuffed inside a Medjool date for a sweet treat. It's also great on toast.

○ Use the toasted nuts and seeds to make your own trail mix, adding superfoods like dried mulberries, goji berries, cacao nibs, or freeze-dried berries.

○ Swirl some thick coconut yogurt into the chia pudding.

DO-AHEAD

○ Check the pantry, fridge, and freezer; make a list; and shop for ingredients.

○ Soak the beans for the pâté.

○ Soak grains or defrost almond pulp for crackers.

PREP LIST

○ Cook the grains for crackers, if needed.

○ Cook the beans.

○ Toast the nuts or seeds for the butter.

○ Toast nuts or seeds for snacking.

○ Toast the seeds for the seeded bars.

○ Make the nut butter (no need to wash the food processor).

○ Make the seeded bars.

○ Make the crackers.

○ Make the bean pâté.

○ Prep the raw vegetables for the pâté (store in airtight containers in the fridge).

○ Prep the garnishes.

Soup and Broth Cleanse

This cleanse is ideal for resetting your system in the cooler months, and it's a brilliant alternative to a juice cleanse. Since it's 100 percent vegetables, most people feel fine when doing it for 3 to 5 days. It's a fantastic way to clean up your diet; to try cutting out dairy, soy, gluten, grains, and sugar; and to infuse your body with the benefits of healing ingredients like burdock, mushrooms, sea vegetables, and plenty of greens. It is not intended for frequent use or for longer periods, as it doesn't contain enough protein.

This plan makes enough soup and broth both for the cleanse itself and to freeze and eat as you transition out of the cleanse (or for later). When transitioning back to normal eating, it's best to start by adding a little protein first and then incorporating whole grains back into your diet. Be sure to drink water between meals, and have some healing herbal teas on hand too. The broth is truly fortifying and perfect for when you're feeling hungry. It's also a great nourishing snack for your everyday diet.

The green Simple and Healing Soups, like the Broccoli Spinach Soup and its variations (pages 128–129) or the Cauliflower Soup with Greens and Dill (page 127), are best for a cleanse, but if you'd like something sweeter in the evening, the Kabocha Squash Soup with Ginger, Turmeric, and Miso (page 134) is a good option. Since most people can't take a week off from work to do the cleanse, the plan includes steamed vegetables at lunchtime to give you something solid. These can be drizzled with a little extra-virgin olive oil and a squeeze of lemon, sprinkled with a pinch of salt, and topped with any of the garnishes to add interest. If you find you're feeling faint during the cleanse, you can add a protein such as plain cooked beans (see the chart on pages 146–147), soaked and drained almonds (see the chart on page 67), or more fat, such as sliced avocado. If you're not used to cleansing and eating so simply, be sure to set yourself up properly and prepare everything ahead so you can relax.

MENU

Morning

Juice of ½ lemon in 1½ cups (360 ml) boiled filtered water

Breakfast

Simple and Healing Soup (pages 126–141)

Snack

Restorative Mineral-Mushroom Broth (page 207)

¼ cup (1¼ ounces | 35 g) raw pumpkin seeds, toasted (see page 390)

Lunch

Steamed vegetables: kale, squash, and daikon (see the chart on pages 170–171) with Essential Garnishes (page 384)

½ cup (2½ ounces | 70 g) fermented vegetables, store-bought or homemade (see pages 192–195)

Instant Miso Soup (see page 383; optional)

Snack

Restorative Mineral-Mushroom Broth (page 207)

Sliced raw radishes

Dinner

Another Simple and Healing Soup (pages 126–141)

DO-AHEAD

○ Check the pantry, fridge, and freezer; make a list; and shop for ingredients.

○ Make sure that you have plenty of glass jars to store the broth and soups.

PREP LIST

○ Start the broth.

○ Make both soups.

○ Prep the steamed vegetables.

○ Toast the pumpkin seeds.

○ Prep the garnishes.

○ Wash, trim, and quarter the radishes (enough for 3 to 5 days).

○ Strain the broth and freeze what you won't drink in 5 days.

○ Blend each soup and freeze what you won't eat in 4 to 5 days.

Restorative Mineral-Mushroom Broth (page 207)

RECIPES TO ROUND OUT YOUR MEAL

INSTANT MISO SOUP
MAKES 1 CUP | 240 ML | SERVES 1

1 tablespoon unpasteurized miso
(chickpea, brown rice, sweet white,
mellow white)

1 cup (240 ml) boiling filtered water

1 teaspoon finely chopped scallions

½ teaspoon finely grated ginger, plus
more to taste

Place the miso in a mug or small bowl and
pour boiling water over the top. Stir until
the miso is dissolved, then add scallions and
ginger, and any other additions (see list).

OPTIONAL ADDITIONS:

½ teaspoon finely grated fresh turmeric

½ teaspoon finely grated fresh horseradish

Pinch of cayenne pepper

Squeeze of lemon juice or lemon zest

1 small garlic clove, finely grated on a
Microplane or pressed

BOILED EGGS
MAKES 4 EGGS

Bring a pot of water to a boil and gently
lower 4 medium eggs into the water, one
at a time, using a slotted spoon. Once the
water returns to a simmer, lower the heat
and cook for 6 to 10 minutes, depending on
how firm you like your egg yolk. Cooking
eggs for 7 minutes will result in a yolk with
a jam-like consistency; 9 to 10 minutes gives
you a sliceable yolk. Drain the eggs and
run under cold water until cool enough to
handle. Roll each egg on your countertop
to crack the shell, then peel and halve. If
the eggs are difficult to peel, place them in
a bowl of cold water; the water will come
between the egg and the cracked shell,
making it easier to peel.

POACHED EGG
MAKES 1 EGG

Fill a small pot of water three-quarters
full and bring to a boil over high heat. Add
a splash of raw apple cider vinegar and a
pinch of sea salt. Once the water is boiling,
break the egg into a small cup, stir the
boiling water to create a vortex, and slowly
drop the egg into the center. Once the
mixture begins simmering again, reduce the
heat a little and simmer gently for 2 to
4 minutes, depending on how soft you want
your yolk. Remove the egg with a slotted
spoon and rest the spoon on a kitchen
towel to drain off the excess water. Serve
immediately.

Caught Out on a Sunday Night?

I'm often caught out on a Sunday night without anything planned for breakfast the next morning, or sometimes even any meals for the next week. So, before bed, I soak two lots of almonds: one for almond milk (see page 71) and one for a Chia Bircher Bowl (pages 20–25); or, if it's winter, I'll soak a grain and some nuts for a Genius Whole-Grain Porridge (pages 34–47). I also soak a cup or so of whatever dried bean catches my eye. In the morning, I get up a little earlier and put the beans on to cook; they take only about 20 minutes in a pressure cooker. Then I make the almond milk and set it aside to drain while I prepare the chia Bircher bowl (or porridge). I get ready for work while the chia Bircher bowl thickens or the porridge cooks. Breakfast is ready in about 20 minutes, and I top the bowl with berries (heated to defrost if they're frozen) and a drizzle of almond milk. I drain the beans, and if I don't have a dressing on hand, I use the Marinated Beans base recipe (page 148) and refrigerate them. They can be eaten with steamed veggies for dinner or in a bowl for lunch topped with avocado, fresh greens, sprouts, if I have them, and fermented vegetables. Then the rest of the almond milk can be used for making vegan lattes (see pages 79–86) and for topping breakfast in the coming days. With items from Always on the Shopping List (opposite), I'm set for a few more breakfasts and have a basis for lunches for the week. Dinners during the week could be either steamed or roasted vegetables with a poached egg, scallions, and avocado; if I have time on Sunday night, I'll make a Simple and Healing Soup (pages 126–141), which gives me enough for several meals plus extra to freeze.

Essential Garnishes

Having a few of these garnishes on hand makes it easy to elevate the simplest ingredients into delicious meals and snacks over the course of a week. They will add flavor and color to steamed vegetables, grain or bean bowls, poached eggs, salads, and soups, and with them in the fridge, you're set for the Instant Miso Soup (see page 383). Store them separately in glass jars or other small airtight containers in the fridge (nuts and seeds can be stored at room temperature if space is tight).

- Thinly sliced scallions
- Fresh cilantro leaves
- Chopped fresh parsley
- Finely grated peeled fresh ginger
- Finely grated peeled fresh turmeric
- Finely grated peeled fresh horseradish
- Toasted nuts and seeds (see the chart on page 390)

Always on the Shopping List

These items are always on the shopping lists for my clients and for my own everyday eating. They help round out breakfasts and other meals and are an important part of a healthy diet.

o Avocados (of varying ripeness)

o Kale and other sturdy seasonal greens

o Baby spinach, for salads and stirring into soups

o A few different types of sauerkraut

o Sunflower sprouts and microgreens

o Brown rice crackers or other gluten-free or whole-grain crackers

o A few different types of unpasteurized miso for Instant Miso Soup (see page 383)

o Coconut yogurt for pairing with Simple Compotes (pages 96–105) for snacks or treats

o Good-quality nut butters when you can't make your own (see Resources, page 393)

o Goat cheese or nut cheeses for snacks

o Your favorite sourdough or sprouted bread, sliced and frozen

Containers and Storing

When you open the fridge to find an array of colorful jars filled with soups, bright dressings, creamy sauces, jewel-like compotes, nut milks, and prepped vegetables ready to go, you're immediately excited for dinner, or for any meal or snack for that matter. This is the reason I think clear glass jars are the best for storage, even for items you may not usually think of, such as prepped greens or wedges of steamed winter squash. Having a range of sizes is very useful when it comes to both advance meal prep and for taking your lunch or breakfast to go. Of course you can buy sets of jars, but I recommend saving the jars from almost anything you buy, because you always need more than you think.

When I first stock a kitchen, I bulk-order widemouthed jars in all sizes: 32 ounces (950 ml), 16 ounces (475 ml), 8 ounces (240 ml), and 4 ounces (120 ml). The biggest jars are for soups, nut milks, drinks, broths, and other items made in large batches. Use the 16-ounce (475 ml) jars for quick pickles, toasted nuts and seeds, and dressings. Use the smaller jars for storing the Essential Garnishes on page 384. Mason jars are probably the best, and most affordable, option. I also like Weck jars, which stack easily and have the option of an airtight seal.

Besides jars, the other vessels I use are ovenproof glass containers. It's handy to get a set of varying sizes so you can portion out individual servings of meals like the Cauliflower Bakes (pages 268–274). Mine have clip-on lids and are also freezer-safe. Then you can simply defrost dishes like the bakes and put them right in the oven. Large reusable plastic containers are great for freezing waffles or sliced bread and for storing large amounts of prepped vegetables. Bees Wrap, beeswax–coated cloth (see Resources, page 393), is good for wrapping loaves of bread and aged cheeses and for covering bowls or containers missing their lids. And I like 32-ounce (950 ml) and 16-ounce (475 ml) plastic containers for freezing, as they are infinitely reusable.

Essential Equipment

This is a list of the equipment I use in my own kitchen. Having these tools on hand means that my time in the kitchen is both efficient and enjoyable. I also check this list when I am setting up a kitchen for a new client.

BAKING EQUIPMENT

Bread pan

Cake pans

Muffin pan

Muffin pan liners

Parchment paper

Rolling pin

Springform pan

Tart pans

COUNTERTOP APPLIANCES

Electric spice grinder

Food processor

High-powered blender

KITCHEN TOOLS

Box grater

Chef's knives (I like Japanese vegetable knives)

Citrus reamer

Digital scale

Glass jars in various sizes

Japanese mandoline

Liquid and dry measuring cups

Measuring spoons

Microplane zester

Mortar and pestle

Nut-milk bag

Rubber spatulas

Serrated knife

Set of stainless steel bowls

Strainers, large and small

Vegetable brush

Whisk

Wooden cutting boards

Wooden spoons

POTS AND PANS

Ceramic or glass baking dishes

Heavy stainless steel or enamel-coated cast-iron pots in a few sizes

Large cast-iron skillet

Large stockpot

Pressure cooker (this could stand in for one of the pots above)

Rimmed baking sheets

Steamer pot with steamer insert (this can stand in for one of the pots above)

The Pantry

A well-stocked whole food pantry has always been a source of infinite inspiration and natural wonder to me. It's the place I turn to when I want to nest and invite people over, or I want to celebrate; when I'm preparing to travel; and, of course, when I'm hungry. A pantry brimming with whole, natural, and organic ingredients is essential to feeling good and at ease in the kitchen. With these items in your pantry (or fridge or freezer), you'll be set to make a multitude of recipes, from simple to truly elevated.

BEANS

Adzuki beans

Black beans

Butter beans/baby lima beans

Chickpeas

French lentils

Heirloom beans (a variety)

Pinto beans or cranberry beans

Red lentils

CANNED/JARRED INGREDIENTS

Artichoke hearts

Capers

Coconut milk

Olives

Tomatoes

FLOURS AND OTHER BAKING INGREDIENTS

Almond flour

Aluminum-free baking powder

Arrowroot

Brown rice flour

Brown rice syrup

Buckwheat flour

Cacao powder

Coconut flour

Dried coconut (shredded and flaked; unsweetened)

Hazelnut flour

Maple syrup (pure)

Medjool dates

Millet flour

Oat flour

Psyllium husks

Vanilla extract and beans

Yacon syrup

FROZEN INGREDIENTS

Berries (blueberries, raspberries, strawberries)

Green peas

Raw coconut meat

FRUITS

Avocados

Lemons

Limes

Oranges

GRAINS (see page 391 for cooking times)

Buckwheat groats

Forbidden black rice

Millet

Quinoa

Rolled oats

Short-grain brown rice

Whole oat groats

Wild rice

NUTS (raw; see page 390 for toasting info)

Almonds

Cashews

Hazelnuts

Macadamia nuts

Pecans

Pine nuts

Pistachios

Walnuts

OILS AND BUTTERS

Coconut butter

Extra-virgin coconut oil

Extra-virgin olive oil

Ghee

Raw cashew butter

Tahini

Unrefined cold-pressed flax oil
(keep refrigerated)

Unrefined sesame oil

POWDERS, FLOWERS, DRIED MUSHROOMS, AND BERRIES

Ashwagandha powder

Bee pollen

Chaga mushroom powder (fine)

Dried organic calendula flower
petals

Dried organic cornflower petals

Dried maitake and shiitake
mushrooms

Dried organic rosebuds

Freeze-dried beet juice powder

Freeze-dried berries (blueberries,
raspberries, strawberries)

Freeze-dried berry and fruit
powders (blueberry, mango,
pomegranate, raspberry,
strawberry)

Goji berries

Golden berries

Maca powder, gelatinized

Mesquite powder

Mulberries, golden dried

Orange blossom water

Organic rose water

Reishi mushroom powder

SEASONINGS AND CONDIMENTS

Fermented vegetables
(sauerkraut and pickles)

Fine Celtic sea salt

Flaky sea salt

Mirin

Nutritional yeast

Tamari

Unpasteurized miso (adzuki bean,
brown rice, chickpea, mellow
white, sweet white)

Whole-grain mustard

SEA VEGETABLES

Arame

Dulse

Kombu (kelp)

Nori

Wakame (alaria)

SEEDS

Black sesame seeds

Brown sesame seeds (unhulled)

Chia seeds

Flax seeds

Hemp seeds

Poppy seeds

Pumpkin seeds

Sunflower seeds

SPICES AND DRIED HERBS

Allspice

Black mustard seeds

Black peppercorns

Cardamom (pods and ground)

Cayenne pepper

Chiles (whole dried)

Cinnamon (sticks and ground)

Coriander seeds

Cumin seeds

Fennel seeds

Ground ginger

Ground turmeric

Red chili pepper flakes

Rosemary

Star anise

Sumac

Whole cloves

Whole nutmeg

TEA

Black

Dried nettle leaf

Earl Grey

Herbal teas

Matcha (ceremonial grade and,
for baking, everyday or culinary
grade)

Roasted dandelion root granules

Sencha

VEGETABLES AND FRESH HERBS

Beets

Carrots

Cilantro

Garlic

Ginger

Greens (varieties that keep well,
such as collards and kale)

Microgreens

Onions

Parsley

Radishes

Scallions

Sunflower sprouts

Sweet potatoes

Turmeric

Winter squash

VINEGARS

Balsamic vinegar

Brown rice vinegar

Raw apple cider vinegar

Red wine vinegar

Umeboshi vinegar

NUT AND SEED TOASTING TIMES

Toasting nuts and seeds is the best way to bring out their delicious flavor. For best results, line your baking sheet with parchment paper and spread the nuts or seeds out on it. You can then use the parchment as a funnel and easily transfer the nuts or seeds to jars once cool; the parchment can be reused for multiple batches. Toasted nuts and seeds keep well for 2 to 3 weeks at room temperature; they can be stored in the fridge for a month or longer. Be sure to rinse the seeds and drain well before spreading over the trays and roasting. Stir nuts and seeds halfway through the times listed to ensure even baking.

2 Cups Nuts/Seeds	Weight	Rinse	Remove Skins	Oven Temp	Time
Almonds, Whole	10 ounces | 280 g	No	No	300°F | 150°C	16 to 18 minutes
Brazil Nuts	9 ounces | 260 g	No	No	300°F | 150°C	14 minutes
Cashews, Whole	9 ounces | 260 g	No	No	300°F | 150°C	8 to 10 minutes
Dried Coconut, Flaked	3½ ounces | 100 g	No	No	300°F | 150°C	6 to 8 minutes
Dried Coconut, Shredded	6 ounces | 170 g	No	No	300°F | 150°C	4 to 6 minutes
Hazelnuts	9 ounces | 260 g	No	Yes	300°F | 150°C	14 to 16 minutes
Macadamia Nuts, Whole	9 ounces | 260 g	No	No	300°F | 150°C	8 to 10 minutes
Pecans, Whole	7 ounces | 200 g	No	No	300°F | 150°C	5 to 8 minutes
Pistachios	9 ounces | 260 g	No	No	300°F | 150°C	6 to 8 minutes
Pumpkin Seeds	10 ounces | 280 g	Yes	No	300°F | 150°C	10 to 12 minutes
Sesame Seeds (Black or Unhulled)	10 ounces | 280 g	Yes	No	300°F | 150°C	20 minutes
Sunflower Seeds	9 ounces | 260 g	Yes	No	300°F | 150°C	10 to 12 minutes
Walnuts, Whole	7 ounces | 200 g	No	Yes	300°F | 150°C	5 to 8 minutes

GRAIN SOAKING AND COOKING TIMES

This chart lists the whole grains I keep on hand and describes how to prepare them. Because whole grains contain phytic acid (see page 66), they need to be soaked before cooking. All grains benefit from being left to sit after they are cooked. Simply turn off the heat and let the pot sit, covered, for 10 minutes before serving. Cooked grains keep well for up to 4 days in the fridge.

1 Cup Grains	Weight	Soaking Time and Amount of Filtered Water	Filtered Water for Cooking	Cook Time	Yield
Brown Basmati Rice	6 ounces | 170 g	10 to 12 hours in 3 cups | 720 ml water with a pinch of sea salt	1¾ cups | 420 ml with a pinch of sea salt	60 minutes	3½ cups | 1 pound, 2 ounces | 510 g
Brown Jasmine Rice	6 ounces | 170 g	10 to 12 hours in 3 cups | 720 ml water with a pinch of sea salt	1¾ cups | 420 ml with a pinch of sea salt	50 minutes	3½ cups | 1 pound, 2 ounces | 510 g
Forbidden Black Rice	6½ ounces | 185 g	10 to 12 hours in 4 cups | 960 ml water with a pinch of sea salt	1¾ cups | 420 ml with a pinch of sea salt	50 to 55 minutes	5 cups | 1 pound, 12 ounces | 790 g
Millet	6¼ ounces | 180 g	10 to 12 hours in 3 cups | 720 ml water with a pinch of sea salt	2 cups | 480 ml with a pinch of sea salt	15 to 20 minutes	4½ cups | 6¼ ounces | 180 g
Quinoa	5½ ounces | 160 g	10 to 12 hours in 4 cups | 960 ml water with a pinch of sea salt	1 cup | 240 ml with a pinch of sea salt	15 minutes	4 cups | 15 ounces | 425 g
Raw Buckwheat Groats	5½ ounces | 160 g	4 to 6 hours in 3 cups | 720 ml water with a pinch of sea salt	1¼ cups | 300 ml with a pinch of sea salt	20 minutes	3½ cups | 1 pound | 455 g
Short-Grain Brown Rice	6½ ounces | 185 g	10 to 12 hours in 3 cups | 720 ml water	2 cups | 480 ml	1 hour	3½ cups | 1 pound, 3 ounces | 540 g
Wild Rice	5½ ounces | 160 g	10 to 12 hours in 3 cups | 720 ml water	1½ cups | 360 ml	30 minutes	3½ cups | 13 ounces | 370 g

Resources

INGREDIENTS

ADAPTOGENS, POWDERS, FLOWERS, BERRIES, AND TEA

Alteya Organics
Organic Bulgarian rose water
alteyaorganics.com

Beet Beet Beet
Organic beet juice powder
Available on Amazon; no company website

Frontier Co-op
Organic spices and herbs, dandelion root granules, essential oils, dried nettle, dried burdock, dried shiitake mushrooms
frontiercoop.com

Furnace Creek Farm
Ashwagandha powder
furnacecreekfarm.com

Karen's Naturals
Freeze-dried berries and fruit and berry powders
shopkarensnaturals.com

Mountain Rose Herbs
Dried organic calendula petals, dried organic cornflower petals, dried organic rosebuds, dried maitake mushrooms, rose powder
mountainroseherbs.com

My Berry Organics
Fine chaga powder
myberryorganics.com

Ranger Select
Reishi powder
healthrangerstore.com

Rishi Tea & Botanicals
Ceremonial-grade matcha, everyday matcha, sencha tea, black tea, Earl Grey tea, herbal blends
rishi-tea.com

Sun Potion
Reishi powder blend
sunpotion.com

BEANS

Rancho Gordo
Heirloom beans
ranchogordo.com

CANNED OR JARRED INGREDIENTS

Bionaturae
Canned and bottled tomatoes
bionaturae.com

Eden Foods
Canned beans cooked with kombu
edenfoods.com

Mediterranean Organics
Capers
mediterraneanorganic.com

Native Forest
Full-fat coconut milk (no gums)
edwardandsons.com

Seggiano
Olives and high-quality Italian ingredients
seggiano.com

COCONUT

Anita's Yogurt
Organic coconut yogurt
anitas.com

Exotic Superfoods
Frozen coconut meat
exoticsuperfoods.com

Let's Do . . . Organic
Coconut flakes
edwardandsons.com

FLOURS AND OTHER BAKING INGREDIENTS

Arrowhead Mills
Buckwheat flour, millet flour, oat flour, coconut flour
arrowheadmills.com

Bob's Red Mill
Blanched almond flour, hazelnut flour, aluminum-free baking powder
bobsredmill.com

Coconut Secret
Coconut flour
coconutsecret.com

Frontier Co-op
Arrowroot powder, aluminum-free baking powder, vanilla beans and extract, almond extract
frontiercoop.com

Nuts.com
Blanched organic almond flour,
hazelnut flour
nuts.com

Organic India
Psyllium husks
organicindia.com

Raw Food World
Yacon syrup
therawfoodworld.com

GRAINS AND PASTA

Lotus Foods
Forbidden black rice
lotusfoods.com

Massa Organics
Organic brown rice
massaorganics.com

Tinkyada
Gluten-free brown rice pasta
tinkyada.com

NUTS, SEEDS, AND SUPERFOODS

Blue Mountain Organics
Organic nuts and seeds, sprouted
nuts and flours, nut butter,
Austrian pumpkin seeds
bluemountainorganics.com

Jaffe Brothers
Bulk organic nuts and seeds
organicfruitsandnuts.com

Massa Organics
Unpasteurized organic almonds,
organic almond butter
massaorganics.com

Navitas Organics
Chia seeds, goji berries, cacao
powder, cacao butter, pomegranate
powder, gelatinized maca powder,
mesquite powder, golden berries,
raw cashews
navitasorganics.com

OILS AND BUTTERS

Ancient Organics
Ghee
ancientorganics.com

Artisana Organics
Coconut butter, raw cashew butter
artisanaorganics.com

Bragg Live Food
Extra-virgin olive oil
bragg.com

Cap Beauty
Bulk coconut butter, and a large
range of adaptogens
capbeauty.com

Flora
Unrefined cold-pressed flax oil
florahealth.com

Nutiva
Bulk extra-virgin coconut oil,
coconut flour, and hemp seeds
nutiva.com

SEASONINGS AND CONDIMENTS

Bragg Live Food
Raw apple cider vinegar,
nutritional yeast
bragg.com

Eden Foods
Mirin, tamari, and other
traditional Japanese products
edenfoods.com

Maldon Salt Company
Flaky sea salt
maldonsalt.co.uk

Miso Master
Unpasteurized organic miso
great-eastern-sun.com

Selina Naturally
Fine Celtic sea salt
selinanaturally.com

South River Miso
Specialty unpasteurized organic
miso
southrivermiso.com

SEA VEGETABLES

Eden Foods
Arame, nori, wakame
edenfoods.com

Ironbound Island
Kombu, wakame
ironboundisland.com

Maine Coast Sea Vegetables
Kombu, nori, wakame, dulse, alaria
seaveg.com

Salt Point Seaweed
Kombu, wakame
saltpointseaweed.com

EQUIPMENT

Bees Wrap
Beeswax-coated cloth
food52.com

Ellie's Best
Nut-milk bag
elliesbest.com

Fermentology
Glass pickle weights
tryfermentology.myshopify.com

Frieling
Milk frother
food52.com

KitchenAid
High-powered blenders and other
countertop appliances
kitchenaid.com

Kuhn Rikon
Pressure cookers
kuhnrikon.com

Kyocera Advanced Ceramics
Ceramic-blade mandoline
kyoceraadvancedceramics.com

Le Creuset
Enamel-coated cast-iron pots
lecreuset.com

Le Parfait
Widemouthed glass jars
leparfait.com

Weck Jars
Widemouthed jars
weckjars.com

ACKNOWLEDGMENTS

My deepest gratitude to my wife, Jacqui Kravetz, for steadily supporting me and continuously easing the burden with every project I take on—I simply couldn't do it without you.

THANK YOU TO

My agent, Sharon Bowers, for an enormous amount of guidance and support all the way from before this book began. You're the best.

Artisan and the incredible team I am fortunate to work with: Lia Ronnen for seeing a brilliantly clear concept for this project, for providing so much flexibility and support, and for truly understanding me and my style of food. My editor, Judy Pray, for going above and beyond for this book. I really appreciate all the time, focus, and diligence it took to get such an unwieldy manuscript into shape. I can't thank you enough!

Michelle Ishay-Cohen for art direction, for a beautiful and unique vision, and for being so collaborative. Sibylle Kazeroid, Jane Treuhaft, Nancy Murray, Zach Greenwald, Allison McGeehon, Theresa Collier, Amy Michelson, Bella Lemos, and Hanh Le, thank you all for your meticulous work on this book.

Toni Tajima for book design; Stephanie Pesakoff for leading us to Jenny Bowers, whose beautiful illustrations grace the cover; and Judith Sutton for copyediting.

The amazing team of people who traveled from afar to shoot this book and were an absolute delight to work alongside. Anson Smart for beautiful photography and effortlessly bringing so much life, warmth, and magic to these recipes. Lucy Attwater for excellent prop-styling skills and a razor-sharp eye, and for being such a pleasure to collaborate with.

Blaine Arin for sharing a connection to really good food and working so hard on another book with me. Mary Wiles for ongoing support, and Russell Horton and Jody Scott for helping make it all happen.

KitchenAid, Le Creuset, Kuhn Rikon, Rishi Tea & Botanicals, Frontier Co-op, Nuvita, Selina Naturally, Navitas Organics, Anita's Yogurt, Furnace Creek Farm, Elisa Waysenson and Lacanche, and Vanessa Bruno for adding so much to this project.

Thank you to my recipe testers and assistants: Arianna Casellas, Kate Carlevato, Natasha Perlis, Theresa Czerniak, Alina Heineke, Colombe Jacobsen, Katherine Lough, Mike O'Malley, and Rita Nakouzi. Rob Sutherland for making so many crackers and Geraldine Devas for finding interesting ways to eat them.

Seung Sui and the Copake General Store for coordinating amazing biodynamic produce from Tavius Sims at Camphill Village Copake and Jeremy Spesard from Miracle Springs Farm.

Special thanks to: Stephen Kent Johnson for helping to shape the vision for this book and for feedback and help the whole way through. Tess Masters for talking me off a few ledges and for supporting me and what I do in so many ways.

Sarah Perlis and Gabriel Riley for true friendship and unending care. Gabrielle Russomagno for empathy and support with the process. Michael Diamond for insight and guidance. Emilie Cresp for being my biggest fan, for inspiring beauty in everything, and for supporting this project. Ellen Boyce for stepping in to help at a moment's notice. John Derian for generosity and inspiration, always. Guinevere Naar for lifelong friendship. Heidi Swanson for great advice early on and for being such an inspiration in this field.

Henry Street Studio for beautiful ceramics. Ozlem and Gaudéricq Robiliard for lending props. The lovely team at Soho House New York, for generosity and support, and for being my office in the city while I was editing this book.

Infinite gratitude to my family—my father, Bill Chaplin, for encouragement and excitement for every project I tackle. My sister, Bonnie Chaplin, for real support and endless feedback (again!), and for stepping in to help no matter what. Damion Lawyer for providing a city home while I was editing, and Cyrus William for loving and hating my food with pure honesty. My mother, Pamela Shera, for all that you do and have done to inspire me to cook and share nourishing food—and for working so hard to help develop the first recipes for this book, stocking the pantry and never complaining about the endless dishes and mess. I love you.

To all the readers of my first book—your enthusiasm and support continue to inspire me. Thank you so much.

INDEX